W9-CUZ-396

WITHDRAWN

PUBLIC POLICY
for
DEMOCRACY

Helen Ingram
Steven Rathgeb Smith
Editors

The Brookings Institution
Washington, D.C.

CARL A. RUDISILL LIBRARY
LENOIR-RHYNE COLLEGE

JK
1764
.P83
1993

May 1994

About Brookings

The Brookings Institution is a private nonprofit
organization devoted to research, education, and publication
on important issues of domestic and foreign policy. Its
principal purpose is to bring knowledge to bear on current
and emerging policy problems.

The Institution was founded on December 8, 1927, to merge
the activities of the Institute for Government Research,
founded in 1916, the Institute of Economics, founded in 1922,
and the Robert Brookings Graduate School of Economics,
founded in 1924.

The Institution maintains a position of neutrality on issues
of public policy. Interpretations or conclusions in Brookings
publications should be understood to be solely those of the
authors.

Copyright © 1993
THE BROOKINGS INSTITUTION
1775 Massachusetts Avenue, N.W., Washington, D.C. 20036

All rights reserved

Library of Congress Cataloging-in-Publication data:

Public policy for democracy / [edited by] Helen Ingram, Steven Rathgeb Smith.
    p.   cm.
    Includes bibliographical references and index.
    ISBN 0-8157-4152-9 (alk. paper) — ISBN 0-8157-4153-7
(pbk. : alk. paper).
    1. Political participation—United States. 2. Democracy—United
States. 3. Policy sciences. I. Ingram, Helen M., 1937–   .
II. Smith, Steven Rathgeb, 1951–   .
JK1764.P83   1993
320'.6'0973—dc20   93-5951
                                                                            CIP

9   8   7   6   5   4   3   2   1

The paper used in this publication meets the minimum
requirements of the American National Standard for
Information Sciences—Permanence of Paper for Printed
Library Materials, ANSI Z39.48-1984.

In memory of Aaron Wildavsky,
in recognition of his pioneering work
in public policy

Preface

THIS WORK IS a testimony to the ability of an ideal—public policy designed to foster democracy—to galvanize a collective effort to overcome barriers of different disciplines, ideologies, institutions, and geographic locations. The common realization of the significance of the impact of public policies upon the capacity of citizens came to a group of scholars attending a public policy panel chaired by Richard Valelly at the 1990 American Political Science Association meetings. It has long been clear that policies affect politics, but there emerged a further insight: much of the distance citizens perceive between themselves and politics is rooted in the contents of public policies.

Further study and deliberation of the effects of policy on democracy were clearly in order, but scholars interested in the topic were scattered in various disciplines and locations. Fortunately, the topic was central to the mission of the Udall Center for Studies in Public Policy at the University of Arizona, which explores better alternatives for resolving public policy problems. At that time, with funding from the Ford Foundation, the Udall Center was examining ways to give residents of the U.S.-Mexico border region a greater voice in environmental protection. Because of the link between that work and the larger issue of public participation in a democratic society, the Udall Center committed a large part of its resources to convene a two-day workshop in spring 1991 in Tucson. Participants included political scientists, sociologists, and policy scientists whose contributions were extremely important to this volume, but some of whom are not chapter authors. Michael Lipsky of the Ford Foundation, Paul Burstein of the University of Washington, James Morone of Brown University, and Richard Rose of the University of Strathclyde, as well as a number of public policy scholars at the University of Arizona and the Arizona State University College of Public Programs, enriched the collective effort.

The intellectual harvest of the workshop might have been confined to the participants had it not been for Donald Chatfield, who contributed many hours to editing the original manuscript, which was typed by Betty Prewitt at the Udall Center and made available to various policy scholars.

The difference between a workshop proceedings and a coherent book worthy of general publication is great indeed, and the editors of this volume are grateful to the contributing authors, in particular Marc Landy, for helping us to give voice to our common themes. Daniel A. Mazmanian and Randall B. Ripley provided many useful suggestions for drawing unity from diverse approaches. The final effort to produce a book would not have been made without the encouragement of our editor at Brookings, Nancy Davidson, and would not have succeeded without her hard work. Patricia Dewey, James Schneider, and Theresa Walker edited the manuscript; David Bearce verified its factual content; and L. Pilar Wyman prepared the index.

HELEN INGRAM
STEVEN RATHGEB SMITH

Contents

1. Public Policy and Democracy

STEVEN RATHGEB SMITH AND HELEN INGRAM

IN MANY ADVANCED industrial countries, a fundamental rethinking is under way about the roles of government, community organizations, and citizens in public policy. After a flood of critiques in the early 1990s that attacked the failures of Western democracies to solve societal problems, scholars and policy analysts are now moving beyond such criticism to consider policies, strategies, and actions to make democracy work better.

A good example of this new approach to public policy is the activist agenda of the Clinton administration. From the beginning of his tenure, President Bill Clinton has been on record in support of national service programs through community organizations, government-voluntary collaborations, and community-based development projects. These initiatives reflect an effort to restructure government to enhance the effectiveness of public policies and make them more responsive to citizens.

Many of these ideas are embodied in one of the first books to make positive suggestions for change, which has become a standard reference work for public administrators at the national, state, and local levels: *Reinventing Government*, by David Osborne and Ted Gaebler.[1] These authors propose that public services be restructured so that government focuses on the business of service management and coordination while private, nonprofit, and for-profit organizations actually deliver the services.

In this context of widespread interest in reforming government and finding new ways to meeting citizens' needs, our book is an attempt to examine the impact of policy on citizenship and democracy. The authors envision a democracy in which policy plays a new role: to empower, enlighten, and engage citizens in the process of self-government. We hope to help set the agenda on the proper role of government, community organizations, and citizens in public policy.

---

1. Osborne and Gaebler (1992).

I

The book's overall aim is to identify and promote more effective public policies, especially those that try to balance or integrate the public and private sectors in new and different ways. The book also has four more specific objectives and themes.

First, the authors in this volume call attention to the need to refocus policy analysis on questions of citizenship and democracy. Policy analysis has tended to concentrate on efficiency concerns and related cost-benefit considerations. Although these studies have usefully pointed to reforms that could improve governmental efficiency, they have generally neglected the effect of public policies or of their reforms on citizen participation and democratic values. Likewise, many policy analysts have steered clear of research on the new community or public-private initiatives.

Second, the essays strive to provide insights into how the social construction of public policies affects the targets of these policies and the success of policy initiatives. For example, the groups receiving public services often become alienated, which then causes low participation rates and program ineffectiveness.

Third, much of the research on government restructuring and community programs has not investigated the effect of these policies from a longitudinal perspective.[2] Some of the authors' work provides insights into the effect of public policies over time. This research will in turn provide guidance to policymakers on policy design and reform.

Fourth, the authors suggest concrete strategies to enhance the role of citizens in the democratic process without sacrificing program effectiveness. Many scholars and policymakers are concerned that reforms designed to promote greater citizen involvement, such as decentralization of program management to community groups or contracting for services, may have unintentional and negative consequences for public policy. The essays in this book address this issue and offer recommendations to policymakers on key considerations for approaching the reform of public services.

Citizenship, Democracy, and Public Policy

The idea of government restructuring and a desire for new forms of public and private collaboration in public service delivery is not a recent development. Many of the major programs of the 1960s, such as the

2. Our research fits into the ongoing debate within political science on the extent to which "new policies create a new politics." See Schattschneider (1935); Lowi (1964); Brown (1983); and Pierson (1992).

community action program, community mental health centers, neighborhood health centers, and Head Start, were community oriented and combined public funding with private administration. These programs were run by predominantly private nonprofit organizations with volunteer citizen boards and, at least initially, a heavy reliance on volunteers. The goal was to provide citizens a greater opportunity to participate in the governance of public services and the policymaking process. Many of the initial hopes for these programs as vehicles for greater citizen participation in the design and implementation of public services were frustrated as local politicians and social welfare professionals intervened to control the programs. Some of these programs, such as model cities, were also attacked as infeasible and poorly conceived.

Nonetheless, the interest in new forms of public service delivery persisted. This was reflected in the appeals to voluntarism and community throughout the 1980s, including the now-famous reference by President Bush to the "1,000 points of light" as central to America's response to social problems.[3]

Relatedly, many scholars and lay persons are interested in the reconstitution and restructuring of civil society as a way of enhancing democracy. The term *civil society* has many meanings and a long intellectual history, but it generally refers to the effort to construct social and political organizations that "represent the values and interests of social autonomy in face of *both* the modern state and the capitalist economy."[4] In this view, voluntary associations and political organizations are especially critical in providing an opportunity for individuals to participate in the life of society unconstrained by either the imperatives of the state or market forces.

Proponents of a vigorous civil society usually suggest the need for a major reorientation of the welfare state. For decades, the growth of the welfare state was based on the assumption that the public sector would gradually expand its responsibilities for the funding and administration of social welfare. Concomitantly, the voluntary sector's role would decline. This expansion is now questioned by individuals on the left and the right. Instead, many policymakers and citizens now regard voluntary associations, self-help groups, social movements, and other intermediary organizations as important alternatives to state social provision that can provide a crucial empowering role for citizens.

3. Boyte (1989); Glazer (1988, pp. 118–39); Bellah and others (1985).
4. Cohen and Arrato (1992, p. 30) (emphasis in original).

4 STEVEN RATHGEB SMITH AND HELEN INGRAM

The recent interest of many scholars in communitarianism also fits with this appeal to community and voluntary organizations as alternatives to rampant individualism and the power of the state.[5] Indeed, communitarians often link more involvement in community service and voluntary organization with greater democracy. They believe community organizations can promote a more active citizenship that in the long run may help invigorate democracy and reverse the decline in voting and increasing alienation from the political system. Ideally, community organizations could also promote greater individual responsibility for personal behavior and community problems. For this reason, many communitarians support "Neighborhood Watch" programs and community efforts to rid their areas of drug abuse.

Alienation from the state, combined with the enduring pull of community, is a major reason to restructure government to increase the role of community organizations in providing public services. This restructuring is part of the push to privatize government by delegating the responsibility for the funding and delivery of public services to private organizations. Privatization encompasses many policies, including reduced public funding of services, government contracting with nonprofit and for-profit organizations, fees for services, vouchers for public education, and a greater role for community organizations in addressing public problems.

These privatization strategies are based at least in part on the belief that democracies produce rigid, inefficient bureaucracies. Privatization offers the hope that private organizations and market competition will empower citizens, increase the efficiency of public services, and reduce the influence of special interests in policymaking. Examples of privatization addressed in this book include government contracting with voluntary organizations, using private organizations as intermediary organizations to manage government-financed programs, the deliberate involvement of private groups in governmental decisionmaking, and the use of nonprofit immigrant advocacy groups to screen and process applications of immigrants for citizenship and residency status.

Most research on privatization tends to focus on concerns about efficiency. Does contracting save money? How can government improve its monitoring of contract agencies? This focus is understandable, given the

5. Michael J. Sandel, "Democrats and Community." *New Republic*, February 22, 1988, pp. 20–23; Etzioni (1991); Galston (1991); and Peter Steinfels, "A Political Movement Blends Its Ideas from Left and Right." *New York Times*, May 24, 1992, p. E6.

fiscal pressures on government. A subject that has received relatively little attention from researchers to date is the impact of privatization on citizenship, which several chapters in this book analyze.

Supporters of greater citizen participation in policymaking often encounter opposition or skepticism from politicians or scholars. This concern about greater citizen involvement tends to be reflected in three different perspectives. Some academics worry that the United States actually suffers from too much democracy. As a result, government is overwhelmed by demands, producing paralysis and poor policy. This view is reflected in books such as *The Crisis of Democracy*, by Michel Crozier, Samuel Huntington, and Joji Watanuki, and the many different proposals advanced in the last fifteen years to restructure American government along the lines of a European-style parliamentary democracy.[6] The rationale for such proposals is that the American government allows too many access points for interest groups and is thus unable to formulate policy adequately. Parliamentary democracies tend to insulate policymakers from public pressure by reducing the opportunities for interest group influence. Party organizations are stronger in parliamentary systems, which also allows more accountability for government officials than the American system of weak, declining parties.

Second, citizen participation through community organizations has been criticized by scholars who fear that community organizations are ill suited to carry the torch of more enhanced political participation. Karen Paget suggests that community organizations are inherently incapable of sustaining political participation.[7] Indeed, citizen participation in community organization can produce fragmented, ineffective responses to public policy problems. She believes that only parties are capable of mounting a serious challenge to prevailing government policy and maintaining accountability for government officials.

Third, some policymakers are concerned that efforts to restructure government, such as decentralization and community coalitions, may empower the wrong people and lead to regressive or ineffective policies.

In this volume, we strive to move beyond the debate on the capabilities of community organizations and the merits of citizen participation by suggesting concrete strategies for policymakers to promote democratic renewal. Although we understand the difficulties involved in enhancing citizen participation, we believe that the empirical research presented in

6. Crozier, Huntington, and Watanuki (1975); Cutler (1980–81); and Rose (1980).
7. Paget (1990).

the following chapters suggests that worthwhile avenues for greater citizen participation deserve consideration.

Implicit in the restructuring of government is a new view of citizenship rights in contemporary society. Until the 1970s, views about citizenship in advanced industrial societies were shaped by the work of T. H. Marshall, who argued that citizenship depended upon the expansion of government-guaranteed civil, political, and social rights.[8] In his view, citizenship was the equal opportunity by all citizens to participate fully in all spheres of society. To achieve this goal, government should assume an increasingly prominent role.

Yet Marshall's work tends to understate or overlook the serious constraints public bureaucracies place on the freedom of individuals and groups.[9] Also, Marshall focuses on rights, rather than duties and obligations that attend membership in a society. In his essay in this volume, Marc Landy argues that one consequence of the emphasis on rights is a weakening of the deliberative process for making decisions. Rights tend to forestall discussion because they can be demanded as absolute claims rather than negotiable items. Landy suggests that our ideas of citizenship need to be revised in order to promote greater deliberation and participation in policymaking, especially at the local level.

An additional criticism of Marshall is that he views the application of citizenship rights as relatively unproblematic. But, as the chapters in this book demonstrate, citizenship rights are often highly controversial and difficult to implement. For many decades, the presumption was that implementation problems could and should be rectified through greater use of state power. But this option is increasingly restricted due to governments' budgetary woes, a backlash against the use of state authority, and citizens' desire for greater involvement in services and programs affecting their lives.

One predominant solution to these problems of citizenship is mixed public-private collaborations, in which the state retains managerial authority and the private organization is responsible for program implementation. The chapters by Steven Smith and by Brinton Milward and Keith Provan suggest that such collaborations can blur the boundaries of the state and create troubling dilemmas of program accountability and citizenship. However, they suggest potential strategies for policymakers to overcome these policy dilemmas. Similarly, the chapters by Susan

8. Marshall (1949, pp. 71–134).
9. These criticisms are based in part on Pierson (1991, p. 202); Dicey (1914); and Hayek (1960).

Baker and Sallie Marston indicate that in certain circumstances voluntary associations can be valuable tools to increase citizen participation and improve the effectiveness of public services.

Marshall was skeptical of markets to achieve social policy goals because he believed that a reliance on markets produced inequalities in citizenship. Kenneth Godwin challenges this argument in his chapter. Drawing upon his research on contraceptive policy in developing countries, he contends that market incentives can improve service access among poor or disenfranchised groups and enhance citizen empowerment. In his view, education vouchers would be a worthwhile application of market principles in the United States.

By rethinking the links between citizenship and public policy, the authors in this volume are also striving to expand the borders of policy analysis. Traditionally, policy analysis has been primarily concerned with questions of efficiency. Analysts examine the choices faced by policymakers and recommend the most efficient course of action. Policy is judged by the outcome of rational processes that can be assayed and corrected if necessary. This focus tends to downplay or neglect the effect of public policy on the citizenry.[10] It also tends to present a snapshot of policy at a point in time. This approach is of course helpful when evaluating alternative courses of action. However, some of the most important effects of policy may be long term or unanticipated.

A longitudinal approach is valuable because it calls attention to long-term effects on conceptions of success and failure. Many policy evaluations of the community action program suggested that it was a failure because it was not implemented according to the expectations of its supporters or program administrators. Yet Marston argues that the community action program in Tucson gets high marks: over a period of many years, the program had major positive effects on political participation in Tucson. As a result, policymaking has been transformed in a more equitable and progressive direction.

Central to this longitudinal approach is the idea that policy is a series of interactions rather than a static entity, as suggested by some policy analysts. The chapter by Helen Ingram and Anne Schneider is consistent with this conception of policy as dynamic. Their chapter represents a major advance in thinking about policy classification and the effect of different types of policy on citizenship. They argue that policy designs "reflect the decisions of many different people often acting in different

10. See Heclo (1974); and Lowi (1992).

contexts and places, and are not necessarily logical, rational, or even coherent." Citizens are subsequently affected in systematic ways by the messages conveyed by policy types.

Policy Design and American Politics

The work of Ingram, Schneider, and the other authors in this volume builds and expands upon the work of political scientists who have argued that policy can have an important independent effect on political mobilization and participation. During the 1960s, the prevailing view within American political science was quite different. Influenced by the work of David Easton, the common view of policy was that the political system was a "system." Inputs such as interest groups' demands would be processed in a "black box" of political institutions. The output would be public policies.[11] This view was typified by the extensive research in the 1960s focused at the state and local level that treated policy as an outcome of certain political and economic factors.[12]

Even at the height of popularity of this state and local research on policy outputs, new approaches to policy analysis were advanced to address what were perceived to be serious explanatory shortcomings. First, several scholars proposed viewing policy as an independent variable that may affect the political process.[13] Theodore Lowi suggested that policies are basically of three types: distributive, regulatory, and redistributive. Distributive policies are what are commonly considered pork barrel projects, such as agricultural subsidies or dams.[14] Regulatory policies are focused on the control of individual conduct by directly coercive techniques. Redistributive policies require politicians to redistribute resources from one group to another. The progressive income tax or the social security program are good examples. Lowi's framework has been widely applied and has generated a number of important insights about how politics vary from one issue area to another. For instance, Randall Ripley and Grace Franklin trace the difficulties some agencies have in generating public support for the type of policies they administer. James Q. Wilson puts forth a model that divides policy into four categories that affect

11. Easton (1965).
12. See Dawson and Robinson (1963); Hofferbert (1966); Dye (1966); and Wilensky (1975). For a discussion of the difficulties of output analysis see Jacobs and Lipsky (1968).
13. See Lowi (1964); Froman (1968); and Wilson (1980).
14. Lowi has subsequently changed the name of his distributive category to *promotional policies*. See Lowi and Ginsberg (1992, p. 656).

politics differentially depending upon the perceived mix of benefits and costs.[15]

A related body of research was the work of Murray Edelman, who argued that the symbolic aspects of policy could directly affect the willingness of groups to mobilize and sustain political activity.[16] Subsequently, Michael Lipsky incorporated Edelman's emphasis on the role of policy symbols into his work on protest movements.[17] This work is consistent with an important theme of this book: policy symbols contained in public programs can profoundly affect political participation.

The implementation literature of the 1970s and early 1980s also contributed to establishing a link between policy design and political participation.[18] Jeffrey Pressman argued that federal poverty and employment programs "created new arenas of political action" that facilitated political mobilization by previously underrepresented groups, especially minority groups.[19] Daniel Mazmanian and Paul Sabatier argued that the characteristics of statutes, including the clarity of goals, greatly affect the politics of implementation by constraining bureaucratic discretion and providing opportunities for legislative oversight.[20]

One well-known characterization of the policy process—incrementalism—also calls attention to the link between policy and politics. Charles Lindblom and Aaron Wildavsky concluded that policymaking tends to be incremental: policymakers start with last year's budget or package of programs and then incrementally adjust it upward, with little effort to fundamentally reevaluate policy priorities.[21] In this sense, previous policies shape the politics of government programs. Subsequently, Hugh Heclo observed that politics is a form of social learning where policymakers collectively puzzle about what to do. This learning process is influenced by previous policy, which helps set the parameters for potential new policies.[22]

In the same tradition, Lawrence D. Brown argued that the growth of government had produced new policies such as expanded health care coverage for the elderly or new urban aid programs. These new policies

15. Ripley and Franklin (1986); Wilson (1980).
16. Edelman (1964).
17. Lipsky (1968).
18. The implementation literature is extensive. See for example, Pressman and Wildavsky (1973); and Derthick (1972).
19. Pressman (1975, p. 58).
20. Mazmanian and Sabatier (1983).
21. Lindblom (1965); and Wildavsky (1964).
22. Heclo (1974, p. 304).

produced accomplishments (such as better health care), but created new problems, such as runaway costs, that lead to a new politics characterized by rationalizing policies such as greater regulation or more market competition. As "rationalizing politics" moves to center stage (as government growth continues), fundamental changes occur in political institutions such as the presidency and Congress as policymakers adapt to changes in public policies and their consequences.[23]

More recently, the "new institutionalist" approach to the study of politics, as represented in the work of James March and Johan Olson, Suzanne Berger, Theda Skocpol, and others, has called attention to the importance of political institutions in structuring politics, including political interactions and participation.[24] Like Ingram and Schneider, these authors note the key role of symbolic politics in affecting citizen interest and participation in politics.

Deliberation, Policy Design, and Policy Studies

An essential aspect of a well-functioning democracy is the capacity for deliberation and discussion. In this sense, we concur with a succession of recent writers who argue that the deliberative functions of political institutions and voluntary organizations are essential to democracy and should be strengthened.[25] In part, deliberation is extolled because it has an educative function that can help empower citizens and increase their investment in public policymaking. For this reason, many recommend national service in local voluntary organizations as a strategy to promote greater understanding among citizens and to foster greater policy deliberation.[26]

In his chapter in this volume, Landy argues that the benefits of deliberation are more likely to materialize in decentralized political systems. Baker and Marston suggest that voluntary organizations can promote greater public debate on key policy questions. Smith calls attention to the potential deleterious effect of government funding and regulations on the political role of nonprofit organizations. One result is a muted, constrained political voice, which may make it more difficult for voluntary organizations to offer alternative political perspectives to the state.

23. Brown (1983).

24. March and Olson (1989); Berger (1981); Skocpol (1992); Evans, Rueschemeyer and Skocpol (1985); and Steinmo, Thelen, and Longstreth (1992).

25. See Mansbridge (1980); Maass (1983); and Barber (1984).

26. See, for example, Barber (1992).

The importance of public discourse is an old concern among scholars. Tocqueville argued in the early nineteenth century that voluntary associations in the United States were critical to fostering and sustaining a democratic way of life because their independence from the state provided an opportunity for a free and open discussion of political issues.[27] We share this concern, especially about the tendency for public policies to depoliticize public issues. In her essay, Deborah A. Stone describes how clinical reasoning has expanded beyond the health care field into education and criminal justice policy and the regulation of gender roles. This major development has defused the political content of these policy areas and masked fundamental distributional questions. Ingram and Schneider argue that the social construction of public policy can affect the likelihood that certain groups will politically mobilize, thus affecting public discourse. Janet A. Weiss discusses the uses of public information campaigns in public policy and their effect on democratic participation. And Richard M. Valelly details specific policy strategies to reinvigorate democracy.

Advocates of greater deliberation have tended to subscribe to a revisionist theory that links citizenship not to Marshall's conception of government-guaranteed civil, political, and social rights but to the freedom to be part of a political community characterized by the free and open discussion of political issues. And, as Landy notes in his chapter, membership in a political community also entails an obligation to participate. The debate fostered by voluntary organizations can help nurture and promote this sense of obligation.

In our view, one of the major challenges for policymakers in the coming years will be to reconcile the desire to foster more public debate and citizen participation in policymaking with the concern of many scholars and policymakers about the potential negative consequences for public policies of community control and responsibility. For example, many communities may decide to reduce social benefits due to insufficient finances or political opposition to certain types of social spending.

We believe that policy analysis and public policy studies can play a useful role in assaying the effects of public policies on political participation and social entitlements. Policy analysis can contribute to an expansion of the criteria to judge the merits of public policies by focusing on questions of political and social citizenship. To be sure, we are not

27. Concern about public discourse is expressed by many contemporary scholars including Mansbridge (1980); Habermas (1989); Boyte (1989); and Wuthnow (1991).

suggesting citizenship issues become the sole criteria by which public policies should be judged. Other criteria such as efficiency are crucial considerations. Nonetheless, we believe that the research presented in this book indicates that citizenship criteria should receive far more attention than they currently enjoy.

A greater role for citizenship issues is particularly timely, given the concern expressed by scholars and journalists about what appears to be declining interest in civic affairs in the United States. Political scientists have for many years been puzzled by the decrease in voting and interest in politics despite the widespread attention to democracy worldwide. The research presented in the following pages suggests that this waning involvement in politics may be related to the unintended consequences of many public policies for citizen participation in politics. As the Clinton administration pushes ahead with plans to invigorate community organizations, support public-private partnerships, and spur new levels of volunteerism in civic life, it would do well to be cognizant of the effect of policy design on political participation and the ways government can work with private organizations and individuals to involve the citizenry in their own governance and public services without diminishing the efficiency or effectiveness of public policies.

References

Barber, Benjamin R. 1984. *Strong Democracy: Participatory Politics for a New Age*. University of California Press.
———. 1992. *An Aristocracy of Everyone: The Politics of Education and the Future of America*. Ballantine Books.
Bellah, Robert N., and others. 1985. *Habits of the Heart: Individualism and Commitment in American Life*. University of California Press.
Berger, Suzanne D. 1981. "Introduction." In *Organizing Intererests in Western Europe: Pluralism, Corporatism, and the Transformation of Politics*, edited by Suzanne D. Berger, 1–23. Cambridge University Press.
Boyte, Harry C. 1989. *Common Wealth: A Return to Citizen Politics*. Free Press.
Brown, Lawrence D. 1983. *New Policies, New Politics: Government's Response to Government's Growth*. Brookings.
Cohen, Jean L., and Andrew Arato. 1992. *Civil Society and Political Theory*. MIT Press.
Crozier, Michel J., Samuel P. Huntington, and Joji Watanuki. 1975. *The Crisis of Democracy: A Report on the Governability of Democracies to the Trilateral Commission*. New York University Press.

Cutler, Lloyd. 1980–81. "To Form a Government." *Foreign Affairs* 59 (Fall–Winter): 126–43.

Dawson, Richard E., and James A. Robinson. 1963."Inter-Party Competition, Economic Variables, and Welfare Policies in the American States." *Journal of Politics* 25 (May): 265–89.

Derthick, Martha. 1972. *New-Towns In-Town: Why a Federal Program Failed.* Washington: Urban Institute.

Dicey, Albert V. 1914. *Law and Public Opinion in England.* Macmillan.

Dye, Thomas R. 1966. *Politics, Economics, and the Public: Policy Outcomes in the States.* Rand McNally.

Easton, David. 1965. *A Framework for Political Analysis.* Prentice-Hall.

Edelman, Murray J. 1964. *The Symbolic Uses of Politics.* University of Illinois Press.

Etzioni, Amitai. 1991. *A Responsive Community: Collected Essays on Guiding Deliberate Social Change.* Jossey-Bass.

Evans, Peter B., Dietrich Rueschemeyer, and Theda Skocpol. 1985. *Bringing the State Back In.* Cambridge University Press.

Froman, Lewis A., Jr. 1968. "The Categorization of Policy Contents." In *Political Science and Public Policy*, edited by Austin Ranney, 41–52. Chicago: Markham.

Galston, William A. 1991. *Liberal Purposes: Goods, Virtues, and Diversity in the Liberal State.* Cambridge University Press.

Glazer, Nathan. 1988. *The Limits of Social Policy.* Harvard University Press.

Habermas, Jürgen. 1989. *The Structural Transformation of the Public Sphere: An Inquiry into a Category of Bourgeois Society.* MIT Press.

Hayek, Friedrich A. 1960. *The Constitution of Liberty.* University of Chicago Press.

Heclo, Hugh. 1974. *Modern Social Politics in Britain and Sweden: From Relief to Income Maintenance.* Yale University Press.

Hofferbert, Richard I. 1966. "The Relation between Public Policy and Some Structural and Environmental Variables in the American States." *American Political Science Review* 60 (March): 73–82.

Jacobs, Herbert, and Michael Lipsky. 1968. "Outputs, Structure, and Power: An Assessment of Changes in the Study of State and Local Politics." *Journal of Politics* 30 (May): 514–16.

Lindblom, Charles E. 1965. *The Intelligence of Democracy.* Free Press.

Lipsky, Michael. 1968. "Protest as a Political Resource." *American Political Science Review* 62 (December): 1144–58.

Lowi, Theodore J. 1964. "American Business, Public Policy, Case Studies, and Political Theory." *World Politics* 16 (July): 677–715.

———. 1992. "The State in Political Science: How We Became What We Study." *American Political Science Review* 86 (March): 1–7.

Lowi, Theodore J., and Benjamin Ginsberg. 1992. *American Government: Freedom and Power.* 2d ed. W. W. Norton.

Maass, Arthur. 1983. *Congress and the Common Good.* Basic Books.

Mansbridge, Jane J. 1980. *Beyond Adversary Democracy*. Basic Books.

March, James, and Johan Olson. 1989. *Rediscovering Institutions*. Free Press.

Marshall, T. H. 1949, reprinted 1965. *Class, Citizenship and Social Development*. Anchor Books.

Mazmanian, Daniel A., and Paul A. Sabatier. 1983. *Implementation and Public Policy*. Scott, Foresman.

Osborne, David, and Ted Gaebler. 1992. *Reinventing Government: How the Entrepreneurial Spirit Is Transforming the Public Sector*. Addison-Wesley.

Paget, Karen. 1990. "Citizen Organizing: Many Movements, No Majority." *American Prospect* 2 (Summer): 115–28.

Pierson, Christopher. 1991. *Beyond the Welfare State? The New Political Economy of Welfare*. Pennsylvania State University Press.

Pierson, Paul. 1992. "From Policy to Politics: 'Feedback Effects' and Political Development." Center for European Studies, Harvard University.

Pressman, Jeffrey L. 1975. *Federal Programs and City Politics: The Dynamics of the Aid Process in Oakland*. University of California Press.

Pressman, Jeffrey L., and Aaron Wildavsky. 1973. *Implementation: How Great Expectations in Washington Are Dashed in Oakland*. University of California Press.

Ripley, Randall B., and Grace A. Franklin. 1986. *Policy Implementation and Bureaucracy*, 2d ed. Chicago: Dorsey Press.

Rose, Richard. 1980. "Governments against Sub-Governments: A European Perspective on Washington." In *Presidents and Prime Ministers*, edited by Richard Rose and Ezra N. Suleiman, 284–347. Washington: American Enterprise Institute.

Schattschneider, E. E. 1935. *Politics, Pressures and the Tariff*. Prentice-Hall.

Skocpol, Theda. 1992. "State Formation and Social Policy in the United States." *American Behavioral Scientist* 35 (March–June): 559–84.

Steinmo, Sven, Kathleen Thelen, and Frank Longstreth. 1992. *Structuring Politics: Historical Institutionalism in Comparative Analysis*. Cambridge University Press.

Wildavsky, Aaron. 1964. *The Politics of the Budgetary Process*. Little, Brown.

Wilensky, Harold L. 1975. *The Welfare State and Equality: Structural and Ideological Roots of Public Expenditure*. University of California Press.

Wilson, James Q. 1980. "The Politics of Regulation." In *The Politics of Regulation*, edited by James Q. Wilson, 357–94. Basic Books.

Wuthnow, Robert J., ed. 1991. *Between States and Markets: The Voluntary Sector in Comparative Perspective*. Princeton University Press.

Part One
Policy Shapes and Citizenship

T IS USUALLY BELIEVED that in a democracy citizens shape policies. It is less commonly realized that the far-reaching policies of modern governments shape citizens and may do so in directions harmful to democracy. The three chapters in this section examine from quite different but complimentary perspectives how policies affect the exercise of citizenship and the performance of civic duties. Citizenship can not be taken for granted in the modern state, but instead must be nurtured by good policy designs.

Defining the core concept of democratic citizenship begins in the chapter by Marc Landy. Like most important political ideas, citizenship is complex and multidimensional. Landy explores the tension between citizens' rights and responsibilities, loyalty to national and local communities, and the welfare of the whole and the good of the individual. Citizenship requires engagement in a process of political deliberation, Landy argues, and good policies establish arenas where the norms appropriate to particular circumstances are explored. According to Landy, the preferred policy designs of both the left and the right are both in error in that neither attends sufficiently to the civic teachings that are embodied in policy. Narrow concerns with effectiveness or efficiency ignore the full range of consequences of policy for citizenship. Some well-meaning policies are fatally flawed because they establish privileged rights and entitlements that remove critical issues from the give and take of the deliberative process. Policies can be thought of as constitutions that establish broad ends, prescribe institutional arrangements, define powers, and delimit membership.

Deborah Stone, whose chapter follows, and Helen Ingram and Anne Schneider, authors of the final chapter in this section, agree with Landy that the civic teachings of public policies are often at odds with the lessons necessary for citizenship in a democracy. Like Landy, Stone questions utilitarian or rational policy evaluations that replace representative and deliberative processes with expertise. Stone argues that clinical reasoning is a form of normative judgment that often conflates deviation with pathology. Clinical reasoning is celebrated for its supposed objectivity in measuring deservedness. Supposedly, the information upon which important policy decisions is based is weighed by independent observers whose work can be verified. Yet, as such reasoning is applied in education, criminal justice, and regulation of gender roles, Stone finds that clinical tests are intrusive and disempowering to the subjects examined because they do not participate in the process of articulating and communicating symptoms. Individual will or preference is no longer the standard for judging how persons should be treated. Citizens are robbed of the opportunity to participate in important policy decisions affecting their lives. And, since the focus of clinical reasoning is on individual deviance from the norm, the structural and relational flaws in the political system are obscured. As a result, the transformation of social problems into clinical syndromes is profoundly antidemocratic.

The disempowering messages of policy design are also the focus of Ingram and Schneider's chapter, but for these authors the greatest threats to democratic citizenship are to be found in the combined influence of political power and social constructions. The elements of policy design send messages about citizenship to target groups. Different target populations of policies receive quite different signals about their status, what sort of game politics is, and how people like themselves are likely to be treated by government. Advantaged groups are reinforced in their pursuit of narrow self-interest, their belief that the obligations of citizenship require little sacrifice, and their lack of empathy with the needs of the less well off. In contrast, dependents and deviant groups are encouraged in their withdrawal and passivity. The participatory mechanisms that are supposed to correct policy errors by reflecting citizen discontent with ineffective or unjust policies simply do not operate. The authors in this section and the entire volume, as the reader will discover, agree about the broad definition of citizenship in a democracy, but differ concerning priorities and emphasis. Landy stresses the collective processes of democracy and the civic duty and self-sacrifice involved in citizenship. For Stone and Ingram and Schneider, democratic citizenship involves individual empowerment, and disempowering effects of some policy designs are identified as particular impediments to citizenship. These authors are skeptical of rights-based claims in policy for different reasons. For Landy, rights claims tend to be absolute, distort policy deliberation, and produce public miseducation. Clinical reasoning, according to Stone, is often used in determining individual eligibility for rights, thus depriving citizens of the opportunity to discover and politically mobilize against discriminatory patterns directed toward entire classes or groups of people, including women, minorities, and the poor. Ingram and Schneider see rights-based policies directed mostly to dependents and criticize such policies for labeling individuals with negative stereotypes, for being mainly symbolic, and for being poorly implemented and funded. Such policies are less empowering than the utilitarian-based policies directed toward advantaged groups.

The authors in this section are attracted to different strategies to improve democratic citizenship. Landy prefers policy designs that decentralize power. Stone favors defining policy issues to highlight value conflicts and engage political processes for conflict resolution. Ingram and Schneider counsel that policy designs should specify policy targets that cut across social divisions and are not easily stereotyped by positive or negative social constructions. Also, they prefer policies that emphasize learning and capacity building. The authors of all three chapters in this section agree that policy analysts can greatly contribute to policies for democracy by critically examining the impact of policies upon citizenship.

2. Public Policy and Citizenship

MARC LANDY

IN THE LAST DECADE the study of public policy has been greatly
enriched by scholars who have refused to limit themselves to the economic assumptions that undergird orthodox "policy analysis."[1] The writings of Deborah Stone, Stephen Kelman, Mary Ann Glendon, Robert
Reich, Lawrence Mead, and James Q. Wilson demonstrate the importance of considering the political effects of policy, and, more particularly,
the influence policy has upon the quality of public life and the character
of the citizenry.[2] These writers are hardly peas in a pod, but each recognizes that policies cannot be evaluated on efficiency criteria alone. Policies
also constitute a teaching: they instruct the public about the aims of government and the rights and responsibilities of citizens. These scholars have
enriched public discourse by reintroducing and legitimizing the use of words
like *character, civic virtue, public spiritedness,* and *deliberation.*

This essay seeks to illuminate further the nature of the relationship
between policy and polity by focusing specifically upon the effects of
policy on citizenship. The Constitution is virtually silent on the obligations of citizenship. This is not accidental. It reflects the Framers' preoccupation with curbing the excesses of popular democracy. But this reti-
cence has been overinterpreted to mean that the governing structures the
Constitution provides are so hardy, and so cleverly designed, that no
serious attention need be paid to the character and quality of the people
over whom they hold sway. In this view, the checks and balances of the
constitutional system work best if, as in a market, each citizen lawfully
and single-mindedly pursues his or her own self-interest. Private vice
produces public virtue. Thus a concern for citizen responsibility was,
until recently, largely written out of the American political and public
policy equation.

1. For a critique of policy analysis in its economistic guise, see Landy (1981).
2. Stone (1988); Kelman (1987); Glendon (1991); Reich (1988); Mead (1986); and
Wilson (1985).

This narrowing of the political field of vision is mistaken, both psychologically and practically. The yearning for a better common life is every bit as real a facet of human personality as the need to satisfy bodily desires. The preservation of the commonwealth depends as much on compassion and sacrifice as it does on the prudent pursuit of private well-being. Of course, public urges are as susceptible to perversion as private ones. The cultivation of citizenship is as much about tempering and moderating excessive zeal as it is about helping people escape the shackles of selfishness.

To the extent that citizenship has been a concern of policymakers and analysts, the emphasis has been upon the rights citizens enjoy and upon how policy can enable them to most fully enjoy and exercise those rights. Although rights are hardly the same as interests, the preoccupation with them can have a similarly corrosive impact. Rights pertain to individuals, not collectivities. They tell people what they are entitled to, not what they owe. A full-fledged concern for citizenship would require policymakers to concern themselves as much with its obligations as with its privileges.

The effort to bring citizenship to the forefront of policymakers' attention owes more to the classical than to the Enlightenment understanding of politics, but it is not, thereby, an exercise in nostalgia. On the contrary, the disrepair of contemporary political life—evidenced by such phenomena as mistrust of representative institutions and low voter turnout—indicates that the constitutional order is badly in need of bolstering and reinvigoration. Fortunately, nothing in the Constitution precludes, or even seriously impedes, such a revitalization. The need is to find constitutionally compatible means for filling the void that noble document has left.

Citizenship

Citizenship is a station that lies between self-absorption and absorption with abstractions. It is tied to sensory experience, hence the meaninglessness of "world citizenship," which is everywhere and thus nowhere. It involves an ongoing effort to synthesize questions of "what is best for the world" with "what is best for me." This task is reducible neither to a narrow utilitarian calculus nor to abstract ethical rumination. It requires a point of reference that is beyond the self and the family but close enough to be apprehended emotionally as well as embraced intellectually. It is tied to place.

The exercise of citizenship involves a distinctive blend of attitudes and skills. Michael Walzer enumerates what one should expect of a citizen: allegiance to the republic, willingness to risk one's life for the national defense, law abidingness, tolerance, and participation.[3] Despite his claim that the list is exhaustive, it is radically incomplete. It ignores the public-spirited impulses needed to promote and sustain the mundane life of communities. Few may be asked to fight in battle, but all will be given an opportunity to sacrifice private pleasures for some public purpose. To do so, one must have the capacity to care about the common good as well as confidence in one's ability to help attain it. Furthermore, these impulses need to be tempered by a healthy egoism lest they impel a futile and disillusioning quest for utopia. Citizens are neither dreamers nor schemers but persons who have the emotional breadth to attach their own well-being to that of a wider community.

Likewise, citizens must develop a strong sense of personal responsibility regarding those public matters over which they have some modicum of control. In private life, one is continually required to take responsibility for addressing problems that one did not cause. It is rare indeed that parents try to escape responsibility for rearing their child on the grounds that they did not cause the child's defects. But such arguments have become quite common in the public realm as people seek to deflect public burdens on grounds of personal innocence.

Walzer rightly stresses the need for toleration in a polity as heterodox as our own. But toleration is too passive a notion to express those qualities needed to enable those of radically different cultural and ideological backgrounds to coexist. Urban life forces different peoples to share common space, whether they like it or not. This can be made tolerable only through the exercise of political arts, the primary one being deliberation.

Deliberation

Deliberation is a collective process for engaging in what Bernard Williams has called "reflective criticism."[4] People work back and forth among the norms and theories they claim to subscribe to and the decisions they have made or are tempted to make. They seek to understand where their ideas conflict and where they are inconsistent with their actual practice. They explore those options they find most compelling as their grasp of the situation improves.

3. Walzer (1980, pp. 54–72).
4. Williams (1985, p. 116).

When people deliberate, they explore what their various ethical ideas imply in a specific context. This acknowledges the possibility that individuals may be wiser than they know—that their decisions may embody ethical insights that their explicit theories have not fully captured. Participants ask themselves, and each other, which norms are relevant to the case at hand: what point of view should be adopted to make a particular decision, recognizing that different definitions of the question imply different answers.

Deliberation is intended to lead to empirical as well as ethical enlightenment. It is an inquiry that profits from the contributions of several minds. It expands available information, enlarges the set of options, and broadens understanding. At its best, it can even improve foresight by encouraging the full discussion of the possible results of alternative courses of action.

Political Deliberation

Many forms of deliberation are possible, including theological, legal, and philosophical. Political deliberation is a quite distinctive form. Although it is not unconcerned with the quest for truth, political deliberation is not simply about the truth. Political deliberators represent particular constituencies and have particular bureaucratic and economic interests. They have particular political goals and ambitions that may be only indirectly related to the subject of a particular deliberation, but their posture in the deliberation will nonetheless be influenced by those other concerns. But they are also listening and learning and trying to fully understand the issues at stake. They may well have a genuine concern for the merits of the question quite apart from practical political concerns.

Political deliberation fosters what Robert Reich terms "civic discovery."[5] Through such deliberation, opinions can be revised, premises altered, and common interests rediscovered. Such discovery does not obviate the need for conciliation and compromise; rather it is a necessary precondition for those activities because it enables the contending parties to determine what it is legitimate to bargain about.

Congressional hearings, or at least some of them, represent a good example of political deliberation. It would be naive to deny that the committee or subcommittee chairman who presides has not orchestrated

5. Reich (1985, p. 1635).

the hearing to produce preordained political and policy objectives. But congressional norms dictate that witnesses representing a wide variety of points of view must be called and that committee members may engage them in real dialogue. Regardless of the preconceptions and aims the participants bring to the occasion, a real possibility exists that as a result of testimony presented and the discussion it provokes, new facts will come to light, understandings will be deepened, and, perhaps, opinions will be changed.[6]

Economic analogies are useful for understanding politics, but this is not to say that the predominant activity of both economics and politics are the same. This unfortunate assumption underlies much of the contemporary analysis of political behavior and institutions, and among its many difficulties is that it has led to underestimation of the importance of political deliberation.

Political life in a democracy, or in a constitutional republic, is dominated by speech. Congressmen, assemblymen, citizen activists, and bureaucrats talk all the time. They sit in hearings, go to meetings, and treat the telephone as if it were an appendage. Would they spend so much time speaking if no one were listening, if their speech would not alter their audience's understanding of the facts and of how those facts should be evaluated? Speech is so omnipresent because speakers have the impression that others are paying attention and that the quality of their speech will influence the outcome of events.

One could imagine the stock or commodities markets functioning without speech. To a large extent they do. Brokers register their buy and sell orders on computers, and transactions take place accordingly. Such a circumstance is unimaginable in the world of republican politics. Voting can be wordless, but voting comes only at the end of the deliberative process, which includes discussion of the issue at hand. In that sense voting is akin to bargaining. It is a crucial mechanism for resolving disputes, but it can occur only at the end of a deliberative chain, after a discussion has occurred about what it is that will be voted on or haggled over.

Much if not most of political speech is composed of appeals to reason and principle. No doubt much of it is hypocritical, disguising claims to naked self-interest. But, in the immortal words of La Rochefoucauld, "Hypocrisy is the homage that vice pays to virtue." These principled appeals would be worthless if there did not exist an audience for appeals to principles and reason. To denigrate the possibility of deliberation in politics one would have to deny the Lincolnian admonition about who can fool whom how much of the time.

Citizenship and the Modern State

To appreciate why public policy is so critical to the cultivation of good citizenship, it is helpful to recognize that for most people, good citizenship, like physical fitness, does not come naturally. It is a regimen and thus requires adherence to a self-imposed, but publicly sanctioned, discipline. The government cannot make good citizens, but its choice of actions makes that regimen relatively easier or harder to follow.

The idea of a republic, and the concomitant notion of republican citizenship, was developed long before the existence of the modern state. The advent of the state poses enormous problems for the practice of citizenship.[7] Inevitably, it centralizes power and creates a class of state agents to exercise that power in ways that are hard to render accountable. And yet the realities of modern life require even those most concerned about the practice of citizenship to acknowledge the need for a strong central state.

The wild fluctuations of the market and the vast increase in the concentration of political and economic power in a small number of hands provided ample justification for the New Deal's expansion of the purposes of government to include income security and the disciplining of corporate power. The inability of states and localities to provide equal protection and due process of law for racial minorities or to cope with a vast array of problems with interstate implications—air and water pollution, welfare, health care—provided additional rationale for the expansion of national policymaking authority in the postwar era.

Citizens cannot function in the wider world of national policymaking as they do closer to home. Jane Mansbridge and Michael Walzer have commented on the need to distinguish among the possibilities provided for citizens by different realms of politics.[8] They argue that decentralization offers the best hope of providing arenas for citizenship. They accept that adversarial goals and tactics will dominate at the national level. Although Mansbridge recognizes that national affairs must retain

7. The most comprehensive discussion of this problem is in de Jouvenel (1962).
8. Mansbridge (1980, p. 89); and Walzer (1980).

some "unitary" component, that is, some sense of common purpose, she expects it to operate only at the level of broad guiding principles and during great national emergencies.[9]

In a previous work my coauthors and I shared Walzer's and Mansbridge's commitment to decentralization as offering the best opportunity for the cultivation of citizenship.[10] But, because we are less sanguine about the results produced by adversarial democracy at the national level, we tried to integrate a concern for civic education and public accountability in this arena as well. We argued that making the state "citizen friendly" requires a reconsideration of the fundamental responsibilities of senior bureaucrats. They must come to see themselves primarily as civic educators. Because they comprise that segment of the expert realm that is most insulated from the adversarial process, they are best situated to take the lead in framing questions so that public debate can be made intelligible. They have the prime responsibility for teasing out the essential social and ethical issues at stake from the welter of scientific data and legal formalisms in which those issues are enveloped.

Thus the nurturance of national citizenship is dependent upon a revised view of leadership, one that enables citizens to exercise their capacities for judgment and deliberation. This view is not inimical to the version of citizenship presented earlier, but it does present a more passive portrait. In the national realm, the citizen has less opportunity for direct involvement in political life, but important rights and responsibilities still attach. Among those rights is the right to demand that the agents of the state remain responsive to citizen concerns and enrich public discourse. Among those responsibilities is the responsibility to provide the state with sufficient resources so that its agents can be sufficiently responsive and educative.

Perhaps the greatest point of tension between a national and a local conception of citizenship is exhibited by the so-called NIMBY (not in my backyard) syndrome, whereby citizens mobilize to protect the quality of life in their own locality by preventing the location of a facility—a prison, hazardous waste incinerator, or a power plant—that is being proposed to further valid national policy objectives. The growing ability of local citizens to successfully block the siting of such facilities is due in large measure to changes in state and federal statutes and regulations requiring that such proposed sites be subjected to intensive local scrutiny.

9. Mansbridge (1980, p. 297).
10. For a discussion of institutional considerations, see Landy, Roberts, and Thomas (1990).

National citizens cannot be expected to function as policy experts, exploring all the ramifications of increasingly esoteric issues. But they cannot escape the responsibility to commit political science, to examine the civic impact of proposed changes in institutional arrangements and of requests to contribute additional resources to the public weal. The rest of this essay explores how policy can be evaluated from a civic perspective.

To consider a particular policy in civic terms, it is useful to abandon a purely instrumental conception of it as a machine designed to spew out specific outputs and to think of it instead as a constitution. The broad enabling statutes that are the cornerstones of public policy do in fact contain all the elements of a "real" constitution. They establish broad ends, prescribe specific institutional arrangements, define powers, and delimit membership. Like the U.S. Constitution, they provide not only a blueprint but a civic teaching. The landmark laws passed during the past few decades impart crucial lessons to citizens about who they are, what rights and duties they possess, and how they are to exercise those rights and fulfill those duties.

Policies as Constitutions: Ends

The American polity is unique in its tendency to consider important public questions as matters of rights. This tendency goes as far back as the Declaration of Independence, which was framed in terms of the securing of rights. Its impact can be seen in the inclusion of a Bill of Rights in our founding document as well as in Lincoln's defense of the Union as a nation "conceived in liberty and dedicated to the proposition that all men are created equal." The Civil War, and Lincoln's rationale for it, constituted a second, rights-based, founding of the Republic. The constitutional underpinning of this rededication of the political community are the Fourteenth and Fifteenth amendments, which provide that the rights outlined in the Constitution would actually be protected by the federal government.

The New Deal expanded upon this revised understanding in two crucial ways. First, as outlined by Franklin D. Roosevelt in his Commonwealth Club address, it explicitly set out to create an economic constitution that would secure economic rights just as the political constitution secured political and civil rights. The content of these rights was not fully elaborated, but they were considered to imply minimal levels of economic security, as provided for by old age pensions and unemployment compensation. Second, the National Labor Relations Act constitutionalized the relationship between unions and management, endowing workers with a right to form unions without fear of reprisal and to compel management to bargain with them in good faith.

The civil rights acts of the 1960s represent both a fulfillment of the Civil War founding and also an extension of the New Deal principle of establishing rights in contexts heretofore viewed as lying outside the purview of government. Protecting the rights of racial minorities to vote, to assemble, and to enjoy a fair trial was simply making good on promises made a hundred years before. But in banning discrimination in hiring and in the provision of certain forms of accommodations, these laws were expanding upon the New Deal effort to endow people with publicly enforceable rights in arenas that had been previously defined as private.

The positive civic consequences of this progression and expansion of rights are almost too obvious to require comment. The very concept of the Republic is predicated upon the ability of all citizens to assemble, speak freely, have their votes recorded fairly, and be protected from discrimination that is based upon their race, gender, religion, or political viewpoint. The extension of such forms of protection from the purely public sphere to the workplace represents a fair recognition that without the ability to earn a livelihood, the possession of political freedom is rendered meaningless. Therefore the exercise of citizenship requires certain forms of economic security and protection from economic discrimination.

The relationship between rights claims and citizenship has become more problematical as a result of the proliferation of such claims since the mid-1960s. Shep Melnick dubs this phenomena "the rights revolution."

> The "rights revolution" refers to the tendency to define nearly every public issue in terms of legally protected rights of individuals. . . . the handicapped . . . workers . . . students . . . racial, linguistic, and religious minorities . . . women . . . consumers, the right to a hearing, the right to know—these have become the stock [in] trade of American political discourse."[11]

A fuller enumeration of rights claims makes Melnick's point even more striking. Claims for the rights of aliens and the unborn extend the uni-

11. Melnick (1989, p. 188).

verse of rights claimants to those not previously considered to be entitled to the full protection of American law and even to those not previously considered persons. The Endangered Species Act expands the universe of rights to the world of plants and animals.

Had the economy continued to grow at the phenomenal rates achieved during much of the 1950s and 1960s, the tensions and conflicts inherent in this proliferation of rights claims might have been more easily suppressed. In the face of declining growth, however, the funds needed to support these claims have become increasingly hard to obtain.

It is of the very nature of these claims to be absolute. A rapidly expanding public budget can avoid placing these claims in close competition with one another or with other valid public goals that are not framed in terms of rights. A shrinking one cannot. The selective introduction of rights-based arguments into the policy formulation process, especially under conditions of austerity, has several anticivic implications: it can distort policy deliberation, produce public miseducation, and threaten the survival of civic collectivities.

The problem of deliberative distortion is illustrated by the recent history of education funding. The percentage of education spending devoted to disabled children has risen dramatically over the past two decades. Despite a decline in total school population, the number of children receiving special education has nearly doubled. In the state of New York, almost 40 percent of students have been defined as in need of "special education." This enormous relative improvement in the educational opportunities available to disabled, as opposed to "normal" or gifted students, is attributable in large measure to the passage of the Education for All Handicapped Children Act of 1975. Among other things, this act creates a right for all handicapped children to receive "a free appropriate education." To ensure that this right is protected, the act mandates that teachers, administrators, and parents meet together each year to devise an "individualized educational program" for each handicapped child. If parents contend that this program does not entirely guarantee their child's lawful right, they may challenge it at an "impartial due process hearing" before an impartial hearing officer. If they are not satisfied by the results of the hearing, they may appeal first to a state review board and then to a federal district court judge.[12]

Federal law establishes no such equivalent right, or procedure for protecting that right, for children who are not disabled. Therefore it is

12. This issue is treated in a masterful fashion by Melnick (forthcoming).

not surprising that state and local education officials strive to protect that portion of the budget devoted to the disabled for fear that the parents of those children will make use of the procedural devices readily available for enforcing their rights claims. In the face of static or declining educational budgets, this ensures that fewer resources will be left for those who are not disabled, who cannot enforce *their* claims in court.

I do not criticize these results. Perhaps this redistribution of educational resources in favor of the disabled constitutes wise policy. But I do criticize the process by which this decision was arrived at. The selective establishment and enforcement of a rights claim made it impossible to conduct a full discussion of the relative merits of apportioning the education budget among the various claimants. Deliberation was forestalled.

In other circumstances, the successful assertion of rights claims renders policy deliberation incoherent and misleads the citizenry about what is truly at stake. For example, the Clean Air Act establishes a right to air quality and, regarding national ambient air standards at least, forbids any consideration of cost in setting standards. Unfortunately, it is impossible to avoid cost considerations when establishing those standards since any reduction in pollution will result in some further diminution in the health risks associated with air pollution. Therefore, in the absence of any concern for cost, pollution standards would require zero emissions and result in the shutdown of all manufacturing and transport. In fact, when regulators set standards they do consider cost but pretend that they do not.[13] By preserving the fiction that there exists a level of pollution above zero that will provide "healthy" air, they are miseducating the citizenry and depriving it of a choice about how much to pay to reduce the risks it has to endure.

As currently construed, rights pertain to individuals, not collectivities. The inability to accord protection to those whose legitimate concerns can only be expressed collectively is poignantly illustrated by the fate of Poletown, a neighborhood in Detroit. As the name implies, Poletown was home to many of eastern European descent. But it was also racially integrated. It contained 1,400 homes, 16 churches, and 144 businesses. In order to enable General Motors to build a new Cadillac assembly plant, the city of Detroit used its powers of eminent domain to acquire the entire neighborhood and raze it to the ground.[14]

Although the move was challenged by an organization of residents,

13. Landy, Roberts, and Thomas (1990).
14. Glendon (1991, pp. 29–30).

30   MARC LANDY

the Michigan Supreme Court denied the petition. It ruled that the city was exercising a valid "public use" in condemning the land in order to create vitally needed construction and manufacturing jobs and therefore it could legitimately take the property of the residents as long as it provided just compensation. The residents had argued that while they could be compensated for their individual tracts of real estate, no amount of compensation could, in Mary Ann Glendon's words, "repair the destruction of roots, relationships, solidarity, sense of place, and shared memory that was at stake."[15] The court could not heed this argument because, in America, property owners do have rights, but communities do not. Therefore Poletown as an entity had no real legal claim. Ironically, if Poletowners had been dusky sparrows or northern spotted owls instead of people, their "habitat" would have had a claim to protection because the law does protect the rights of endangered species, but not human communities, to survive.

One response to the Poletown story, and perhaps to the education funding story as well, would be to try to promote greater deliberative inclusiveness by conveying rights upon an ever greater array of individuals and collectivities as well. Congress could pass an "Endangered Communities Act" that would confer a right to survival upon those neighborhoods or towns that meet the criteria. Or it could pass a "Students Bill of Rights" guaranteeing that the full panoply of rights and procedural guarantees available to disabled students would also be available to those without disabilities.

This would be the wrong lesson to draw. Sad as the story is, and poor as the court's reasoning was, it is far from clear that the wrong decision was made. Detroit is a very poor city. Auto assembly jobs are highly prized by just the kind of person living in Poletown. Community solidarity and remunerative employment are both goods, as is education for the disabled child, the gifted child, and the average child. When goods collide, resort to rights claims prevents the sort of reasoned deliberation required to sort out the actual stakes involved and to clarify the concrete choices that have to be made. Was Poletown really the best or indeed the only site that would have enabled GM to build a plant in Detroit? How solid were the economic prospects for this particular plant and therefore how secure were the jobs being promised? How valuable was Poletown, both to its residents and to the life of the greater metropolitan area? And most important, how could the value attached to the survival of Poletown

15. Glendon (1991, p. 30).

be compared with the value to both Poletowners and other Detroiters of the jobs that the plant promised to produce? In order to be able to ask such subtle and provocative questions, one must first acknowledge that a judgment is being made on the *relative* merits of the different goods at stake, a judgment that the absoluteness of rights claims precludes.

Policies as Constitutions: Powers

The statutory equivalents of constitutional powers are the specific means provided to accomplish the specified ends. The last quarter century has produced extraordinary innovations in this realm. As diverse as these changes are, they have a common source: disillusionment with two preexisting powers, regulation and public provision.

The form of regulation developed during the Progressive Era and widely deployed during the New Deal establishes rigid standards against which to measure the actions of private parties, who are subject to fines or other penalties if they fail to abide by those standards.[16] Critics have charged that this approach is, at best, inefficient and, at worst, counterproductive and have proposed alternatives means to the same ends.

One alternative approach might be called ends-directed. Instead of specifying what to do, the government requires that certain results be achieved. For example, in response to industry's claim that it could not meet stringent new air quality standards, government responded by adopted a "technology-forcing" approach, requiring industry to develop the new technology that would be required to meet those standards. The law assumed that if industry put its mind to the problem it would be able to make whatever engineering breakthroughs would be required to get the job done.

A second strategy specifies not the ends themselves, but the nature of the deliberation that private parties must engage in when arriving at certain decisions. Two good examples of this approach are the affirmative action provisions of the Civil Rights Act and the environmental impact requirements of the National Environmental Protection Act (NEPA). Affirmative action does not require employers to hire anyone in particular, but it does insist that they make a serious effort to solicit applications from minority groups and to give serious and fair consideration to those applications. Likewise, NEPA does not specify what sorts of projects should or should not be built. But it does force developers to demonstrate

16. Schultze (1977).

that they gave thorough consideration to the environmental consequences of alternative design options.

From a citizenship standpoint, these seemingly opposite approaches actually have a great deal in common. If an industry can demonstrate that its strenuous efforts to invent new technology have not panned out, neither Congress nor the bureaucracy is likely to punish it. On the other hand, if an employer's seemingly fair procedures *never* actually lead to the hiring of minority candidates, he is unlikely to escape sanction. In both cases, therefore, the emphasis is really neither on result nor procedure but upon good-faith effort. This bespeaks a qualitative change in the relationship between the citizen and the government in that one is now accountable not just for one's actions but for one's intentions as well.

Evaluating intentions is a legitimate, indeed a necessary, aspect of political deliberation and of legal deliberation as well. When citizens gather, they must make a judgment about the character of various speakers in order to judge the validity of the competing recommendations they are presented with. The law distinguishes among crimes on the basis of the intent of the perpetrator. But these are determinations to be rendered by assemblies and juries, not bureaucrats. A constitutional democracy provides no basis for granting government agents the power to read people's minds.

Because American bureaucrats still think of themselves as citizens, they are uncomfortable with such power. Therefore they tacitly or overtly abandon the considerations of intentionality they are supposed to employ. They will evaluate an environmental impact statement in terms of the comprehensiveness of the consultant reports it contains rather than try to determine whether serious consideration was actually given to the alternatives that were rejected. Likewise, they will subtly transform affirmative action guidelines into quota systems rather than have to determine whether a good-faith effort to hire minorities was actually made. These subversions of statutory intent may have dire policy consequences, but, seen in another light, they represent a great victory for republican rule.

Action Forcing

A single statute, the Clean Air Act, contains two different action-forcing provisions that neatly illustrate how similar means can have dissimilar consequences when they are placed in the service of different ends. One provision of the act requires the Environmental Protection Agency (EPA) to ban new construction and to cut off certain federal funds in states that fail to institute acceptable automobile inspection and maintenance programs. Although this is, by historical and comparative standards, a very draconian policy tool, its use is readily justifiable in view of the end it serves. Reducing auto pollution emissions requires that car engines burn properly and that their emissions controls devices work properly. The requirement that states conduct periodic inspections to make sure that cars are working properly constitutes a readily defensible aim of policy. In fact, strong consensus did exist in Congress regarding the legitimacy of this requirement. When the EPA announced its intention of applying the ban on new construction to two states that had failed to institute inspection and maintenance programs, those states, sensing that the weight of public and congressional opinion was against them, did indeed comply.[17]

A very different situation has developed regarding the broader requirement of the act, which insists that states face the same sort of construction ban and cutoff of funds if they fail to meet the various air quality standards the act imposes by the deadline it specifies. Originally the act required that these standards be achieved by 1975. Then the deadline was deferred to 1982. When many metropolitan areas failed to meet that deadline, the act's strongest congressional supporters, as well as key environmental leaders, joined in an effort to pass an appropriations bill rider preventing the EPA from imposing a construction ban on those states that had failed to comply. As of 1992 there has still been no effort to impose the action-forcing penalties the act requires.[18]

The key to this embarrassing failure is the illegitimacy of the ends this policy purports to serve. Originally the air quality standards were defended on the grounds that they were required to protect the public health. This rationale was undermined by the inability of public health science to discover actual thresholds below which the public was safe and above which it was endangered. Although, from a health standpoint, less pollution is always better than more, no strong rationale could be established for picking a specific numerical standard and punishing states or communities for failing to achieve it. Given the continuous nature of pollution risk, a much stronger rationale could be established for taxing

17. Melnick (1992, p. 93).
18. Melnick (1992, pp. 91–94).

all emissions, thereby giving polluters an incentive to continuously lower the amount of pollutants they emitted. The willingness of even the most zealous environmentalists to accede to postponing the imposition of mandated penalties for noncompliance is a tacit acknowledgment that the goals they are supposed to accomplish are simply not worth the extremely high price, both political and economic, that would have to be paid to attain them. For political reasons, however, they are unwilling to support abolishing the standards. In Melnick's apt depiction,

> Deadlines—or, perhaps more accurately, the ghost of deadlines passed—constitute a reminder of how much remains to be done. In a very real sense, deadlines are made to be broken. . . . Perpetual failure to meet deadlines gives those who advocate more pollution control a key rhetorical advantage. Why is the government still refusing to do what is right?[19]

These political advantages come at a high civic price. By giving credence to the notion that government is once again failing to meet its responsibilities, stretching out the deadlines hastens the spread of public cynicism that has already reached pandemic proportions. All too much of this cynicism is well justified. However, in this case the ends of policy have been inappropriately framed in a manner that more or less guarantees that they cannot be attained. In fact, as Melnick also points out, many aspects of the government's attack on air pollution have been quite successful. The high degree of public cynicism is in fact unwarranted, and yet by promoting an uncritical acceptance of the notion that government can do no right, the act's proponents help to undermine the capacity of citizens to critically evaluate government action.[20]

Deliberation Forcing

Deliberation forcing is a laudable, yet very subtle and delicate, policy tool. Its ostensible purpose is not to obtain any particular result but rather to change the way decisionmakers think and the processes by which they reach decisions in order to ensure that previously underemphasized values and principles are given their proper due. Thus it does not dictate any particular substantive outcome, but rather requires that more careful

19. Melnick (1992, p. 98).
20. Melnick (1992, pp. 99–100).

and sustained attention be paid to certain attributes of outcomes. Its virtue is in enriching the quality and character of the decisionmaking process itself. Because the objectives of this policy device are so subtle, those who must implement and evaluate are placed in a very difficult situation. In search of clear-cut standards for evaluation they are sorely tempted either to substitute their judgment about outcomes for those of the ostensible deliberators, thus turning deliberation forcing into just another form of action forcing, or to establish purely procedural standards of evaluation, thereby enabling sophisticated decisionmakers to merely "go through the motions" without deliberating about alternatives.

Both these distortions entail serious civic consequences. As I have shown above, action forcing is a technique that can readily be justified. But it also highly coercive and disruptive. In a liberal regime, responsibility for its deployment should rest with elected representatives who can articulate to the public why it is necessary and can be held accountable for its success or failure. When action forcing takes place surreptitiously, under the guise of enhanced deliberation, the public is at a loss as to what is actually going on and whom to hold responsible.

On the other hand, when deliberation forcing degenerates into mere form filling, it heightens public cynicism. "Everybody knows" that all one needs to do to meet seemingly stringent environmental impact statements or affirmative action requirements is to place the right advertisements, put a token African-American or woman on your "short list," and hire sophisticated consultants to prepare your documentation. This has a particularly serious impact upon those who participate in such shenanigans. The citizens' groups who find that all the seemingly serious consideration given to their environmental concerns actually leads to no real change in the outcome and the minority group members who find that being interviewed never seems to actually result in getting a job become even more convinced that playing by the rules is a waste of time. Those who master the game of procedural charades lose respect both for themselves and for a government that would force them to expend their time and energy in such a demeaning fashion.

Even at its best, deliberation forcing can only ensure that a partial form of deliberation will occur. It can provide that previously underrepresented perspectives will be taken into account, but not that all relevant concerns will be accorded their proper weight. In certain circumstances, forcing deliberation about one set of ends renders the attainment of other ones all the more difficult and unlikely.

Suppose that a state desperately needs a new hospice for AIDS victims.

Although it is still important that the hospice be located where it will cause the least environmental and social disruption, those goals are subordinate to the broader social objective of building the hospice. It is at least arguable that it is better to build the hospice in the "wrong" place than not to build it at all. Under such circumstances, the potential for delay inherent in an environmental impact process can well serve to undermine that objective as community after community presents well-documented arguments about why it is poorly suited to serve as the host for the hospice and the agency responsible for constructing it must demonstrate that it has fully accounted for and considered these myriad arguments. It might well be that every community in a state can demonstrate its environmental unsuitability, but does this mean that the hospice should not be built? Rather, such partial deliberations must give way to fuller ones, ensuring that valuable but limited objectives are subordinated to broader and even more valuable goals.

Deregulation, Privatization, and Managed Markets

Analysis of the more conservative forms of policy innovation has likewise suffered from inattention to the relationship between means and ends. When the ends to be served are truly well suited to marketlike means, palpable efficiencies can be realized. Unfortunately, such techniques are too often advocated as means for attaining ends for which they are wildly inappropriate. For example, a key argument in favor of markets is that, unlike regulation, they do not appear to be coercive. If government orders one to leave town, one is likely to resist. But if market forces deprive one of a job, and the unemployment rate in town is high, one is very likely to leave town on one's own.[21]

This argument is true as far as it goes, but it makes the unwarranted assumption that coercion, or, to be more accurate, the perception of coercion, is always a bad thing. From the standpoint of citizenship, public coercion can be highly desirable. Citizens are not saints. They are prone to be law abiding and public spirited, but they do not like to be taken for chumps. If they observe others flouting the norms that they are struggling to abide by, their reserves of law abidingness will be sapped and eventually they too will disobey. For the well intentioned there is no more bracing tonic than the sight of miscreants being punished.

21. Schultze (1977, pp. 17–19).

Another virtue of market mechanisms is their flexibility. If installing a new piece of abatement technology is too expensive for a particular firm, it can choose to pay higher pollution taxes instead. But, however much such flexibility may contribute to economic efficiency, it may well hamper civic education. Strict standards enable citizens to know when they are doing right and when they are doing wrong. The freedom to pay the tax instead of cleaning up means that no moral onus is being cast upon the behavior in question.

These caveats do not imply that old-fashioned "command and control" regulation is always to be preferred to the use of economic incentives, but rather that the choice be made with an eye toward its civic implications. Ironically, the case that has aroused the most attention and debate, the use of incentives to control air and water quality, would survive such a civic test. With regard to most forms of pollutants, the public interest involves the total amount of the pollutant to be found in the air or water, not the amount of emissions from a particular source. Under such circumstances, pollution should be conceived of as a residual of the manufacturing process, not an antisocial phenomenon. A factory emitting sulfur into the air is not committing a sin. It is simply using resources (in this case, air) that it is not paying for. Because causing such residuals is not morally abhorrent, the public need not apply moral sanction against individual polluters as long as they are paying the appropriate amount for the privilege.

In this context, citizens would want to pursue the goal of economic efficiency since it is hardly in their best interest to squander resources. That goal is best served by allowing polluters to sort themselves out in terms of how much to invest in abatement and how much taxes to pay. If such a process does not result in the optimum level of overall reduction, then it is sufficient to raise the taxes until that level is attained.

But consider industrial accidents. One might argue that, unlike air pollution emissions, lax safety conditions are an unacceptable violation of public norms. Therefore guilty firms deserve punishment regardless of their economic circumstances. Even if rigid standards impose excessive economic burdens, they provide a salutary emblem of civic intolerance of such practices.

The same logic applies to deregulation and privatization. Trucking deregulation has few civic implications. Despite the self-serving arguments of the Teamsters Union, its major impact has been to improve the economic well-being of the nation by lowering shipping costs. But the savings and loan fiasco has quite different implications. Savings and loans were established to provide a crucial civic function, the provision of mortgage money for home purchase and other forms of community improvement. The deregulation of other forms of banking placed them at a competitive disadvantage in acquiring deposits. The lifting of the ceiling on the rate of interest they could pay depositors removed that obstacle, but only at the cost of displacing the savings and loans' original mission. In order to make high enough returns to pay those high rates of interest, the savings and loans were forced to look for more lucrative and speculative forms of investment than home mortgages. Therefore, even if the unique combination of deregulation and subsidy (in the form of federal deposit insurance) they were accorded had not resulted in massive losses, it could not have been justified on civic grounds.

Likewise, the privatization of garbage collection survives the civic impact standard, while the voucher system for providing primary and secondary education does not. Economic efficiency considerations are paramount in determining how to pick up trash but not in how children are schooled. A voucher system encourages parents to think like shoppers, choosing the best product from the array they are being offered. It is precisely because a public school system limits "shopping" that it encourages parents to think like citizens.[22] Since they are "stuck" in a particular school district, they have very strong incentives to exercise their political skills to make it better. And, because it is a *public* school, they are guaranteed the right to exercise those skills.

Also, school is one of the primary locations in which citizen education takes place. Therefore the entire citizenry, not just the parent body, has a legitimate interest in the character and quality of what goes on there. Although the market is an excellent mechanism for providing a wide variety of alternatives, it is incapable of ensuring that crucial common principles are taught. A public school board, and its parent-teacher organizations, provide excellent deliberative forums for determining what those common principles are and how they are most effectively transmitted.

Critics of the public schools are right to point out that they have too often turned into "state schools," governed not by local communities but by national accrediting and testing organizations, the U.S. Department of Education, and the national trade unions of teachers and supervisors. However, given the transcendent importance of the schools in the process of civic education, it would be a mistake to respond to this disheartening

22. For the definitive treatment of this problem, see Hirschman (1970).

situation by abandoning the principle of public education itself. It is not too late for parents and neighbors to reclaim their local schools and insist on governing them according to their lights.

Membership

As the writings of Grant McConnell and Theodore Lowi have so amply documented, the welter of federal policies that arose during the New Deal conferred special participatory privileges upon specific segments of the populace. For example, farm organizations are involved in the implementation of farm policy, and ranchers help determine the allocation of federal grazing land. Although these grants of special access to decisionmaking are justified on the grounds of efficiency, they also serve to confer a privileged, quasi-official status on these same private parties.[23]

Federal policy initiatives of the 1960s and 1970s represent departures from the New Deal pattern in two important senses. Although certain of these, especially those connected with the war on poverty, do convey privileged decisionmaking access to special groups, the rationale for this grant of authority was different. These groups form some of the most economically deprived and politically dispossessed elements of the population. It was hoped that by involving them in decisions affecting their lives those decisions would not only be more conducive to their needs, but that this opportunity to participate would in fact change their lives by giving them a new sense of efficacy and diminishing their feelings of anomie.

The environmental and consumer statutes enacted during the 1970s serve to confer new participatory privileges on everyone. They make bureaucratic decisionmaking far more open to public scrutiny and involvement. They compel the holding of public hearings at various stages of the regulatory process and require that agencies elicit public comments, and respond to those comments, before issuing regulations. Many also include citizen suit provisions that enable virtually anyone to sue the government for failure to implement the law adequately. Some even award grants to groups seeking to develop their own data resources on the basis of which they can determine if in fact the law is being enforced.

These new initiatives have had mixed results from a citizen perspective. Community action programs (CAPs) did serve as political mobilizers and

23. McConnell (1966); and Lowi (1969).

recruitment vehicles. Active involvement and scrutiny by public interest groups undoubtedly provided safeguards against bureaucratic arbitrariness and parochiality. But neither of these efforts have been able to achieve the broad expansion of citizen involvement they promised. The CAPs made no detectable impact upon low participation rates or other indices of social isolation and anomie. The participation resulting from the new environmental and consumer laws has been limited, for the most part, to the staff-dominated Washington "public interest" groups that have sufficient expertise to overcome the barriers to participation erected by the highly esoteric nature of environmental and other forms of judicial and bureaucratic regulatory proceedings. As Sidney Milkis has pointed out, this failure is due to the inability of participatory politics to cope successfully with the vagaries and complexities of a political world dominated by administration. These participatory efforts self-consciously sought not to restrain administrative power but to make it more democratic. They underestimated the degree to which the very nature of administration renders it a poor venue for democratic life. In Milkis's words, "They [consumer and environmental laws] devolved public authority to a less visible institutional coalition of bureaucratic agencies, courts, congressional subcommittees and public interest groups. . . ."[24] By doing so, they underscore the problem of sustaining democratic citizenship within an institutional arena extensively insulated from the vagaries of public opinion, elections, and legislative deliberation. To the extent that these approaches serve as substitutes for enlivening the traditional avenues of representative government—such as town councils, state legislatures, and Congress—and for rendering those institutions more accountable, they actually undermine the capacity of a democratic citizenry to flourish.

A more fruitful avenue for empowering citizens is that of full-fledged political decentralization. The centralization of policy direction at the national level is inimical to citizenship because it deprives local civic forums of weighty matters to deliberate about. Citizens are unlikely to expend the painstaking effort civic participation requires if they have the sense that all the really important decisions are being made in Washington. Centralization also encourages citizens to be irresponsible. If the funds to handle a particular problem are attainable from Washington, then there is no reason for the local citizenry to fix it themselves.

As I argued earlier, the conditions of modern existence make govern-

24. Milkis (1989, p. 170).

ment centralization inevitable. But not all forms of centralization are equally necessary. The problems posed for citizenship provide a strong rationale for considering each new centralizing initiative on its own merits. Some claims about the benefits of centralization may well prove spurious ("the states can't be trusted to deal with this question"). Others involving economies of scale, the need for national uniformity, or the existence of significant interstate spillovers may well prove genuine. But then it is still necessary to determine whether the gains they provide outweigh the civic losses they incur.

An Illustration: Superfund

An examination of a single federal statute provides a clearer sense of how these diverse "constitutional" elements combine to affect citizenship. Superfund, passed in 1980 and reauthorized and expanded in 1986, is the federal statute governing cleanup of abandoned hazardous waste sites. It mandates that all eligible sites be cleaned up to meet federal air, water, and hazardous waste standards. The cleanup is to be conducted either by those responsible, at their expense, or by the government (state or federal), also at the responsible parties' expense. If the responsible parties cannot be found, the government conducts the cleanup with funds obtained from a tax imposed on chemical feedstocks.[25]

The goal of uniform cleanup to meet all applicable standards does not frame the issue in a way that enables citizens to think intelligently about it. It appears to establish a right to total freedom from risk, but there are far too many eligible sites, and the costs of this high level of cleanup are far too great, to make this goal obtainable. However, since the right to full cleanup has been proclaimed, the EPA must pretend that all eligible sites will in fact receive such complete attention. Therefore the agency is constrained from establishing sensible guidelines and procedures for setting priorities among sites and for determining how much money and effort to expend on each one. This is bad policy, but, more important, it miseducates the public about the true nature of the problem at hand and the choices at stake.

President Jimmy Carter, as well as Superfund's congressional supporters, defended the fee on chemical feedstocks on the grounds that business, not the public, would pay for the program. This is untrue. Chemical feedstocks are the building blocks of the plastics industry and

25. Landy, Roberts, and Thomas (1990, pp. 204–37).

are thus to be found in virtually all consumer products. The industry passes this tax directly to the customer in the form of higher prices for Scotch tape, compact disks, and computer games. The universe of consumers of such products is virtually identical with that of the taxpaying public, and so the chemical feedstock tax is really a form of sales tax. Yet citizens received the impression that the program is free.

Superfund's most serious impact upon citizenship is embedded in the structure of the program itself. The very decision to handle this problem on a national basis vastly reduced the degree of responsibility to be taken by the citizens of an affected community and the deliberative capacity of the citizens of the several states. Sites do not move. The spillover rationale for federal involvement that is so compelling with regard to waterways and airsheds is largely absent. Because cleanup is perceived to be free, local citizens have no incentive to deliberate about how much cleanup a site actually merits. More is always better. No claim is made on their sense of responsibility. After all, they did not make the mess, so why should they have to contribute to cleaning it up?

Conclusion

This examination of policy in constitutional terms provokes a reconsideration of policy objectives and policy design on the basis of each of the three key constitutional components: ends, means, and membership.

The tendency to consider policy aims in terms of rights should be checked and a broader deliberative framework established in which rights claims are balanced against considerations of duty and obligation. De Jouvenel compares "the dissonance of rights to the consonance of duties."[26] The enhancement of citizenship requires the achievement of new harmonies based on greater concern for the good of the whole and the responsibilities each should bear to achieve it. This does not involve abandoning the rights-based liberalism upon which this country was founded, but it does involve tempering and modulating the cacophonies to which it has fallen prone.

The consideration of which policy means to employ must extend beyond concerns for efficiency and effectiveness. Policy analysis is too important to be left either to the economists or to the advocates. It must include a broad consideration of the relationship between ends and means, on the basis of which the full civic consequences of alternative design techniques can be evaluated.

26. de Jouvenel (1957).

The new definitions of membership contained in modern antipoverty, environmental, and consumer legislation do not provide an adequate substitute for older geographically based notions of citizenship. The key to empowering citizens as well as rendering them more responsible is to enliven local forms of government by devolving greater power to them. However, advocates of decentralization too often obscure its dangers in a haze of nostalgia for community life gone by. Communities can be despotic. Decentralization must be limited to those policy spheres where minority rights can be fully protected.

If policies may be conceived of as constitutions, then their designers are, in some important sense, founders. Like their illustrious predecessors, policymakers must reconcile specific policy objectives with a concern for the long-term political health of the Republic. The Founding Fathers fashioned a set of institutions whose purpose was to sustain both liberty and order. Only by emulating both their breadth of vision and their skills as institutional architects will it be possible for their descendants to strike the proper balance between protecting individual rights, accomplishing important public objectives, and promoting civic responsibility.

References

Glendon, Mary Ann. 1991. *Rights Talk: The Impoverishment of Political Discourse*. Free Press.

Hirschman, Albert O. 1970. *Exit, Voice, and Loyalty: Responses to Decline in Firms, Organizations, and States*. Harvard University Press.

de Jouvenel, Bertrand. 1957. *Sovereignty: An Inquiry into the Political Good*. Translated by J. F. Huntington. Cambridge University Press.

———. 1962. *On Power*. Boston: Beacon Press.

Kelman, Steven. 1987. *Making Public Policy: A Hopeful View of American Government*. Basic Books.

Landy, Marc. 1981. "Policy Analysis as a Vocation." *World Politics* 33 (April): 468–84.

Landy, Marc K., Marc J. Roberts, and Stephen R. Thomas. 1990. *The Environmental Protection Agency: Asking the Wrong Questions*. Oxford University Press.

Lowi, Theodore J. 1969. *The End of Liberalism: Ideology, Policy, and the Crisis of Public Authority*. Norton.

McConnell, Grant. 1966. *Private Power and American Democracy*. Knopf.

Mansbridge, Jane J. 1980. *Beyond Adversary Democracy*. Basic Books.

Mead, Lawrence M. 1986. *Beyond Entitlement: The Social Obligations of Citizenship*. Free Press.

44   MARC LANDY

Melnick, R. Shep. 1989. "The Courts, Congress, and Programmatic Rights." In *Remaking American Politics*, edited by Richard A. Harris and Sidney M. Milkis, 188–212. Westview Press.

———. 1992. "Pollution Deadlines and the Coalition for Failure." In *Environmental Politics: Public Costs, Private Rewards*, edited by Michael S. Greve and Fred L. Smith Jr., 89–103. Praeger.

———. Forthcoming. "Separation of Powers and the Strategy of Rights: The Expansion of Special Education." In *The New Politics of Public Policy*, edited by Marc Landy and Martin Levin. Johns Hopkins University Press.

Milkis, Sidney M. 1989. "The Presidency, Policy Reform, and the Rise of Administrative Politics." In *Remaking American Politics*, edited by Richard A. Harris and Sidney M. Milkis, 146–87. Westview.

Quirk, Paul. Forthcoming. "Regulatory Policy in the New Congress." In *The New Politics of Public Policy*, edited by Marc Landy and Martin Levin. Johns Hopkins University Press.

Reich, Robert B. 1985. "Public Administration and Public Deliberation: An Interpretive Essay." *Yale Law Journal* 94 (June): 1617–41.

———, ed. 1988. *The Power of Public Ideas*. Cambridge, Mass.: Ballinger.

Schultze, Charles L. 1977. *The Public Use of Private Interest*. Brookings.

Stone, Deborah A. 1988. *Policy Paradox and Political Reason*. Scott, Foresman.

Walzer, Michael. 1980. "Civility and Civic Virtue in Contemporary America." In *Radical Principles: Reflections of An Unreconstructed Democrat*, edited by Michael Walzer, 54–72. Basic Books.

Williams, Bernard. 1985. *Ethics and the Limits of Philosophy*. Harvard University Press.

Wilson, James Q. 1985. "The Rediscovery of Character: Private Virtue and Public Policy." *Public Interest* 81 (Fall): 3–16.

3. Clinical Authority in the Construction of Citizenship

DEBORAH A. STONE

IN THIS VOLUME, the authors turn the traditional question of democratic theory on its head and ask not what kinds of policies a democratic society should or does produce, but rather how public policies shape the processes of democracy. Does a policy encourage citizen participation? Does it create structures of influence that enable "little people" to express their views and see them translated into future policy? Does it tell citizens that political participation might be worthwhile? Does it enable citizens to participate in formulating the central political questions, or does it bring them into decisionmaking when they can only ratify preselected choices?

To talk about how and whether public policies empower citizens, one needs a definition of power. Political scientists have evolved a complex notion of power that is neatly captured in Steven Lukes's imagery of "three dimensions of power."[1] The first dimension of power is the ability to influence the outcome of specific decisions. The second dimension is the ability to influence the agenda, or the menu of choices from which any specific decision is made. The third dimension (and the one least adequately addressed by empirical studies) is the ability to influence consciousness—to define core ideas, shape people's wants and tastes, frame issues, and define the standards of proof for evaluating claims to knowledge. Any inquiry into the effects on democracy of public policies must consider all three dimensions of power.

This essay addresses the third dimension, the one most neglected in analyses of citizen participation and democracy, and focuses on one particular form of third-dimension power: clinical reason. Clinical reason, I will try to show, is a pattern of thinking derived from clinical medicine and used to evaluate and classify citizens in many areas of social policy far removed from medicine and health. This mode of reasoning

1. Lukes (1974).

45

has attained such enormous cultural authority and widespread popular acceptance that it has come to be a dominant mode of resolving social conflict and exercising social control. Further, I will argue, clinical authority often removes power from individuals, placing it instead in the hands of clinicians and professional researchers, and it defines political issues in ways that highlight individual behavior and ignore structural and relational understandings.

There are other forms of third-dimension power whose analysis is germane to democratic theory and public policy. Perhaps the most hegemonic idea-belief system in contemporary political and policy thinking is the nexus of rational choice theory, microeconomic efficiency models, and cost-benefit analysis, which might be called "the rationality project."[2] Another powerful form of cultural authority is the concept of rights and legal reasoning at the heart of a broad range of political issues and policy arenas where discrimination and civil rights are the inspirational metaphors: issues of race relations, gender relations, generational conflict, prisons and mental health institutions, and disability, for example.[3] A third domain of cultural authority is certainly religion.[4] Thus I do not pretend that clinical reason is the only form of cultural authority in contemporary politics, but it is probably the least recognized and the least well understood.

The Model of Clinical Reason

Clinical reason is a way of thinking about and acting on human problems. It derives from clinical medicine but has expanded far beyond the domain of medicine to be incorporated by a variety of professionals who process human beings. As I define it, clinical reason has three key components. First, it is based on observations of individuals, the derivation of norms from these observations, and the reapplication of the norms back to an individual. Second, clinical reason bases its observations of individuals on imaging techniques, that is, modes of observation and measurement that claim to render visible something that is invisible to the ordinary person. Third, it uses measurement and quantification to describe the characteristics of individuals and, through measurement, promises objectivity.

2. This is my own term (Stone 1988).
3. Scheingold (1974); Horowitz (1977); and Glendon (1991).
4. Wuthnow (1988); and Hunter (1991).

CLINICAL AUTHORITY 47

From Statistical to Normative Normality

Clinical reason begins with an examination of the individual. It expects to find the source of trouble in the individual, and it promises to locate and define problems by measuring something inside the boundaries of the person. At the same time, trouble is identified by comparing the individual to previously established norms. Those norms, in turn, are derived by compiling measurements of a large number of individuals. Thus clinical reason is simultaneously individualistic and comparative.

In this intellectual schema, trouble is defined as deviance from a group norm. As Michel Foucault noted about nineteenth-century medicine,

> Medicine must no longer be confined to a body of techniques for curing ills . . . it will also embrace a knowledge of the *healthy man*, that is, a study of *non-sick man* and a definition of the *model man*. In the ordering of human existence it assumes a normative posture, which authorizes it not only to distribute advice as to healthy life, but also to dictate the standards for physical and moral relations of the individual and the society in which he lives. . . . Nineteenth century medicine . . . was regulated more in accordance with normality than with health.[5]

The orientation of clinical reason toward *statistical* normality is still a prominent feature of contemporary medicine. Every new diagnostic technology requires calibration of norms, and at the time of introduction of a new technology, clinicians often have difficulty distinguishing mere statistical abnormality from pathological (harmful) abnormality. As breast mammography was introduced, for example, radiologists saw a high number of abnormalities in the statistical sense, simply because there is normal variation in breast tissue, and physicians did not know what to make of these abnormalities because they had never before had this kind of visual (radiologic) image to correlate with malignancy. Women with these abnormalities were (and are) treated as "cancer suspects," and subjected to further diagnostic testing to determine whether the abnormal visual findings were true malignancies. This is typically true of new clinical technologies (whether they are physical diagnostic tests or psychological tests): statistical deviations are considered pathological until proven otherwise. With diagnostic tests for cancer, it is easy to see the

5. Foucault (1973, pp. 34–35).

virtue of this assumption. Imagine a standardized test for intelligence or personality disorder, however, and the assumption becomes more troubling.

Observation as Imaging

Clinical reason promises to render visible something hidden. Its aim is to reveal the characteristics that define people's abilities to function biologically and socially. This aspect might be called imaging. All forms of diagnosis entail making visible what is going in the body or mind and comparing the features thus revealed with population norms.

Diagnostic technique in medicine rests on three kinds of imaging. The earliest form was testing things extracted from the body, such as blood, urine, feces, air, or bone marrow, to measure the performance of organ systems. (Freudian psychiatry applies this same form of diagnosis, using slips of the tongue, word associations, dreams, and other "verbal excretions" to reveal what is happening in the psyche.) A second kind of diagnostic test invades the body with instruments or particles to render the inside visible. Examples of imaging technologies are cardiac catheterization, fiber optic examinations (for example, of stomachs, joints), X rays, ultrasound, sonograms, and magnetic resonance imaging. All these technologies produce literal pictures of the inside of the body. A third type of diagnostic test challenges the body and measures how it responds. Examples are the glucose tolerance test for diabetes (in which a patient drinks a highly concentrated sugar drink and subsequent blood tests measure how well the body can metabolize it), liver clearance tests, cardiac stress tests, and the various signs for pain (in which a physician moves a patient in a certain way to see whether the patient responds with "pain behavior" such as a scream or a grimace or a sudden stiffening). These tests are all based on the idea of forcing the body to perform in some way that reveals its true capacities.

Diagnostic imaging techniques liberate physicians from the subjective knowledge and reports of the patient. They give doctors direct access to what is going on inside the patient, so they are no longer dependent on the patient's description and interpretations. In the jargon of clinical medicine, they provide doctors with "signs," which are objective indicators of disease, and make them less reliant on "symptoms," which are only experiences and interpretations of the sick person.[6] Embedded in

6. Resier's (1978) study of the historical development of medical technology shows

the use of imaging techologies is a claim that they reveal an objective truth about the person, and that when there is a discrepancy between the subjective claims of the individual and the data provided by imaging, the imaging information is correct.

Clinical imaging technologies are often used precisely in political situations where there is a dispute between a citizen and an agency over some characteristic of the citizen. Indeed, several early medical technologies, such as the ophthalmoscope and the spirometer (a device for measuring lung capacity), were touted as means of detecting malingerers among military recruits who claimed to be unable to serve.[7] Pain has proven to be a particularly nettlesome phenomenon in agencies that use disability as a criterion (for example, disability insurance programs or courts presiding over injury claims) because so far there is no uncontested means of translating pain into a visual image. Thermography, a technique of measuring heat waves generated by body tissues, is currently a major object of conflict in American courts. Its proponents say it is a sort of pain thermometer, a device that translates true pain into physical and visual correlates, and thus could indicate whether plaintiffs are exaggerating their "pain and suffering" to increase monetary damages they are awarded.[8] Alcoholism is another area of social policy conflict for which imaging technology is offered as a resolution. Disputes over drunkenness and the prosecution of car drivers, ship and plane pilots, or workers for causing accidents turn on whether the defendant was "really" drunk. State laws generally use a measure of blood alcohol level as a standard and set a fixed standard for the entire population. Defense attorneys, naturally enough, argue that alcohol affects people differently and that only a behavioral—not a chemical—standard is fair. A new technology uses computer analysis of sound waves from tape-recorded speech to produce pictures of the speech patterns of people who are known to be either sober or drunk. Then speech patterns of individual defendants are compared with these norms.[9]

The imaging aspect of diagnosis is central to political and social au-

that new diagnostic technologies were extolled and promoted specifically for their ability to free the physician from dependence on the patient. For another excellent essay on the political import of diagnostic imaging, see Petchesky (1987).

7. Resier (1978, pp. 44, 47).

8. Boyce Rensberger, "Heat 'Pictures' of Pain Expected to Aid Sufferers, Detect Fakers," New York Times, October 21, 1980, p. C3.

9. Katherine Bishop, "Leaps of Science Create Quandaries on Evidence," New York Times, April 6, 1990, p. B6.

thority because it seems to bring private information out into public. Clinical imaging not only appears to reveal bodily truths that a person might knowingly or willingly conceal; it also seems to be able to reveal truths of which the individual may have no consciousness.

Objectivity and Reification

Clinical reason is rooted in quantification and measurement. Through measurement, it promises objectivity. The assumption of clinical reason is that some feature of the person, such as tissues or organs, mental capacity, learning ability, or physical capacity, has measurable characteristics. These characteristics are relatively fixed properties of the person, and their measurement, if done correctly, remains stable across different observers.

A great deal of professional effort is expended in developing objective measurement technologies that are not susceptible to manipulation by the patient or client. For example, some measures of breathing capacity, known as lung function tests, measure the amount of air a person can inhale or exhale in a fixed time. Lung function tests are key diagnostic measures in occupational disability assessments and fitness examinations, but clinicians have always understood that these tests are "effort-dependent": different readings result depending on how hard the person tries. Therefore, the test results are also somewhat sensitive to the interaction between the tester and the person being tested, since testers can coach, encourage, cajole, or provoke people into trying harder. Because respiratory difficulties are one of the three or four most common disabling conditions in work disability, clinicians are always searching for a new technique that is less subject to manipulation by the tester or testee.

Clinical reason actually claims two kinds of objectivity. First, there is objectivity in the measurement of individual characteristics, traits, or behaviors. And second, with proper statistical techniques, there is objectivity in the combination of multiple measurements into a predictive diagnosis. There is a branch of decision science and cognitive psychology that seeks to make clinical judgments more accurate, essentially by using mathematical formulas instead of individual judgment to derive the aggregate group norms from individual measurements and to make predictions about individuals based on the group norms. In this literature, the term *clinical judgment* is often juxtaposed with *actuarial judgment*, where *clinical* denotes reliance on intuition and *actuarial* denotes use of formal statistics. I see these approaches as aspects of the same method: both rely on comparisons between individual characteristics and group norms to determine the diagnostic classification of the individual.[10] The push to bring formal decision science into clinical work is a way of bolstering the authority of clinical reason by giving it more statistical rigor.

Despite some realization that clinical measurements are in part subject to the influences of the person being tested and the tester, the assumption (or perhaps wish) that clinical measurements are objective often leads to reification of the qualities that are measured. They are taken as fixed, stable capacities of individuals. To see the import of this reification, imagine the opposite assumption—that physical capacity is the product of interaction between people and their social environment. Under this assumption, a worker does not have a fixed, static capacity for physical exertion. He or she might be able to lift a greater weight, for example, when the supervisor is encouraging, respectful, and humorous rather than punitive, degrading, and morose; when the worker feels part of a team; or when the worker can determine the pacing of the work, rather than accommodating to a pace set by someone else.[11]

The Political Properties of Clinical Reason

Inside medicine, new diagnostic technologies are celebrated and promoted for their ability to yield objective information and to liberate physicians from the subjective reporting and claims of patients. Outside medicine, social institutions are eager to use clinical techniques and reasoning in various forms of the construction of citizenship: the allocation of social roles and statuses; the assignment of guilt, innocence, and punishment; the determination of eligibility for entitlements and monetary compensation; and the regulation of conflict more generally. Clinical reason seems to have important political properties that make it a desirable instrument for these purposes.

First, clinical reason purports to measure something in the individual, be it traits, capabilities, or behaviors. Since it is part of liberal ideology that individual status and rewards should depend on individual characteristics and achievements, clinical reason offers a seemingly objective way to measure deservingness that is consistent with liberal ideology.

10. See, for example, Dawes, Faust, and Meehl (1989) and literature cited therein; Elstein, Shulman, and Sprafka (1978); Schwartz and others (1973); Eddy (1982); and Sjoberg (1982).
11. For evidence on this score, see studies cited in Karasek and Theorell (1990).

Second, clinical reason purports to be objective, to rest on knowledge that is produced by independent observers, replicable, and unaffected by the subject of measurement. Liberal ideology also requires that people should not be able to claim statuses or resources merely because they *want* them. Claims must be based on merit or need. Clinical reason seemingly provides a way to validate individual claims objectively, using the knowledge of outside observers and insulating decisions from the will of the claimant.

Third, clinical reason seems to bridge the gap between the public and the private spheres. It is a form of power that makes the individual yield up private knowledge to the public domain. Through imaging, information previously available only to the individual in the form of experience is rendered accessible to others in the form of visual pictures, numbers, or precise verbal pictures. It is precisely the (alleged) technical ability of the clinical professions to reveal the hidden that gives them their claim to control citizen classification on behalf of society.

The Expansion of Clinical Authority

Clinical authority—the kind of knowledge used to define and identify diseases—is increasingly used as a mode of social power that defines the citizen's relationship to the state. It is not just that clinical methods are used to classify people into roles and statuses, but that government recognizes, indeed seeks out, clinical authority as the preferred method of legitimating social classification. I will consider three key areas of social policy and political conflict—education, criminal justice, and the regulation of gender roles—that are rich domains in which to explore various aspects of clinical authority in politics.

Clinical Reason in Education

Schools have always been the premier institution for sorting a population into future occupational (and consequently socioeconomic and to some degree political) statuses. Schools in the United States are at the center of controversy over two forms of social classification, apart from tracking by social class. First, schools were institutions of formal legal racial segregation until 1954 and continue to perpetuate some de facto racial segregation. Second, schools were the first arena where the conflict over segregation of people with disabilities was fought. The two kinds of sorting come together in the new concept of identifying disabled children. (In the American penchant for euphemism, we often refer to these children as "special" or "exceptional" or "special needs" children.)

Under the Education for All Handicapped Children Act of 1975, public school systems are required to identify children with disabilities, to make special accommodations for them, and to educate them in the "least restrictive environment," meaning that they are to be integrated in regular classrooms whenever possible. Because the statute also provided for federal funds to local schools on a per–handicapped child basis, it created enormous incentives for the development of personnel and methods to identify handicapped children. The law had the ironic (but entirely predictable) effect of leading to the identification of *more* children as handicapped and of having more children educated for at least part of the day in separate classrooms apart from the "mainstream."[12]

The definition of "handicapped" was considerably broadened. Originally, this category contained primarily children with severe mental retardation, emotional disturbances, or physical disabilities, such as deafness, blindness, or cerebral palsy.[13] It was these kinds of disabilities that were envisioned by legislators who passed the 1975 legislation. Because of the new fiscal incentives attaching to handicapped children, school systems employed learning specialists, psychologists, and other gatekeepers to identify such children. They placed children with behavioral and learning difficulties into this category and created medical "syndromes" to aid in diagnosis of these disorders. Thus disruptive children were identified as hyperactive (and sometimes treated with drugs).[14] Children who could not concentrate and who formerly would have been blamed for not spending enough time doing their assignments were diagnosed as having "attention deficit disorder." Now, most children who are determined to be handicapped are classified on the basis of social and psychological criteria, including intelligence, achievement, social behavior and adjustment, and communication and language problems.[15] The general category of "specific learning disabilities" named in the original statute

12. See Granger and Granger (1986, pp. 52–53) and sources therein.
13. The Education for All Handicapped Children Act of 1975 named eleven different handicaps, most of which were indeed medically identifiable: deaf, deaf-blind, hard of hearing, orthopedically impaired, other health impaired, speech impaired, visually impaired, seriously emotionally disturbed, multihandicapped, mentally retarded, and learning disabled. See Gartner and Lipsky (1987, p. 372).
14. The classic study on the creation of hyperactivity as a medical syndrome is Conrad (1976).
15. Wang, Reynolds, and Walberg (1986).

became the tail that wagged the dog. Thus, in the decade from 1976–77 to 1986–87, the overall special education population grew by 20 percent but the learning-disabled population increased 142 percent, so that at the end of the period learning-disabled students made up 44 percent of the total.[16]

Imaging is central to educational gatekeeping. The various forms of testing used by teachers, school psychologists, and vocational and rehabilitation counselors, for example, are all forms of imaging. They purport to reveal some inner characteristics of the individual by eliciting answers, responses, and performances in a structured way. The enormous resources and attention these professions devote to "validating" their testing instruments all serve to promote a faith in these instruments as objective and beyond manipulation by interested parties. Meanwhile, some scholars of special education have found that tests are often designed and administered and sometimes even redesigned to confirm the referral decisions of teachers and the diagnostic decisions of educational testers.[17] Specialized educational tests are supposed to reveal a truth that ordinary teachers cannot see and that parents might be all too prone to deny. In this way, the scientific imagery of the tests adds weight to the school system's side in conflict between the school and parents. When parents protest the placement of their child in a special class, their intimate knowledge of the child is pitted against and made inferior to the objective knowledge revealed by the tests.[18]

True to the model of clinical reason, the education profession deems learning disabilities to be qualities inherent in the individual. There has been a strong tendency to treat learning problems as biologically determined, especially as neurological defects or malfunction. Dyslexia, for example, is conceived as a discrete diagnostic entitity with a neurological basis, although a recent study suggests that dyslexia is just the lower tail of a normal distribution of reading ability, and therefore there is no clear boundary between dyslexia and normal reading ability.[19] Dyslexia is thus perhaps another example of how clinical reason finds pathology in deviation from a statistical norm.

Once children are designated with the label "special needs" or "learning disabled," important consequences follow. They can now be legiti-

16. Gartner and Lipsky (1989, p. 9).
17. Gartner and Lipsky (1987, p. 372).
18. For a gripping first-person account of such a struggle, see Granger and Granger (1986, chaps. 1–5).
19. Shaywitz, Escobar, and Shaywitz (1992).

mately separated from other children for at least part of the day, pulled out from regular classrooms and taught separately in special classes. They are magnets for federal funds, so that the school has a fiscal incentive to maintain the classification of the child as handicapped, quite in contradiction to the nominal purpose of the program, namely, to render these children unhandicapped. To the extent that the very disabilities identified in children are conceived as neurologically or biologically based, moreover, professionals have less expectation that the children can be "cured" or made normal and so set lower educational goals for them.

As happens so often in American social institutions, black children are disproportionately classified as inferior or, in this case, disabled. Although black students constitute only 16 percent of public school students, they make up 35 percent of the children classified as educable mentally retarded, 27 percent of those classified as trainable mentally retarded, and 27 percent of those classifed as seriously emotionally disturbed.[20] Add to this disproportionate shifting of black students into the handicapped categories the fact that nearly three-quarters of students so classified spend some or all of the schoolday in separate classrooms or programs,[21] and it becomes apparent that the system of special education reestablishes or exacerbates old patterns of racial segregation.

Until 1986, special education, with all its labeling and segregation, was limited to children of school age. However, 1986 amendments to the 1975 act require states to provide services for disabled children aged three to five and give states the option to provide "early intervention" services for children from birth to age three. These early intervention services can be targeted to children who already show signs of developmental delay, who have physical or mental impairments associated with delays, or—the most intriguing part for the social construction of citizenship—who show no signs of problems but are deemed "at risk" of behavioral, learning, or physical disabilities.[22] In the field of infant developmental psychology, the dominant wisdom is that multiple risk factors contribute to the ultimate development of the child, and interestingly, most of the risk factors used to identify infants at risk are

20. M. Hume, "Despite Progress, States Have Problems to Overcome in Special Education," *Education Daily*, March 15, 1988, pp. 1–3.

21. Gartner and Lipsky (1987, p. 374). They note that this overall figure masks substantial state-by-state variation, so that in some states almost no children in some categories spend any time in the regular classroom. In Mississippi, for example, zero percent of speech-impaired children are in regular classrooms.

22. Hauser-Cram and others (1988).

characteristics of the mother, the family, or the home environment, rather than of the infant itself. Prominent among these social and environmental risk factors are parents' or mother's education (the lower the education level, the higher the infant's risk); parents' or mother's income (low income is associated with higher risk); parents' occupation (with lower-skilled jobs creating higher risk); and parents' race (with minority status generating a higher risk for infants via prejudice and segregation); and absence of a father.[23] Through clinical reason, the socioeconomic disadvantages of parents are thus translated into individual risk factors for their children. Through a system of scoring to aggregate these factors, the parents' disadvantages become traits of the child. By identifying high-risk infants in this way, the early intervention system assures that the children of the poor and of minorities will be heavily recruited into the world of special education, where the cycle of disadvantage may repeat itself.[24]

Clinical Reason in Criminal Justice

Clinical reason is often called upon to arbitrate claims of truth in the criminal justice system. "Rape trauma syndrome" is a good example of how clinical authority mediates power relations between large groups, in this case, between men and women and between accusers and defendants. The syndrome was first reported in a psychiatry journal in 1974 and eventually included as a subspecies of posttraumatic stress disorder in the psychiatrists' *Diagnostic and Statistical Manual of Mental Disorder* in 1987.[25] While rape trauma syndrome is widely accepted among clinicians as a reliable diagnostic category, its use as evidence in rape trials is still disputed.

Rape represents in some sense the most fundamental form of gender conflict, and a legal system's treatment of rape sets a society's norms for how it regulates this conflict. The American legal system (like others) has historically been quite distrustful—if not hostile—toward women's claims of rape, so that it has been very difficult for rape victims to win convictions of their assailants, and ultimately, the power of the state is

23. Sameroff and others (1987); and Hauser-Cram and others (1988).
24. Of course children might be helped by being drawn into the world of special education and given extra services, and many probably are. However, there is substantial evidence that segregated special education programs do not help students and may in fact harm them. See Gartner and Lipsky (1989, pp. 13–14) and studies cited therein.
25. Burgess and Holstrom (1974).

not used to deter or punish coercive sexual abuse of women. There is a widespread male cultural assumption that women often desire to be raped, which is embodied in the legal requirement that a woman plaintiff prove she did not consent to sexual intercourse with the defendant. This is an extraordinarily difficult evidentiary hurdle, since there are usually no witnesses to a rape and since if the assailant threatens the woman with a weapon, the threat leaves no physical traces and she is likely not to struggle for fear of injury or death. Thus the entire rape case often turns on conflicting stories of consent.

Rape trauma syndrome was created as a clinical category by a coalition of psychologists, psychiatrists, rape counselors, and legal advocates for women rape victims. The first clinical report of the syndrome came from a study of self-reported rape victims who sought help at a Boston hospital emergency room.[26] In this study, as in all the subsequent ones, researchers and counselors observed the behavior of these self-identified victims over a period of at least several months and formulated a clinical picture of symptoms common to them. The cluster of symptoms includes recurrent nightmares about the event, recollections, hallucinations, or flashbacks; numbing of emotional responses; inability to recall aspects of the rape; efforts to avoid thoughts, situations, and stimuli associated with rape; and persistent symptoms of arousal such as difficulty sleeping or concentrating and an exaggerated startle response. Most of the studies also compared self-identified rape victims with a control group of female emergency room patients who had not experienced rape. Legal advocates began trying to introduce expert testimony about rape trauma syndrome as evidence that a woman did not consent. By now, several states have accepted the syndrome as evidence of nonconsent, while courts in other states have not, so the legal status of the syndrome is still very much in flux.[27]

Rape trauma syndrome illustrates the use of clinical reason as a political resource in a major social conflict. In this conflict, advocates for the weaker side (weaker both physically and legally) used the observational methods and logic of clinical reason to bolster the truth claims of women. Rape, like so many of the situations in which clinical reason is called to bear witness, has been constructed as a contest about truth, and the gatekeepers (in this case, judges who dispense the power of state authority to punish and deter rape) are exquisitely concerned about deceit. (Women

26. Burgess and Holstrom (1974).
27. For a review of state law through 1988, see Cling (1988).

might lure men into sex and then charge them with rape, or willingly engage in sex and then bring a rape charge to save their own reputations.) The rape trauma syndrome is a form of imaging. It creates a clinical picture with precise, graphically described symptoms. Experts hold up this picture to courts to bear witness that a woman is telling the truth. Such a cluster of symptoms, the experts maintain, cannot be faked.

The use of clinical reason as a device to arbitrate claims of truth in political conflict is a double-edged sword. On one side, the construct of rape trauma syndrome has empowered women rape victims by giving them more credence in some courts. But at another level, the substitution of clinical knowledge for lay or experiential knowledge denigrates women as witnesses. The substitution of clinical observations for women's own claims still denies them credibility in the courts. Clinical experts—not women themselves—are constituted as the bearers of truth.

Rape trauma syndrome is just one of many clinical syndromes developed by clinicians in cooperation with legal advocates to create evidence of victimization. Clinical syndromes can be useful in getting around difficult evidentiary problems when victims are very young or incapable of speaking, or when their victimization occurred without witnesses. Child abuse first began to be taken seriously by state welfare agencies and the legal system only after physicians defined a medical diagnosis called "battered child syndrome."[28] The diagnostic criteria were rather straightforward—bone fractures, bruises, and burns and frequent visits to a hospital emergency room for these symptoms. Of course physicians in emergency rooms had been seeing these symptoms for a long time, but packaging them as a syndrome turned child abuse into a medical condition more easily reportable to authorities. Other examples of medical syndromes created by clinicians in conjunction with lawyers to prove victimization are "post-traumatic stress disorder" (to prove that soldiers were indeed injured by combat duty, but now expanded to include several varieties of traumatic stress), and "survivor's syndrome" (to prove psychic damages caused by a community disaster such as flood and thereby increase the monetary awards going to victims in a tort liability suit).[29]

Used in this fashion, as a sort of corroborating evidence for a person's own story, clinical authority can enhance citizens' power in an instrumental sense: parties that would otherwise be weak are more likely to

---

28. For the political history of this issue area, see Nelson (1984). The seminal medical article that first defined the syndrome is Kempe (1982).

29. On the original development of "survivor syndrome" in the context of the Buffalo Creek flood in West Virginia, see Erikson (1976) and Stern (1984).

prevail in disputes. They gain influence over specific decisions. On the other hand, clinical authority does not enhance their "third-dimension" power—clinical professions, not ordinary citizens, gain influence over the broader public's understanding of a social conflict.

Clinical syndromes can function not only as evidence of victimization, but also as defenses or excuses on the side of defendants. The best-known example is the insanity defense, a legal move where the defendent admits to a criminal action but claims either a lack of intent to commit the crime or a lack of knowledge that his or her behavior was criminal, on account of insanity at the time of the crime. Psychiatrists are the gatekeepers for this kind of defense.

In the United States, there has been an expansion of what I would call clinical defenses, that is, the definition of syndromes whose chief function is to excuse otherwise criminal actions. These syndromes are behavioral patterns shown to be deviations from a norm. One example is the concept of "paraphilic rapism" articulated by the psychiatry profession as a defense to rape charges.[30] Another is the battered woman syndrome articulated by some women's legal advocates.[31] When a woman assaults or kills a man, one of the few defenses available is "self-defense." Since these activities are generally done quite privately, without witnesses, it is very hard for a woman to prove that her victim threatened her severely enough that she assaulted him truly in self-defense. Some legal advocates observed many battered women involved in violent relationships and constructed a constellation of typical behaviors called the "battered woman syndrome." By showing that an accused defendant exhibited these behaviors, they could offer more convincing proof that she felt threatened and had good reason to believe her life was in jeopardy.

The creation of exculpatory syndromes follows the standard logic of clinical reason: examination of individuals known to behave a certain way (for example, committing rape); identification of behavioral, physiological, or psychological traits; comparison of these traits with a group of "normal" individuals known not to exhibit the deviant behavior; and ultimately, comparison of a particular individual with the population norms as the basis for legal classification.

Clinical syndromes serve additionally as legal devices to mitigate punishment. In states where capital punishment is permitted, insanity and mental retardation have been used as criteria to stop a capital sentence.

30. See Money (1990). Paraphilic rapism has the status of an experimental diagnostic category in the latest version of the psychiatry profession's diagnostic manual, DSMIII-R.
31. Schneider (1986); and Rhode (1989, pp. 241–44).

Indeed, upon hearing an appeal by a man said to have become mentally ill after committing the crime but before the sentence was carried out, the U.S. Supreme Court articulated a rather bizarre notion of "competence to be executed" and concluded that insanity may render a person incompetent for this purpose.[32] Criminal defense lawyers have created the syndrome of "fragile offender" to identify and designate people who are not capable of withstanding normal prison life. One of the most widespread uses of clinical reasoning to mitigate punishment is in predicting dangerousness, where psychologists use statistical models to determine whether an offender should be granted parole or put on probation.

As clinical authority enters the criminal justice system, citizens no longer tell their stories directly to each other, to judges, and to lay witnesses. Instead, clinical authorities construct "good guys and bad guys" by applying the tools of clinical reason. They become the arbiters of innocence and guilt, responsibility and incapacity, and truth telling and lying.

Clinical Reason in the Regulation of Gender Roles

Societal expectations and norms about the proper roles for women have been changing dramatically since World War II. Many conflicts center around motherhood: what it means to be a good mother, whether mothers should engage in paid labor or have careers, what kinds of jobs are appropriate for good mothers, and whether women should be able to choose whether to become mothers in the first place. These are highly politicized conflicts in which the sides tend to have intense feelings and are unwilling to compromise or adopt incremental reforms. Interestingly, clinical reason has become the dominant mode of discourse in these areas.

Social norms about good mothers are nothing new. The settlement house movement at the turn of the century was largely aimed at inculcating immigrant women with middle-class, white, Anglo-Saxon, Protestant values about household management and childrearing practices. Today there is a tremendous emphasis on a woman's behavior during pregnancy as the indicator of proper motherly behavior, and to some extent, the mother-child relation has been drawn as one in which two people's interests clash. States have begun to impose standards of good

32. *Ford* v. *Wainwright*, 477 U.S. 399 (1985).

motherhood on pregnant women that come directly from the clinical sphere. The most notable example is the prosecution and occasional imprisonment of pregant women for taking cocaine or drinking alcohol excessively. The justification for legal enforcement of standards of maternal alcohol consumption is a clinical syndrome known as "fetal alcohol syndrome." Fetal alcohol syndrome is a cluster of symptoms, behaviors, and physical characteristics of infants or children, said to be diagnostic (and therefore probative) of excessive drinking during pregnancy. As yet, there is no consensus in the scientific literature about how much drinking is necessary to cause the syndrome, nor about the periods during pregnancy when a fetus is vulnerable to alcohol. There is, however, a consensus that a certain pattern of serious mental and physical damage is caused by fetal exposure to alcohol in the mother's bloodstream.[33]

Outside the realm of motherhood, alcohol consumption is not regulated with such stringency. Alcoholism is generally tolerated so long as it does not harm others, and even the legal treatment of drunk driving is relatively lenient. In most states, people convicted of drunk driving, even when they cause accidents that kill children, receive reprimands, temporary license suspensions, small fines, and orders to attend classes for alcoholics. Convicted drunk drivers are often given several warnings before any real sanction is imposed. Fetal alcohol syndrome, however, has been used as a justification for regulating the drinking of pregnant women much more harshly, especially imprisoning them.[34] Thus some people would hold mothers to a much higher standard of care than other members of society.

Clinical reason is also used as a means of mediating conflict over women's access to high-paying jobs in industry. Women could be and were formally barred from certain job categories until 1964, when Title VII of the Civil Rights Act prohibited discrimination in employment on the basis of sex. After that point, an employer or trade union could not designate jobs as "for men only" unless they could prove, under a fairly rigorous legal test, that gender was a bona fide occupational qualification for the job. Women began to bid for higher-paying production jobs in the chemical, metal, and electronics industries, where they had formerly been restricted to clerical, packaging, laundry, and janitorial positions. Not long thereafter, many companies began instituting "fetal protection

33. For a review of the literature, see Davis (1992, chap. 4).
34. Dorris (1989).

62   DEBORAH A. STONE

policies," the essence of which was to restrict certain jobs to men on the ground that these jobs could be dangerous to the fetuses of pregnant women. Restrictive fetal protection policies have been implemented almost exclusively in industries and job categories where women already constituted a small minority of the work force, and they have not been applied to men, despite evidence that offspring can be harmed by paternal exposure to toxic substances.[35]

This issue crystallized in the widely publicized case of Johnson Controls, a battery-manufacturing concern that excluded fertile women from its high-paying jobs involving lead exposure. The company presumed that all women between ages 15 and 70 are fertile and potentially pregnant and required female employees to produce medical documentation of infertility as a prerequisite to the desirable jobs. The terms of the legal conflict illustrate another use of clinical reason. Essentially, the debate was framed so that the question had a clinical answer: can pregnant women work in certain jobs without medical harm to their offspring? Or, slightly more broadly, can pregnant women work safely? That question requires the application of clinical reason to the individual, an inquiry into whether each female worker is pregnant or (as in some fetal protection policies) even merely fertile.[36] An alternative framing of the question—one that does not take as a starting assumption that the model or normal worker is a man—might ask whether the job can safely be performed by any worker. That question would require an examination of all workers, not merely some to see if they deviate from a (restrictive) norm. Moreover, by making doctors the arbiters of a woman's potential pregnancy, the company treated women as if they were not agents in their own pregnancy, as if they were powerless to decide whether they wanted to become pregnant or to control their conception. A woman's knowledge that she was infertile, menopausal, sexually inactive, lesbian, or using birth control counted for naught in the company's eyes.

Finally, abortion is one more area where the regulation of conflict over gender roles has relied heavily on clinical reason. The availability of abortion determines whether women have choice about adopting the role of mother; restrictions on access to abortion obviously constrain that choice. Because most of the work of childrearing falls on women, as-

35. Draper (1990, pp. 71–75).
36. This was the framing used by the majority justices in the 7th circuit, in *International Union, UAW* v. *Johnson Controls, Inc.*, 866 F.2d 871 (1989). The appellate court ruled for Johnson Controls, but its decision was overturned by the U.S. Supreme Court in *International Union, UAW* v. *Johnson Controls, Inc.*, 111 S.Ct. 1196 (1991).

sumption of the motherhood role curtails women's ability to adopt other roles. Thus the conflict over access to abortion is largely a conflict over what roles women are allowed or enabled to have.[37]

This is a fundamental issue of the distribution of status—almost caste—and it is striking to what degree it is regulated on the basis of clinical reason. The Supreme Court decision that protected abortion rights during the first two trimesters (*Roe* v. *Wade* in 1973) was based on two clinical questions: First, what are the medical consequences of abortion, compared with carrying a pregnancy to term? And second, when does a fetus become viable, or able to live outside the womb? To find a constitutional right to abortion in the first trimester, the Supreme Court used clinical evidence that women have a higher statistical chance of dying from childbirth than from abortion during the first trimester. To find a constitutional right to unrestricted access to abortion in the second trimester, but not the third, the Court used clinical evidence about the point of viability of the fetus.

The clinical construction of the issue of abortion rights has meant that the fight about major social divisions according to gender was transformed into narrow disputes about clinical evidence: Does abortion cause psychological damage to mothers? Is the point of viability twenty-four weeks or twenty-six weeks? Is it possible to test fetuses in utero to determine their viability? The clinical construction displaces and masks the profound sociopolitical issue at stake: What roles can women have, and what degree of choice do they have in assuming those roles?

An alternative sociological construction of the abortion issue highlights the narrowness of the clinical construction. If one assumes that "viability" of a child entails not just sheer biological existence, but physical, mental and emotional development, then it is obvious that adult care is critical for viability. Assessing the availability of a willing adult caretaker would become a relevant question, and even questions about the quality of the relationship between mother and child would become relevant.[38]

All three examples of the regulation of gender conflict entail profound social conflict over the roles available to women, the authority to decide who may enter which roles, and the standards of behavior permitted to women in both the motherhood and work roles. In all three cases, clinical reason is invoked—by both sides—because of its important political

37. Luker (1984, especially chap. 8).

38. For a thoughtful and extensive *relational* analysis of motherhood and child development (quite explicitly contrasted with a clinical construction), see Goldstein (1988).

properties. It seems to reveal uncontrovertible truths, it seems to be apolitical and objective, and it holds the potential for defusing intense political conflict. At the same time, however, clinical reason drastically narrows the terms of debate in areas of major social conflict. For that reason, it is likely to contribute to maintenance of the status quo.

Conclusion

These widely disparate examples of the rise of clinical authority in education, criminal justice, and the regulation of gender conflict elucidate different aspects of the use of clinical reason in the construction of citizenship. Clinical authority, when substituted for other forms of authority, profoundly changes the way social problems are defined, the political instruments used to resolve them, and the relative power of social groups. Through the rise of clinical authority, many of America's deepest social conflicts have been transformed into issues of clinical definition, classification, evidence, and judgment. It is worth speculating about why this transformation has occurred and what its consequences are.

Clinical reason has certain political properties that make it especially attractive to policymakers as a mode of conflict resolution. It accords with the liberal tradition of justifying differences in status and rewards by differences in individual achievement, merit, and even need. Clinical reason seems to give an independent source of knowledge to social and political authorities, rendering them less vulnerable to the (manipulative) desires of individuals; it offers a way to compel individuals to yield up socially relevant knowledge.

One question that has concerned social scientists is whether the medicalization of social problems is the result of professional imperialism— professionals seeking to enlarge their domains of power—or alternatively, whether social forces beyond the control of professionals are responsible. There is probably a grain of truth in both explanations. Because of its political properties, clinical reason offers politicians, judges, and other arbiters of dispute an attractive escape, or a way of defusing intense political conflict. These people are often all too eager to hand over a conflict to clinicians for resolution. There are many policy domains where clinicians are extremely reluctant to be drawn into political disputes, and where they resist providing clinical evidence for these purposes.

At the same time, once the pattern of conflict resolution through clinical reason is established, there are enormous incentives for professionals to service the state, both by developing clinical paradigms of social problems and by applying clinical investigation to individuals. The state has become a major client for professional services, not just in its obvious role as payer and employer, but in its role as the ultimate political authority that now relies on clinical classifications and judgments as a major form of gatekeeping and conflict resolution.

The transformation of social problems into clinical syndromes is profoundly antidemocratic. It elevates a particular type of expert knowledge and denigrates or even ignores the knowledge, perceptions, and interpretations of ordinary citizens in their relations with other individuals and with social institutions. This sort of medicalization is also antiliberal. When clinical definitions of normality and deviance prevail, individual will or preference is no longer the standard for judging how a person should be treated. Citizens are prevented on the one hand from self-expression, and on the other, from using their own understanding and social experience to interpret the authenticity of other people's motives and claims.

The rise of clinical authority also constricts the realm of choice for individuals. The more clinicians define standards of healthy behavior—whether in learning styles, work roles, parental roles, or relations with others—the smaller the realm of deliberation and choice for individuals. To the extent that clinical authority constructs individual behavior as biologically determined or biologically limited, the importance of human will is also diminished.

Ultimately, the most profound consequence of the rise of clinical authority is that it disguises or displaces conflict in the first place. Once a situation is defined as a matter of health and disease, of normality and pathology, both the problem and its treatment appear to be dictated by nature and no longer a matter of value choice and political resolution.

References

Burgess, Ann Wolbert, and Lynda Lytle Holmstrom. 1974. "Rape Trauma Syndrome." *American Journal of Psychiatry* 131 (September): 981–86.
Cling, B. J. 1988. "Rape Trauma Syndrome: Medical Evidence of Non-consent." *Women's Rights Law Reporter* 10 (Fall): 243–59.
Conrad, Peter. 1976. *Identifying Hyperactive Children: The Medicalization of Deviant Behavior.* Lexington, Mass.: D.C. Heath.
Davis, Robert. 1992. "Epidemiology on the Agenda." Ph.D. dissertation, Heller School, Brandeis University.

66   DEBORAH A. STONE

Dawes, Robyn, David Faust, and Paul Meehl. 1989. "Clinical versus Actuarial Judgment." *Science* 243 (March 31): 1668–74.

Dorris, Michael. 1989. *The Broken Cord.* Harper and Row.

Draper, Elaine. 1990. *Risky Business: Genetic Testing and Exclusionary Practices in the Hazardous Workplace.* Cambridge University Press.

Eddy, David M. 1982. "Probabilistic Reasoning in Clinical Medicine: Problems and Opportunities." In *Judgment under Uncertainty: Heuristics and Biases,* edited by Daniel Kahneman, Paul Slovic, and Amos Tversky, 249–67. Cambridge University Press.

Elstein, Arthur S., Lee S. Shulman, and Sarah A. Sprafka. 1978. *Medical Problem Solving: An Analysis of Clincial Reasoning.* Harvard University Press.

Erikson, Kai T. 1976. *Everything in Its Path: Destruction of Community in the Buffalo Creek Flood.* Simon and Schuster.

Foucault, Michel. 1973. *The Birth of the Clinic: An Archeology of Medical Perception.* Translated by A. M. Sheridan Smith. Vintage Books.

Gartner, Alan, and Dorothy Kerzner Lipsky. 1987. "Beyond Special Education: Toward a Quality System for All Students." *Harvard Educational Review* 57 (November): 367–95.

————. 1989. *The Yoke of Special Education: How to Break It.* Rochester, N.Y.: National Center on Education and the Economy.

Glendon, Mary Ann. 1991. *Rights Talk: The Impoverishment of Political Discourse.* Free Press.

Goldstein, Robert D. 1988. *Mother-Love and Abortion: A Legal Interpretation.* University of California Press.

Granger, Lori, and Bill Granger. 1986. *The Magic Feather: The Truth About "Special Education."* Dutton.

Hauser-Cram, Penny, and others. 1988. "Implications of Public Law 99–457 for Early Intervention Services for Infants and Toddlers with Disabilities." In *Social Policy Report* 3 (3). Washington: Society for Research in Child Development.

Horowitz, Donald L. 1977. *The Courts and Social Policy.* Brookings.

Hunter, James Davison. 1991. *Culture Wars: The Struggle to Define America.* Basic Books.

Karasek, Robert, and Töres Theorell. 1990. *Healthy Work: Stress, Productivity, and the Reconstruction of Working Life.* Basic Books.

Kempe, C. Henry, and others. 1982. "Battered Child Syndrome." *Journal of the American Medical Association* 181 (July 7): 17–24.

Luker, Kristin. 1984. *Abortion and the Politics of Motherhood.* University of California Press.

Lukes, Steven. 1974. *Power: A Radical View.* Macmillan.

Money, John. 1990. "Forensic Sexology: Paraphilic Serial Rape (Biastophilia) and Lust Murder (Erotophonophilia)." *American Journal of Psychotherapy* 44 (January): 26–36.

Nelson, Barbara J. 1984. *Making an Issue of Child Abuse: Political Agenda Setting for Social Problems.* University of Chicago Press.

Petchesky, Rosalind Pollack. 1987. "Fetal Images: The Power of Visual Culture in the Politics of Reproduction." *Feminist Studies* 13 (Summer): 263–92.

Resier, Stanley Joel. 1978. *Medicine and the Reign of Technology.* Cambridge University Press.

Rhode, Deborah L. 1989. *Justice and Gender: Sex Discrimination and the Law.* Harvard University Press.

Sameroff, Arnold J., and others. 1987. "Intelligence Quotient Scores of 4-Year-Old Children: Social-Environmental Risk Factors." *Pediatrics* 79 (March): 342–50.

Scheingold, Stuart A. 1974. *The Politics of Rights: Lawyers, Public Policy, and Political Change.* Yale University Press.

Schneider, Elizabeth M. 1986. "The Dialectic of Rights and Politics: Perspectives from the Women's Movement." *New York University Law Review* 61 (October): 589–652.

Schwartz, William B., and others. 1973. "Decision Analysis and Clinical Judgment." *American Journal of Medicine* 55 (October): 459–72.

Shaywitz, Sally E., Michael A. Escobar, and Bennett A. Shaywitz. 1992. "Evidence that Dyslexia may Represent the Lower Tail of a Normal Distribution of Reading Ability." *New England Journal of Medicine* 326 (January 16): 145–50.

Sjoberg, Lennert. 1982. "Aided and Unaided Decision Making: Improving Intuitive Judgment." *Journal of Forecasting* 4(4): 349–63.

Stern, Gerald. 1984. *The Buffalo Creek Disaster.* Videocassette.

Stone, Deborah A. 1988. *Policy Paradox and Political Reason.* Scott, Foresman.

Wang, Margaret C., Maynard Reynolds, and Herbert J. Walberg. 1986. "Rethinking Special Education." *Educational Leadership* 44 (September): 27.

Wuthnow, Robert. 1988. *The Restructuring of American Religion: Society and Faith since World War II.* Princeton University Press.

4. Constructing Citizenship:
The Subtle Messages of Policy Design

HELEN INGRAM AND ANNE SCHNEIDER

$\mathbf{M}$ODERN DEMOCRACY IS beset with a number of ironies. The members of groups that gain the most from governmental policies do not support activist government. Instead they credit themselves, rather than government, for their advantages and criticize government's attempts to help others. Rather than providing general support for a political system under which they prosper, such persons often pursue narrow self-interests, even at the expense of the system. In contrast, those most disadvantaged by public policies and who might have the most to gain by participation, including the poor, minorities, and young people, are the least likely to vote, mobilize, or try to influence government officials. As others in this volume note, there is massive dissatisfaction with governmental performance yet high levels of indifference about political activity.

This chapter argues that the seeds of many of the contradictions related to public participation and citizenship are sown by public policy. Along with other authors in this volume, we share the perspective that policy creates politics and affects citizen orientation and participation. Policy design sends messages about what government is supposed to do, which citizens are deserving and undeserving, and what sort of participation is appropriate in democratic societies. Different target populations receive quite different messages. Policies that have bad effects on the members of some target groups or are ineffective in solving their problems may not produce a political reaction because such policies also deliver affective messages that encourage withdrawal and passivity. Other target populations, however, receive messages that encourage them to pursue narrowly construed interests.

Our argument begins with a discussion of past research relating policy content to patterns of politics. Politically feasible policies are designed to assure sufficient support among legislators and the public to become law. We build upon an important policy literature that associates policy characteristics with political mobilization. Next we suggest how the pathologies that plague citizenship and participation are reinforced by policy characteristics. Finally we suggest some changes in policy design more favorable to democratic participation.

Previous Research

We are not the first to observe that policy designs often discourage democratic processes. The best known theory relating policy to politics is Theodore Lowi's contention that different types of policies attract different patterns of political participation.[1] Lowi argues that distributive policy, which confers benefits directly on identifiable groups, tends to encourage patterns of mutual noninterference and will result in the production of policies serving private rather than public interests.[2] Redistributive policy is characterized by competing elites, and regulatory policy is the only one likely to attract a wider audience and result in the competitive group participation envisioned by pluralist democracy. Lowi was quite explicit about the normative implications:

> We can also judge public policy as good or bad in still another sense, a sense that leads toward fundamental questions about the relationship between public policy and democracy. If we want an open and public politics, we are limited to certain kinds of policies—regardless of whether the manifest goals of these policies are fulfilled. Again we would try to avoid distributive policies, because nothing open and democratic can come of them.[3]

Lowi's prescription for creating more democratic patterns of political mobilization is to rely on regulatory policy designs with clear standards that have general applications across broad categories of winners and losers. Such clear and general effects could be easily anticipated and would generate broad political mobilization.[4]

James Q. Wilson doubts whether the type of policy design recommended by Lowi is politically feasible or would have the desired effect. Policies with clear standards subject legislative leaders to attacks from losers, limit the power of strong bureaucracies, and displease client groups. Wilson notes that "making choices means creating losers; and

1. Lowi (1964, 1972).
2. Lowi (1964, 1972, 1985).
3. Lowi (1972, p. 308).
4. Lowi (1979).

our political system thrives on maintaining the illusion that no one need ever be a loser." For Wilson there is no solution to the problem of interest group liberalism that Lowi criticizes, and "if there is . . . it is not the one that Lowi recommends."[5] Reducing the mischievous effects of interest group liberalism, he argues, requires reducing the role of politics in our lives.

Further, Wilson observed that the predictions about political mobilization and participation made by Lowi's theory are sometimes wrong: distributive policy may produce intense conflict and pluralist-type reactions, and regulatory policy sometimes does not produce the kind of pluralism anticipated.[6] He proposed an alternative typology in which the concentration of benefits and costs expected from the policy determines whether organized groups will emerge. For instance, when costs are heavily concentrated but benefits are widely dispersed, policies will be difficult to enact because those who bear the costs will mobilize to thwart the policy, whereas the beneficiaries will be less attentive. Yet legislation that distributes costs to focused powerful interests does pass, and Wilson suggests how. The media can be used to mobilize the broader, more diffuse, public by labeling the situation as a public crisis, and the groups in opposition can be portrayed as undeserving or utterly self-serving.[7]

Politicians are not oblivious to the possibility that broad publics can be mobilized by symbolic appeals, and Douglas Arnold believes that policymakers are motivated to look beyond narrow group interests to calculate the broad public's potential policy preferences.[8] Public officials recognize that inattentive publics may become attentive and potential preferences may be shaped by the actions of opponents or the media. Should the policy become a broad public issue, politicians want to be aligned with politically compelling values and avoid association with politically repellent ones.

Of course, governmental officials are not simply passive reflectors of prevailing values; instead, they actively participate in values' formation and perpetuation as they design and justify policy. Critical theorists, though not especially interested in the specifics of policy design, have added to an understanding of the need for government to fashion convincing justifications. Habermas argues that modern societies are founded

5. Wilson (1990, p. 571).
6. Wilson (1973).
7. Wilson (1973).
8. Arnold (1990).

mainly upon the communication of shared norms and that people do what government wants only when it reflects shared norms.[9] Consequently, government is constantly having to justify its actions and to explain the continuing inequalities in societies that are based on the idea of equal opportunities. Technical explanations are frequently employed, and government officials argue that they are not making political judgments but simply applying technical standards. Deborah Stone (chapter 3) argues that clinical reasoning is used in policy because it provides a convincing rationale for distinguishing among people who have different clinically identified characteristics and then treating them differently in policy. Unfortunately the consequences of clinical reasoning for mobilization and citizenship can be detrimental to democracy.

Other authors have emphasized the role of language and symbols in manipulating broad public support and justifying policy.[10] Governmental actions can be made much more publicly palatable through association with favorable or unfavorable images. A skilled political industry fashions the right "spin" on events or proposals. While the credulity of the public and its willingness to be manipulated are great, political merchandizing is competitive, and politicians and their handlers take care not to align themselves against prevailing values. They want to appear to do "good" things for "good" people and "bad" things to "bad" people. Of course, in anticipating public reactions on the basis of prevailing values, politicians perpetuate those values and create images and stereotypes for the groups associated with them.

Our intent in this chapter is to further define policy content to include the symbolic images or social constructions that are mechanisms for assuring support and political feasibility. Further, we trace consequences of policy beyond mobilization, which were of primary interest to Lowi and Wilson, to include participation and citizenship. Our central purpose is to identify policies that foster democratic participation.

Policy Design and Citizen Participation

Policy design refers to the elements found in the content of policy that affects target populations and other citizens.[11] The term *design* has been used by some to infer a mechanistic and rationalistic approach to reach-

9. Habermas (1975).
10. Edelman (1988); and Luke (1989).
11. Schneider and Ingram (1990); and Ingram and Schneider (1991).

ing goals, but as we employ it the idea includes the attributes of policy that affect the orientation and behavior of target populations.[12] Designs reflect the decisions of many different people, often acting in different contexts and places; they are not necessarily logical, rational, or even coherent. The elements of design that are most important to an understanding of the effect of policy on citizen participation are:

—The definition of target populations, including the social construction conveyed.

—The political attributes of policy (for example, beneficial or burdensome).

—The location of target groups within the chain of effects implicit within the policy "logic" (proximate or remote).

—The tools through which policy attempts to motivate target populations to take the actions envisioned by policy (such as authority, incentives, capacity building, and self-learning).

—The rationales for justifying and explaining policy (such as merit, need, equality, efficiency, or effectiveness).

—The messages implicit within the policy.

Citizens encounter and internalize the messages contained within policy designs through their numerous experiences with public policy, and through these experiences they develop perceptions of how they are viewed by government and by society. Policy implies attitudes about the groups within which people are placed, for example, whether the groups are "good," "bad," "intelligent," "stupid," "deserving," "undeserving," "respected," "feared," "hated," or "pitied." The messages indicate whether the problems of the target population are legitimate for government attention, what kind of "game" politics is (public-spirited or the pursuit of private interests), and who usually wins. Experiences with public policy affect citizen orientations and influence attitudes toward government and self-images, as well as images of other groups. These experiences tell target groups whether they are viewed as "clients" by government and bureaucracies or whether they are treated as "objects." Experience with policy tells people whether they are atomized individuals who must deal directly with government and bureaucracy to press their own claims, or whether they are participants in a cooperative process joining with others to solve problems collectively for the common good.

12. Linder and Peters (1992).

Definition of Targets

The definition and characterization of target groups embodied in policy is of critical importance. There is great contention over who is and who is not included in the groups targeted by policy, and over what sort of people targets are. Even after the selection of goals, wide latitude is available in the choice of targets. For instance, targets of AIDS policy include not just homosexual men but heterosexuals, drug users, educators, medical researchers, doctors, dentists, and immigrants. Targets are not the same as interest groups, since targets are selected in policy design that specify who will do what, how, and for what reason. Much of the discussion about targets is likely to be particular to the policy issue under consideration. However, two dimensions of targets are central to our argument. First, the political power of the target group is important, that is, whether it is large, united, easy to mobilize, wealthy, skilled, or well positioned. Also important is the social or cultural valence of the group, that is, whether its values are mainstream American values and whether the members of the group are deserving, virtuous, respectable, attractive, or likable.

The characterization of groups embedded in policy design is often grounded in objective reality, especially the aspect of the definition related to power. Elderly social security recipients, for instance, are portrayed as powerful, a reputation based on their growing numbers and high levels of political activity. Value constructions may also be grounded in verifiable attributes of people (for example, users of cocaine or people convicted in courts of law), but they go beyond these empirical attributes and assign evaluative images to people ("addict" or "criminal"). Constructions of target groups reflect stereotypes that have been created not just by politics but also by culture, media, history, and religion.

Many kinds of social constructions of target groups exist. For simplicity of discussion, four ideal types will be portrayed here: the advantaged, contenders, dependents, and deviants.[13] The discussion will include examples of policy targets that fit each description, whether benefits or costs are directed toward each, the sort of tools employed, and the location of the target group in the chain of policy relationships.

---

13. Schneider and Ingram (1993).

The Advantaged

Whenever possible, target populations that are defined as both powerful and positive are selected for beneficial policy and are seldom chosen for policies that allocate costs. As Lowi observed, distributive policies that contain only benefits usually go to politically powerful groups and arouse little opposition.[14] The lack of contention can be attributed not only to the lack of visible costs to others, but also to the positive image of the group. It is unlikely that a public can be mobilized against policy that helps strong and well-regarded people.

Positive incentives such as subsidies or grants are intended to coax the behavior from advantaged targets that is necessary to fulfill policy goals. Whenever possible, policymakers try to build the capacity of targets through the distribution of information and training. When benefits are being distributed for some public purpose, advantaged groups are chosen even when other groups may be logically more closely related to the achievement of the goal. For instance, in the name of alleviating poverty, money is first distributed not to the poor, but to advantaged groups. Employment policy selects industrial employers as a first-order or proximate target. Similarly, housing policy allocates money to home builders and housing investors as a means of ultimately benefiting the homeless. The proximate position of the advantaged as targets in the policy chain is important. The fewer the decision points or links involved, the more likely it is for policy to deliver on its promises.

Advantaged groups are not often selected as targets for policies that allocate costs. Because of the ability of advantaged groups to wield political power and to mobilize others, policies unfavorable to advantaged groups are usually what Arnold calls "politically infeasible."[15] Costs are ordinarily unspecified when they are directed toward powerful groups or remote targets far down the chain of effects. For instance, regulatory policy aimed at powerful, popular groups often leaves to regulatory agencies the political burden of deciding who pays. When burdens are unavoidable, the tools chosen to achieve policy goals will employ a minimum of coercion, often relying on voluntary compliance and self-enforcement. In almost every instance where burdensome policy is directed to advantaged groups as proximate targets, there are also other advantaged target groups intended as beneficiaries. The policy chain is such that one target

14. Lowi (1964).
15. Arnold (1990).

group must take action so that others can benefit and it is possible to portray the burden as a fair or equitable share or an unavoidable condition of accomplishing a desired end. During periods of droughts, for example, rationing policy that limits water use in urban areas is politically most acceptable if it applies to all categories of users and is voluntary. Even highly valued uses like toilet flushing and bathing are forgone if lack of water is viewed as a natural disaster in which saving every drop counts.

The power and positive construction of scientists, in this case high-energy physicists, as a target group of research and development policy reached superhuman proportions in the proposal to construct the superconducting supercollider (SCC). Monetarily, the benefits of the policy are projected to be enormous. The SCC would be the world's largest and most expensive scientific instrument, an oval underground tunnel more than fifty-two miles in circumference, costing more than $8.4 billion.[16] Justifications of the project are based on social constructions that exaggerate the power and social significance of science. Such justifications perpetuate a myth of rationality that supposes that science, practically by definition, serves higher reason that is beyond self-interest.

The purpose of the project is "to make important discoveries" and to pursue a grand unified theory of physics. The positive image of science allows such aspirations to be taken by the public at large as an obvious good, not just to scientists but to society as a whole. Therefore, scientific discovery is nearly impossible to oppose. In the course of developing the proposal for the SCC, the welfare of the nation and the competitive position of American physicists have been constructed as one and the same. From 1950 until the end of the 1980s, Americans had made virtually every discovery and won every Nobel Prize in high-energy physics. In 1983 a European physicist, Carlo Rubbia, produced signs of several highly sought-after elementary particles, W's and Z's, which physicists had been looking for for decades. The *New York Times* ran an editorial demanding revenge with a headline, "Europe 3, U.S. Not even Zero." One week after the *Times* editorial, an advisory panel of physicists to the Department of Energy voted to cancel the work on one technologically troubled accelerator then under construction and to go full speed ahead with a machine that would be a hundred times more powerful than anything the Europeans could conceivably build in the future. President

16. Thomas C. Hayes, "A Big but Delicate Digging Job," *New York Times*, February 19, 1992, pp. A1, A7.

Ronald Reagan's science adviser, George Keyworth, told Congress, "I won't conceal my opinion that it would be a serious blow to the U.S. scientific leadership if that facility were built in another country."[17]

High-energy physics researchers are the direct target and beneficiary of SCC construction. If the project is built, nearly all members of the subnuclear physics community will be engaged in one way or another. But the sheer size of the project involves promises to many other groups. In 1987 a commentator wrote, "In fact, the physicists' most staunch allies are the states vying to be the site for the accelerator. If it is completed, the SCC will command a $200 million operating budget and create some 3,000 jobs."[18] Competition among various contractors to bid on many of the technical systems to be used in the facility will be held on a national basis. However, the secondary beneficiaries or targets of the SCC are to be specified in implementation. Congress instructed the Department of Energy to make decisions, including its ultimate choice of Texas as the project site, solely on the basis of objective, scientific criteria.[19] The negative stigma of pork barrel politics that so large a construction project might involve was strategically avoided by cloaking the choices in the pristine and protective mantel of science.

Contenders

Populism has always been a powerful force in American politics, but to have acknowledged political power is not the same as having a positive social construction. The promise of democracy is such that inequality and domination draw resentment and suspicion. Privileged and elite groups that appear to be abusing power are vulnerable to being cast in a negative light. Big business, Wall Street bankers, big labor unions, the gun lobby, veterans, and minority rights groups have been portrayed as special interests with too much power in government or with one or another political party.

Contenders are only occasionally the recipients of directly beneficial policy, because to serve their interests too blatantly is to risk countervailing mobilization. Instead, contenders are more likely to be positioned as remote targets for whom positive effects will be difficult to trace because they are only one of a number of beneficiaries, some of whom

17. Taubes (1986, pp. xiv–xix).
18. Emily T. Smith, "Can Scientists Sell Washington on a Dream Machine?" *Business Week*, October 14, 1985, p. 100.
19. 101 Stat. 404.

are more popular and more visible. Contenders are not often the recipients of burdensome policy because they usually have sufficient power to fend off the imposition of costs, but when they are, they are more likely to suffer symbolically than substantively.

Policy tools directed toward contenders will use both positive and negative incentives. Unlike tools directed toward the advantaged that build capacity and often assume that targets will voluntarily comply with policy directives, contenders are recipients of tools that are more coercive. Administrative agencies are given the latitude and thus the blame for including contenders as targets for beneficial policy, while legislators themselves may explicitly specify contenders as targets of regulatory tools. The actual application of such regulations may be more symbolic than real. For instance, federal legislation aimed at firearms merchants regulated "assault" weapons, leaving untouched most weapons easily usable for illegal purposes.

Automobile manufacture executives, though powerful, have a negative image. The film *Roger and Me* gained a wide public audience because it portrayed the chief executive officer of a big automaker just as many imagine: narrow, irresponsible, selfish, insensitive, and unconcerned with the welfare of ordinary people. It was a political mistake in 1992 for President Bush to ask Big Three automaker executives to accompany him on a trade trip to Japan in order to demonstrate his concern about the domestic economy in his handling of foreign policy. Regardless of the facts of trade imbalances, it proved difficult for Americans to identify their interests with those of the auto executives.

The contender status of auto companies is reflected in air pollution policy. The 1970 Clean Air Act symbolically identified automobile manufacturers as polluters who had to be controlled. Reaching the required air quality standards was portrayed as a good deal easier than it turned out to be because the major burden was to be borne by the auto manufacturers who had been lagging in their cleanup efforts. The act required companies to pay more than $10,000 for every car that rolled off the assembly line without meeting the draconian standard by 1975. The necessary technology required further feasible development, and legislators refused to believe that automakers would engage in the necessary development effort voluntarily. They wished to hold the automakers' feet to the fire by targeting them with action-forcing policy.

Henry Jacoby and John Steinbruner note that the negative construct of the auto industry as a target for air pollution policy began in 1965 when Ralph Nader charged the industry with carelessness and the attempt by General Motors to silence him backfired spectacularly. The reputation for recalcitrance and bad faith was amplified when a 1969 Justice Department investigation into possible industry collusion to keep clean technology off the market ended with a consent decree in which automakers admitted no guilt but paid a large fine.[20]

The actual burdens imposed on auto manufacturers by the Clean Air Act turned out to be not nearly so harsh as they appeared. The Environmental Protection Agency was given the discretion to postpone the 1975 deadline through a low-visibility loophole provided in the act, because to do otherwise was economically unthinkable. Ford Motor Company claimed that a suspension denial would cause a shutdown of their factories; this drastic move would have resulted in a reduction of the gross national product by $17 billion, an increase in unemployment by 800,000 persons, and a decrease in tax receipts of $5 billion at all levels of government.[21] Twenty years after the passage of the Clean Air Act, automobile emission goals still have not been reached. Auto manufacturers have been able to exploit procedural loopholes and petition for legislative extensions in order to escape meeting the standards set by the law.

Dependents

Dependent targets have little political power. Their fragmentation, limited numbers, lack of organization, and lack of material resources contribute to their powerlessness. There may be structural barriers to participation; children under age 18, for example, cannot vote. Native Americans on reservations are clustered into only a few state legislative districts. Other groups are gerrymandered, resulting in even less representation. Dependent targets tend to have very little economic power or position. These groups may share common interests, but they seldom mobilize for effective action.

Dependents are viewed as incapable, by themselves, of changing their powerless situation or solving their own problems. They are perceived to lack the capacity, skills, character, discipline, and will to manage their own destiny. Some persons constructed as dependents have less physical power, which then is accompanied by lack of access to arenas where physical power is not even important, such as in economic productivity

20. Jacoby and Steinbruner (1973, pp. 10–11).
21. Ingram (1978).

in an advanced society. These people are often the wards of others: parents make decisions for their children; in much of society, married men make decisions for their families; Native Americans are under the trust responsibility of the federal government; and disabled people are reliant on others for assistance in their daily routines.

Although the construction of dependent people is positive, it is not complimentary. Dependents are viewed as deserving of assistance because their problems are not their fault in the sense that they themselves cannot solve them. They have no choice but to be dependent. However, these are not bad people and they have not done anything to deserve punishment.

Dependent populations are the recipients of beneficial policies, but less so than one would expect, given the magnitude of their problems. This is because their situation is seen as a "natural" product of their lack of capability and productivity. Also, their problems are viewed as the proper prerogative of private-sector groups, such as churches, local volunteer organizations, and philanthropists. When material resources are committed, they are usually not sufficient to address the problem.

Baker (chapter 7) describes how long-standing illegal residents in the United States were more positively constructed by the 1986 immigration legislation and given amnesty. The legislation required English literacy tests in the second phase of legalizing those targeted for amnesty. However, as is typical of policy directed at dependent groups, the provision of English classes was left to underfunded state and local education agencies. The programs directed to dependents may be mainly to salve the conscience of others and to ensure that the community is not to blame for obvious injustice and neglect of dependent people. Benefits are most likely to be given when dramatic events or publicity heightens peoples' awareness of their plight. The recipients may be made to appear pitiful and those who ignore them as selfish and uncaring.

Dependents also are subject to burdensome policy, which is usually justified because they are unable to do things for themselves, may harm themselves, and need regulations for their own protection. The young, for example, are so heavily regulated that self-report studies indicate that by the time they reach the age of 18 upwards of 90 percent of all persons will have broken one or more laws that could have led to their contact with the juvenile justice system.[22] Illegal immigrants applying for amnesty under the 1986 immigration legislation were made ineligible for public

22. U.S. House of Representatives (1986).

welfare and some other public services for five years. Presumably this was to encourage self-reliance and to relieve the burden on the welfare system.

Policy tools directed at dependents seldom employ incentives, since it is not assumed that dependents can respond rationally. Instead authority tools are used to direct targets to perform in a particular manner. Sanctions and force are frequently applied to assure that dependents perform as specified. Rather than tools that build the capacity of dependents through the delivery of balanced information, dependents are often on the receiving end of hortatory and symbolic messages, such as the "Just Say No" campaigns aimed at teenagers through which sports and movie stars portray abstinence from drugs as the socially correct behavior.

Dependent target groups are viewed as being unable to do things for themselves. And because they tend to have few organizations of their own, they usually are the secondary target, rather than the proximate target, even when beneficial policies are directed toward them. Their negative constructions and isolation even from one another are impediments to organization. Leadership from within the group is not trusted. Battered women and homeless people, for example, are customarily the secondary target population for assistance because they usually have no self-help organizations that are viewed as responsible enough to be the direct recipient of funds. Instead, the funding goes to local government agencies or nonprofits operated by more powerfully viewed persons. Further, as Smith (chapter 9) notes, contracting out of services to private enterprise, rather than using government-operated services, marginalizes clients even further from governance.

Juvenile justice systems were initially separated from the adult criminal system in the late 1800s in an effort to separate young people—who, even though they had committed "crimes," were not fully responsible for these acts—from adults who were responsible and therefore should be punished. This separation served the useful purpose of enabling beneficial policy to be directed at juveniles instead of having them endure punishments that were intended for adult criminals.

Before 1974, jurisdiction at the federal level for programs directed at youth was in the Department of Health, Education and Welfare. Congress was displeased with the fact that HEW refused to allocate even the funds that legislation had earmarked for delinquency and instead focused on the more positively viewed segments of their target population such as elementary school children. The delinquent groups, then, could be portrayed as neglected.

In 1974 Congress passed the Juvenile Justice and Delinquency Prevention Act, which shifted responsibility from HEW to the Department of Justice and created the Office of Juvenile Justice and Delinquency Prevention. The construction within the statute was that although juveniles were responsible for half the serious crime in the United States, juvenile crime was due to the massive failures of state and local juvenile justice systems that were not providing the necessary services to thousands of neglected and dependent children. Responsibility also was attributed to schools that were expelling children desperately in need of education. Congress wrote into the act an interesting theory of delinquency that enabled policy to direct resources at status offenders and dependents, who were the most sympathetic of the subpopulations covered by the act. The reasoning was that delinquency arises from status-offending behavior, dependency, and neglect. Thus, by providing services to status offenders, dependents, and neglected children, delinquency could be avoided and juvenile crime reduced.

Even though the status offenders were chosen for more resources than delinquents, none of these were the proximate targets in the sense that usually is found with advantaged groups: the funds were all channeled through state and local agencies and nonprofits, which became the primary proponents of the legislation. Over time, the legislation has been expanded to include missing children. This target group initially was constructed as the victim of vicious kidnappers; but in fact kidnapping by strangers is extremely rare and most of these children are either runaways or have been taken by the parent without custody.

One of the techniques that the juvenile justice system uses to maintain the positive and blameless construction of persons under its jurisdiction is to waive "serious" and "violent" offenders to the adult court, thereby ensuring continued support for provision of helpful services to less serious delinquents.[23]

Deviants

Targeting people for punishment is much more prevalent in public policy than is often acknowledged. The explanation offered by critical theory is that as capitalist societies fail more and more to deliver on the promise of equality and justice, it becomes more and more difficult to justify the distribution of privileges to advantaged groups. Further, it is

23. Bortner (1988).

increasingly necessary for government to deflect criticism from itself by placing the blame for problems on others. Some powerless groups offer easy scapegoats for societal problems. For whatever reason, legislators anticipate an outpouring of public support by punishing negatively constructed targets. Baker (chapter 7) notes that illegal immigrants are portrayed as deviants, lacking political power and favorable images. Waves of deportations have followed cycles of economic downturns as joblessness is blamed on permeable borders. The Immigration Reform and Control Act of 1986 separated those immigrants who had become well settled in the United States from new illegal entrants or visa abusers so that more draconian sanctions could be effectively applied and the flow of illegal border crossings could be stopped by the Immigration and Naturalization Service, which was given new enforcement powers. Predictably, legislators will direct highly coercive policy toward deviant target groups such as flagburners or crossburners. It is increasingly popular in legislative circles to make various acts punishable by death, even though there is little research support linking deterrence and the death penalty.

The policy implications for powerless people with negative images who are constructed as deviants are surprisingly similar to those of advantaged groups, except that they receive burdens instead of rewards. Such policies will be high on the legislative agenda, especially during election campaigns. Sanctions and force are preferred policy tools when dealing with deviants. These groups will usually be proximate targets of punishment policy, and the extent of burdens will be out of proportion to any putative purpose of policy. The negative social constructions make it likely that these groups often will receive burdens even when it is illogical from the perspective of policy effectiveness. Among the sanctions directed at deviants are suspension of civil rights: felons are not allowed to vote; the right of assembly is denied targets who are constructed as "gangs." Such tools have direct implications for democratic participation.

Targets regarded as deviant rarely receive beneficial policy, and then only as secondary beneficiaries. It is extremely difficult to pass policies to construct prisons, even when the courts find overcrowding to be inhumane and experts testify that the conditions in jails perpetuate criminality. Even when support comes, it is usually indirect and deviants are at best remote targets. Thus one of the advantages to policymakers of privatizing prisons is that private firms rather than departments of correction can be identified as beneficiaries of prison construction funds.

Mandatory random drug and alcohol testing for safety-sensitive employment is an example of policy directed at what is constructed as a deviant group. The public very much dislikes being subjected to risks, and target groups suspected of acting irresponsibly in matters of public transportation receive strong sanctions. Pilots, motor carriers, and railway engineers, who have the potential for abusing drugs, are viewed as persons capable of inflicting great harm and are therefore carefully licensed and regulated. In the 1980s several terrible transportation accidents involving alcohol and drug use on the job built upon concern about drug use in society at large. Despite the lack of data to suggest that any sizable proportion of transportation workers were substance abusers, and despite doubts about the fairness and dependability of testing procedures, federal laws were enacted in 1991 that allow for extraordinary invasion of personal rights. Without any evidence of probable cause, transportation workers were subjected to preemployment, random on-the-job, and postaccident drug testing.

The impetus for regulation came initially from the National Transportation Safety Board, which was concerned with assessing blame for the growing number of transportation accidents. At first Secretary of Transportation Elizabeth Dole hesitated to act without the support of both management and labor, but after a serious train accident the Department of Transportation swiftly issued rules.[24] Dole's action came when authorities announced that testing indicated an engineer and brakeman had used marijuana before a collision of a Conrail freight locomotive and an Amtrak passenger train, killing 16 and injuring more than 170. Administrative rules were quickly followed by Senate proposals for random drug and alcohol testing for safety-sensitive employment. These regulations added little to what the administration had already done, but put the Senate on record as strongly in favor of testing. Some Senate members warned against acting in haste. One who voted in favor of testing explained, "We had an accident, and this place is run by emotion."[25]

Opposition came from labor and civil liberties groups. The legislative counsel for the Washington office of the American Civil Liberties Union argued, "The secretary of transportation and the sponsors of this bill have exploited the tragic Amtrak-Conrail collision and the public's ig-

24. Ernest Holsendorph, "U.S. Urged to Curb Alcohol Use by Rail Crews," *New York Times*, March 8, 1983, p. A13.
25. Drew Douglas, "Senate Floor Fight Possible: Panel Approves Drug Testing for Transportation Workers," *Congressional Quarterly Weekly Report*, March 14, 1987, p. 476.

norance about urine drug testing to divert attention from their failure to tackle the systematic safety problems that plague the major transportation industries." Republican John Danforth, who sponsored the bill, conceded that random drug testing was an infringement of privacy, but justified the requirement as reasonable. "It is such a small requirement to give a urine sample when scores, maybe hundreds, of people's lives are in your hands."[26] Even though testing could place transportation workers under a cloud of suspicion, and flawed tests could erroneously ruin a career, these were not sufficiently persuasive arguments to thwart the legislation.

Opponents to drug testing without cause were powerless in the face of a strong public outcry. A group of friends and families of the Amtrak-Conrail victims formed a group named Safe Travel, which lobbied against the members of the House of Representatives who held up the bill. During the 1990 election campaign, Roger Horn, whose 16-year-old daughter died in the wreck, appeared at a press conference in the Cincinnati district of Democratic Representative Thomas A. Luken and blasted Luken for systematically blocking action for fifteen months at the behest of the powerful railway union. Shortly thereafter, Luken announced a change of heart and insisted that alcohol be added to random testing. In 1991 a New York subway crash believed to have been caused by a drunken motorman swept aside remaining House opposition to random testing.[27]

The tools employed against substance abusers among transportation workers were almost entirely negative. One provision in the drug regulations was credited with holding up conference agreement for some time. House members wanted to suspend workers who tested positive and refer them to drug rehabilitation programs. The Senate version provided that they be fired outright.[28] The lack of power and protection afforded to transportation workers resisting the testing programs was underscored by a Supreme Court decision upholding administrative regulations. Justice Kennedy wrote for the majority, "The government interest in testing without showing of individualized suspicion is compelling. . . . Employees subject to the tests discharge duties fraught with such risks of injury

26. Paul Starobin, "Airline Flight Records Would Be Public: Senate Attaches Drug Testing to Consumer-Protection Bill," *Congressional Quarterly Weekly Report*, October 31, 1987, p. 2691.

27. Mike Mills, "Conferees Require Drug Testing in Transportation Bill," *Congressional Quarterly Weekly Report*, October 5, 1991, p. 2855.

28. "Drug-Testing Rift Emerges Again," *Congressional Quarterly Weekly Report*, June 10, 1989, p. 1394.

to others that even a momentary lapse of attention can have disastrous consequences."[29]

Dynamics and Pathologies of Social Construction

When the policy design process operates with reasonable fairness, different interest groups within society—including social, racial, and employment groups—are subject to different constructions when they are the targets of different policies. The process of specifying targets and constructing their power and deservedness is dynamic and constantly changing as new policies are made and others are modified. Social constructions are manipulated and used by public officials, the media, and the groups themselves. New target groups are created and images developed for them; old groups are reconfigured or their social constructions changed. New information and events alter public perceptions of the causal linkages creating public problems and thus the appropriate targets of policy.

The AIDS issue provides a striking illustration of how perceptions of issues evolve as targets are identified and variously constructed. Before 1983 AIDS was presented by the media as a medical research problem, and most news stories originated in science journal articles. The only active participants perceived as involved in the issue besides medical researchers were gay men, who, as a potential target of policy, stirred little sympathetic response. The *New York Times*, for instance, provided little coverage of the issue until 1987, in part because one editor believed that stories about gays did not belong in his newspaper.[30] Perceptions of the issue began to change as victims came to be identified as real people, an occurrence associated with Rock Hudson's death from AIDS.

As long as the likely effects of AIDS were limited to negatively constructed groups, ongoing medical research, isolation, and quarantine were viewed as appropriate policy tools. Government targeted immigrants and prisoners for mandatory drug testing. After AIDS was found to occur in babies and among individuals who had received transfusions of infected blood, both attention to the issue and policy tools began to change. Doctors, dentists, and other medical workers were counted

29. Joan Biskupic, "Court Ruling May Give Impetus to Drug-Testing Measures," *Congressional Quarterly Weekly Report*, March 25, 1989, p. 652.
30. Rogers, Dearing, and Chang (1991).

among the stricken, and solely burdensome policies did not seem appropriate. The story of Ryan White, a 13-year-old schoolboy in Indiana who was banned from his classroom, added a civil rights dimension to the story. Gay men's political activism identified more public funding of research and more adequate health care as appropriate policy tools. The cohesion and bravery displayed by the groups began to alter the previous very negative construction of gays.

AIDS emerged as a major policy issue when potential target groups grew broader and were more positively constructed. Public support for spending on the issue increased enormously as the disease was revealed to affect heterosexuals whose behavior was no different from millions of other Americans. The announcement that basketball star Magic Johnson tested positive and then the death of tennis champion Arthur Ashe demonstrated that the disease could affect practically anyone, including the famous and well liked.

Americans' commitment to fairness operates against always placing the same people among advantaged targets. The media, popular culture, and other carriers of social constructions respond to stimuli other than government and begin to portray the advantaged targets as "greedy" rather than "deserving." Movies, books columnists, and dramatic events serve as catalysts for changes in social constructions. The credibility of policies that offer benefits to advantaged groups declines when there are too many objective reasons, verifiable with personal experiences, showing that policy is ineffective in solving problems, or that important problems are not even being addressed, or that the design of policies is illogical and not actually intended to serve the stated goals.

The social constructions of scientists and universities, for example, are not always positive. After Texas was chosen as the site for the SCC and the coalition of physicists with other state and local areas vying for the project no longer existed, doubts were raised in Congress about whether the SCC really was a high national priority. Scientists were sharply questioned about the immediate payoff from the proposed research for ordinary Americans, and doubts were expressed about whether the nation could really afford the project in light of other national needs. Government auditors have embarrassed universities by exposing inappropriate uses of indirect cost charges associated with federal research grants. After newspapers revealed that one university president had used such funds to buy a yacht, other universities voluntarily returned overcharges in order to save their reputations. Such events were shortly followed in the press by a number of books and journal articles criticizing universities for lobbying Congress for pork barrel research appropriations. Such examples illustrate that even high-status groups and institutions are vulnerable to negative constructions when it appears that they are getting more than their fair share from government.

Inflicting punishment upon powerless, negatively viewed groups ultimately has limits as a means of building political support. When common behaviors of large numbers of ordinary people become subject to negative stereotyping, the public does not automatically acquiesce. The 1986 immigration legislation had to give amnesty to millions of longtime undocumented residents not only because expulsion was impossible to enforce but also because it was politically infeasible. Although it was possible to impose mandatory drug testing upon transportation workers, the legislation was stalled for a number of years by controversy. Further, the number of different targets for such invasions of privacy rights has grown quite slowly from the initial base of clearly deviant groups such as prisoners. Enlargement of target groups to include others such as sports figures changes the distribution of resources in the political process. Sports stars have power not available to transportation workers, including access to the press, and are able to argue the case against unreliable tests that unfairly spoil careers.

As long as social constructions are dynamic, self-correcting forces in the system prevent any group from becoming permanently disenfranchised. When these mechanisms do not work, democracy suffers. Stereotypes of privilege and deservedness and stigma of deviance and culpability have settled upon some groups in American society and stick with them regardless of policy area. Social constructions are increasingly a matter of pigeonholing rather than diagnosis or creativity.

There are a number of reasons social constructions of target groups are becoming less flexible and dynamic. Most important are the tensions resulting from the growing social stratification in American life and the widening gap between the rich and the poor. Some scholars have maintained that modern governments in nations with growing inequalities have a legitimation crisis and must explain why democracies concentrate wealth in the hands of the few rather than the many.[31] The rationales governments commonly use for the uneven allocation of goods and services exploit and reinforce stereotypes and stigmas. When policymakers allocate benefits to well-off and powerful groups, they stress the close instrumental link of the group to some social good, such as national

31. Habermas (1975); and Offe (1984).

defense or economic competitiveness. Helping "good" people is not favoritism, it is serving the public interest.

The rationales policymakers use to explain why policies continue to levy costs on those who have not fared so well in the capitalist economy reinforces images of dependents and deviance. The rights of dependents are restricted for their own good and because they cannot be expected to use good judgment. Deviants are punished because they are evil by nature. Even when dependents and deviants benefit, the rationales are alienating and disempowering. Justice-based explanations, including equity, need, or rights, are commonly used. Landy (chapter 2) argues that there has been a proliferation of rights-based claims in policy, which discourages democratic deliberation. Our point is that rights rationales reinforce dependence and powerlessness. The poor receive welfare because of social compassion. Poor defendants are given counsel in court because the Constitution requires it. Such explanations separate powerless groups from any positive, instrumental connection with the public interest. Rationales also remove both the government and the advantaged from culpability for social and racial strife. Blaming the victim is increasingly common in rationales for urban decay and riots: inner-city residents do not get ahead because they are undeserving.

The growing importance of lifestyle questions in American politics, such as family values, fortifies unvarying and uniform positive or negative images of certain groups in society. Flaws in moral behavior are identified as the root of America's problems. Bad things are happening to people because they have made incorrect choices. For instance, some conservative spokespersons have suggested that divorced and working mothers and those who choose abortion are responsible for their own difficulties.

The decline of political parties as a means for rallying and disciplining policymakers has meant that support for policies must be built individually. It is more convenient and simple for policymakers to rely on stereotypes and prejudices in designing policy and selecting targets than to create separate images for the targets of each policy. Just as party labels once signaled which side of a question held the least risk for a legislator, the prevailing social construction of targets now signals the politically correct stance. The results are static portrayals of targets in which the same socioeconomic classes or geographic groups are persistently treated as advantaged, contenders, dependents, or deviants.

The growing involvement of the mass media in politics has resulted in the tendency to fall back on conventional and popular stereotypes in selecting policy targets and policy design. Whole classes of people are tarred with the words and actions of extreme spokespersons such as David Duke or Sister Souljah because such persons provide dramatic, simplified sound bites. New and changed social constructions of targets require more time and thought than is ordinarily communicable on television.

Agencies and state and local governments implementing policies can also reinforce stereotypes and persistent images. Often pressed to distribute inadequate resources, they engage in "creaming" or redefining targets to include those groups that are constructed most positively. Marston (chapter 6) notes that in Tucson the target populations of community action programs gravitated toward middle-class or advantaged neighborhoods and away from the poor minorities for which the program was designed in the 1960s.

Persistent Construction, Citizenship, and Participation

When the process of social construction is competitive and dynamic, the experience citizens have with government is likely to vary over time and from one policy area to another. Each person will receive a reasonable share of benefits and costs and will be subject to a variety of tools, including authority and capacity building. In dealing with government, whether people are solicited by outreach programs or must present themselves and press for service, their experiences will not vary greatly from one person to another. However, when people are consistently given the same image or stereotype as targets of policy learning, their experience with government is very different.

Persistent construction of certain classes of people as distinct types of targets imparts messages that relate to citizenship and participation. The unvarying experience people have with policy informs them of their status as citizens and how they and people like themselves are likely to be treated by government. Such information becomes internalized. These continually reiterated messages people receive tell them whether they are viewed as active participants in government and bureaucracy or whether they are passive recipients in the process. Experience with policy tells people whether they need to deal directly with government and bureaucracy as individuals to press their own claims, or whether they can join with others in solving problems collectively for the common good.

The messages for the consistently advantaged targets are that they are good, intelligent people. Government appears responsive to them. Policies often involve outreach and seldom require needs tests; thus the advantaged do not see themselves as claimants or as dependent on government. Instead, they are a crucial part of the effort to achieve national goals, such as national defense or economic vitality.

Advantaged groups see government as a responsive forum for pursuing their own purposes, and they often win. There is little difference between their interests and the public interest, and so there is nothing wrong with purely self-interested behavior. The signals they get from policy design seldom indicate that sacrifice or deferring to others serves a larger purpose. When other groups are singled out for benefits, especially those who are less powerful or negatively constructed, the advantaged believe that the government is on the wrong track. Change in leadership is needed. When policies are ineffective, they blame government rather than themselves and they mobilize for change. When government does not work, these groups are likely to organize and devise private alternatives to public services, such as private schools, security systems, or mental health services.

Those regularly selected by policy as advantaged are participants in traditional ways, such as voting, interest group activity, and campaign contributions. There are clear rewards for mobilization, and advantaged targets pursue their self-interest in participation. They are resistant to appeals to sacrifice for others, whom prevailing social constructions have portrayed as undeserving.

Those who are treated consistently by policy as contenders receive very different messages and have contrasting orientations toward government. Politics is a game of raw competition in which they must wield their power with skill or lose. They are likely to resent being treated as scapegoats and to distrust popular government. Clandestine power is preferable, especially when it can be used to alter the symbolic and vague costs to which they are regularly subjected by policy. Even though contenders often profit from government when their behind-the-scenes manipulation pays off, their experience is inconsistent. Consequently, such groups are generally antigovernment and prefer weak agencies with low capacity to administer laws. Those regularly targeted as contenders will participate through lobbying and campaign contributions.

The messages to those regularly labeled as dependents are that they are poor, helpless, and needy. Their problems are their own, and it is not in the public interest to address them. They get attention only through the generosity of others. Income testing and the typical requirement that they must apply to the agency for benefits (rather than being sought out through outreach programs) requires them to admit their dependent status.

Those regularly treated as dependents view government with disinterest and passivity. The game of politics is a bureaucratic game, where they wait in line and eventually get what others want them to have. There is little sense in voting or other conventional kinds of participation since government and politics are matters that concern others, not people like themselves.

Persons who are consistently characterized as deviant targets will have mainly negative experiences with government. The overwhelming messages are that they are "bad" people whose behavior constitutes a problem for others. They will be punished unless they change or avoid contact with the government. Accordingly, these people will frequently fail to claim government benefits for which they are eligible. On the other hand, they are often able to escape law enforcement or they observe others avoid punishment, and so government appears to be arbitrary and unpredictable. The rule of law and justice have no meaning. They are angry and oppressed people who have no faith in government's fairness or effectiveness. They see themselves as alone and as individual players who have no chance of "winning" in a game that they view as essentially corrupt. Even if those characterized as deviant are legally eligible for conventional forms of participation such as voting, running for office, and interest group activity, they will view these forms of participation as irrelevant. Participation, when it occurs, is likely to be in more disruptive and individualized forms, such as riots and protests.

While the reasons for self-interested behavior, cynicism about politics, alienation, and low participation are many, we believe that part of the explanation is to be found in the persistent stereotypes and stigmas cast on targets by policy design. Consistent experiences with policy teach powerful lessons, especially when social constructions that play on emotions and affect self-concept are involved. The high- and middle-income tax breaks regularly extended to the advantaged and contenders in order to help the economy probably teach recipients more about government and citizenship than do elections. Similarly, the long lines in front of welfare offices that are frequently closed tell dependents more about government than short lines for the voting booth.

When policies stray far from equal treatment of citizens, the consequences are damaging to democratic citizenship and participation. Advantaged target groups are not likely to have empathy with the dependents' complaints about an uncaring government because their interests are regularly served. Further, the advantaged are helped by government themselves and have no experience with a government that neglects, burdens, or punishes. Conversely, it is difficult for dependents and deviants to comprehend the utility of actively mobilizing, lobbying, or voting.

Policy Design for Democracy

If, as we argue, the source of some of the problems with democratic participation as evidenced in American government today can be traced to policy designs that reinforce damaging messages about citizenship and the role of government, what is the correct prescription for better policy design? Certainly some recommendations would seem to be misguided. Lowi's juridical democracy, under which policies are designed with clear rules so that the beneficiaries and the burdened can be clearly identified, does not hold much promise. If benefits are mainly directed at targets that come from groups habitually benefited by policy, advantaged groups are reinforced in self-interested behavior. Mark Petracca argues that Lowi's theory is deficient because it suffers from the same underlying problems currently being experienced: people pursue their private interests through politics, and policy designs do not reeducate them to become more involved, public-spirited citizens.[32] If burdens are clearly associated with groups ordinarily constructed as deviant, alienation and disengagement among such groups will increase.

Policy designs that base the identification and treatment of targets on more objective, technical criteria would alleviate some of the difficulties encountered in targets selected on the basis of social construction, but would also create other problems. There would be the problems of political feasibility and gaining public support such as those that many critics of policy science have identified.[33] Rational policy designs depend very much on perspective, and what may make perfect sense from an engineering point of view makes none from that of an economist. Further, as Stone (chapter 3) points out, technical standards for choosing targets carry their own social constructions. Targets identified by clinical diagnosis may be stigmatized as abnormal and discouraged from political mobilization.

32. Petracca (1990).
33. Wildavsky (1987); and Stone (1988).

Modifying our expectations about activist national government policy and expecting more from lower levels of government and nongovernmental institutions removes the invidious messages conveyed by persistent policy designs that serve prepackaged stereotypes. However, it is not at all certain that policies designed by these institutions are likely to be more empowering and less prejudiced. Renouncing federal policy, which seems to be the prescription of Wilson and many critical theorists, would seem to ignore an instrument of positive social change.

Conscious changes in policy design can avoid many of the present dysfunctional messages and resulting negative citizen orientations toward government and participation. Policies should be designed with appropriate attention to their effect on citizenship, as well as attention to technical and political feasibility. Policies with generalized policy targets in which everyone is treated the same are appealing. There are many advantages of policy tools that build capacity and teach, rather than sanctions or negative incentives, including the potentially positive effect upon citizenship. In specifying target groups through policy, old divisions of geographic areas, race, class, gender, and sex can be avoided, and new boundaries set among target groups that break down previous stereotypes. Community service as an option to student loans for all college students, basic health care insurance guaranteed to all Americans, tax and budget cutting plans requiring broad and balanced sacrifice, as well as policy options discussed by Valelly (chapter 11), are examples. Of course, policies must be designed to fit particular contexts, and there are few general rules of design that fit all cases. However, policies must be sensitive to multiple goals and concern, and surely one overarching concern must be strengthening citizen capacity and participation.

References

Arnold, R. Douglas. 1990. *The Logic of Congressional Action*. Yale University Press.

Bortner, M. A. 1988. *Delinquency and Justice: An Age of Crisis*. McGraw-Hill.

Edelman, Murray J. 1988. *Constructing the Political Spectacle*. University of Chicago Press.

Habermas, Jürgen. 1975. *Legitimation Crisis*, translated by Thomas McCarthy. Boston: Beacon Press.

Ingram, Helen. 1978. "The Political Rationality of Innovation: The Clean Air Act Amendments of 1970." In *Approaches to Controlling Air Pollution*, edited by Ann F. Friedlaender, 12–64. MIT Press.

Ingram, Helen, and Anne Schneider. 1991. "The Choice of Target Populations." *Administration and Society* 23 (November): 333–56.
Jacoby, Henry D., and John D. Steinbruner. 1973. *Clearing the Air: Federal Policy on Automotive Emission Control*. Cambridge: Ballinger.
Linder, Stephen, and B. Guy Peters. 1992. "The Study of Policy Instruments." *Policy Currents* 2(2): 1, 4–7.
Lowi, Theodore J. 1964. "American Business, Public Policy, Case Studies, and Political Theory." *World Politics* 16 (July): 677–715.
———. 1972. "Four Systems of Policy, Politics, and Choice." *Public Administration Review* 32 (July–August): 298–310.
———. 1979. *The End of Liberalism: The Second Republic of the United States*. Norton.
Luke, Timothy W. 1989. *Screens of Power: Ideology, Domination, and Resistance in Informational Society*. University of Illinois Press.
Offe, Claus. 1984. *Contradictions of the Welfare State*, edited by John Keane. MIT Press.
Petracca, Mark P. 1990. "Politics Beyond the 'End of Liberalism.' " *PS: Political Science and Politics* 23 (December): 566–69.
Rogers, Everett M., James W. Dearing, and Soonbum Chang. 1991. "AIDS in the 1980s: The Agenda-Setting Process for a Public Issue." *Journalism Monographs* no. 126.
Schneider, Anne, and Helen Ingram. 1990. "Policy Design: Elements, Premises, and Strategies." In *Policy Theory and Policy Evaluation*, edited by Stuart S. Nagel, 77–101. Greenwood Press.
———. 1993. "Social Construction of Target Regulations: Implications for Politics and Policy." *American Political Science Review* 87 (June): 334–47.
Stone, Deborah A. 1988. *Policy Paradox and Political Reason*. Scott, Foresman.
Taubes, Gary. 1986. *Nobel Dreams: Power, Deceit, and the Ultimate Experience*. Random House.
U.S. House of Representatives. Committee on the Judiciary. 1986. *The Immigration Reform and Control Act of 1986*. P.L. 99-603. Serial 14. 99 Cong. 2 sess.
Wildavsky, Aaron. 1987. *Speaking Truth to Power: The Art and Craft of Policy Analysis*. New Brunswick: Transaction Books.
Wilson, James Q. 1973. *Political Organizations*. Basic Books.
———. 1990. "Judicial Democracy versus American Democracy." *PS: Political Science and Politics* 23 (December): 570–72.

Part Two ————————————————————————
Informing and Mobilizing Citizens

GOVERNMENT CAN, BY design or unwittingly, use policy to trigger consciousness of public problems, create constituencies, and affect the behavior and influence of individuals and groups. Authority wielded through policy may be helpful or damaging to democratic participation. The ability to mobilize outside the state in order to exert influence upon government policy is critical to citizen independence in a democracy. Yet government has an obligation to inform citizens on civic matters, especially when lack of information is an impediment to participation or access to information is unequal. The three chapters in this section examine the kinds of citizen involvement that may be activated by policy.

Janet Weiss considers the possible effects of public information campaigns. The kind of information transfers she examines are very different from the subtle messages that Stone and Ingram and Schneider analyze in their chapters. Unlike clinical reasoning or social constructions, public information campaigns overtly attempt to change what people think and what they think about. By taking up one particular policy instrument and tracing the patterns of activity that may follow from it, she offers a prospective analysis that is different from the historical cases in the two chapters that follow. The influence of any tool is much affected by the intent and skill of the user, and so it is not surprising that Weiss finds public information campaigns both good and bad for democracy. More important than such mixed conclusions are the wealth of examples she cites from previous research about the use of the tool and its effects. Particularly useful are the strategies she suggests for enhancing the positive consequences of public information campaigns for citizen participation.

Both Sallie Marston and Susan Gonzales Baker provide case

examples of policies that created new demands and encouraged a more participatory brand of citizenship. In Marston's study, government acted with intent. Drawing upon the history of the war on poverty and the community action program as it evolved in Tucson, Arizona, Marston finds that the widely acknowledged failure of the Great Society's policies to eliminate poverty is only part of the story. These federal programs left what they were supposed to have provided, a lasting legacy at the local level of changed political terrain and institutionalized opportunities for neighborhood participation. The sort of decentralized, public arenas for deliberation idealized by Landy in chapter 2 were only partially realized in Tucson, however. Over the 1980s, middle-class neighborhoods have become powerful political forces, but these gains have ironically come at the expense of the poor, disorganized minorities whom the war on poverty originally intended to help.

The creation of a new constituency with enhanced opportunities for participation was an unexpected consequence of the amnesty provisions of the Immigration Reform and Control Act, according to Baker. The relation of economic and political rights to the full exercise of democratic citizenship become an issue in this chapter, as they are in chapters 8 and 9 below. Oddly, it is the pursuit of economic well-being that attracted many immigrants to seek amnesty status. In the process of granting amnesty to 1.7 million people, however, a new legalized constituency and associated intermediary nonprofit groups gained a significant political foothold. The increased political power afforded immigrants decidedly affected their social construction and their treatment by governmental bureaucracy.

Citizenship is both an individual and associational activity, as these chapters related to mobilization illustrate. Public information campaigns are attempts by government to reach individuals directly over the heads of intermediary groups. Undemocratically exploited, such campaigns can transform a structural problem, like pollution, into an individual sin, like littering. But carefully designed campaigns can facilitate interaction and deliberation, as Weiss suggests. The isolated character of dependent and deviant groups has long disempowered immigrant populations. Yet the process of granting amnesty, designed as a right granted to individuals on a case-by-case basis, was transformed through the intervention of nongovernmental organizations into a potential political advocacy movement.

Political mobilizations fostered by policy may both enhance and threaten democracy, depending upon the context. Immigrant groups previously portrayed as deviants gained political power and status through the advocacy of nonprofit organizations. However, the neighborhood movement in Tucson tended to benefit powerful middle-class interests rather than the poor and disadvantaged. Although it is unlikely that interests can be adequately expressed and represented in a pluralist political system without mobilization, association can foster either the assertion of narrow self-interest or a vehicle for the promotion of the general welfare.

5. Policy Design for Democracy: A Look at Public Information Campaigns

JANET A. WEISS

POLICY ANALYSTS search for appropriate tools to move society in the direction of desired objectives. Thus, for example, they might weigh the relative merits of taxes or regulation to reduce reliance on imported oil. Or they might consider several generic strategies to raise student achievement in public schools, including national standards, grants to local districts, or equalizing school funding. Which tool will achieve the most progress toward the objective? Which tool will be least expensive? Which tool can be implemented most reliably? Which tools are compatible with the ideology of powerful political leaders, can attract the requisite support among elected officials to be adopted in the political process, or will muster enthusiastic support from the staff of the government agencies who will administer the resulting policies? Asking such questions alerts policymakers to the effectiveness, efficiency, and political feasibility of alternate policy instruments. Evaluations of various instruments along such criteria help to inform policy deliberations and promote better public policy.

In this volume, the authors have directed attention to another criterion for evaluating the choice of policy instrument: the consequences of using that instrument for subsequent participation by citizens in democratic processes. This criterion has been largely neglected in the literature on policy design and instrument selection in favor of efficiency, effectiveness, and feasibility of adoption and implementation. In weighing the advantages and disadvantages of different instruments, some authors have noted that some policy instruments are more politically appealing than others.[1] But few have asked how the use of particular policy instruments affects subsequent political relationships.

I am grateful to Helen Ingram and the other authors in this volume for useful comments and suggestions, and to Mary Tschirhart, who provided capable research assistance, good advice, and collegiality.

1. Salamon (1981).

In this chapter, I examine one instrument to see what can be learned by explicit analysis of the consequences of the use of that instrument for citizenship and democratic participation. The instrument is the public information campaign: a government-directed and -sponsored effort to communicate to the mass public or a segment of the public in order to achieve a policy result. Public information campaigns (PICs) are one way that government officials deliberately attempt to shape public attitudes, values, or behavior in the hope of reaching some desirable social outcome. In other words, they are an instrument of government action. In more specific terms, information campaigns are "intend[ed] to generate specific outcomes or effects in a relatively large number of individuals, usually within a specified period of time and through an organized set of communication activities."[2] I include government campaigns that are aimed at producing policy results, such as advertising to get people involved in government services or activities (such as family planning, crime prevention, or military recruitment) or designed to influence household behavior (such as energy conservation, eating habits, or alcohol consumption) that is linked to policy goals (such as reducing dependence on oil imports, reducing health care costs, or reducing alcohol-related accidents). I exclude advertising for political parties or candidates, for these are not official acts of government. I also exclude the direct promotion of government products, such as postage stamps or lotteries, for these are primarily revenue-raising strategies and only indirectly designed to achieve policy goals.

By looking at a generic instrument and predicting the patterns of activity that may follow from its use under diverse circumstances, I offer a different angle on citizenship and democracy than is possible by looking at historical cases. Prospective analysis of this type may inform policymakers of the opportunities and threats of various courses of action or may justify and legitimate the choice of any given policy instrument.[3]

Public Information Campaigns in Action

In the repertoire of government instruments, public information campaigns are unusual in that their implications for citizenship and democracy have attracted some attention from social scientists outside of policy

2. See Rogers and Storey (1987, p. 821).
3. Majone (1989).

studies. My analysis does not, therefore, need to begin from scratch. Public information campaigns also present in sharp relief some of the policy design quandaries that arise when policy analysts attempt to introduce issues of democracy. As this chapter shows, assessing consequences of policy choices for citizenship and democracy is not straightforward. Subsequent analyses of other instruments may find some of the same quandaries of mixed effects in different forms.

Public information campaigns offer an interesting case for the analysis of political consequences because they attempt to change what people think and what they think about.[4] While most policies are directed at changing the incentives or rules governing institutions, other levels of government, or business, for example, public information campaigns are directed at individual members of the public. PICs bypass the institutions in which individuals are embedded and communicate directly with citizens. This characteristic makes them especially useful when people are not organized around the behavior of interest. For example, public information campaigns may ask individuals to refrain from drinking and driving, trying to influence individual choices made at home, at work, at the homes of friends, and in a variety of public places.

However, apparently autonomous people are always embedded in powerful social institutions, such as community, place of employment, occupation, racial or ethnic group, religion, or other meaningful collectivities. Any policy instrument that ignores this embeddedness may overlook opportunities for influence over target behavior and may be vulnerable to counterpressures from these mediating institutions.[5] For example, drinking drivers may be influenced by community norms or by the practices of establishments that serve alcoholic beverages. Therefore PICs may seek to detach individuals from the norms and practices of their social groups (counteracting the norm that drunken driving is socially acceptable or shows courage) or to strengthen those attachments ("friends don't let friends drive drunk"). Alternatively, PICs may be used in combination with other policy instruments designed to change social institutions, such as sobriety checks on highways or laws making bartenders legally liable for accidents caused by inebriated customers. Whether used alone or to complement other policy instruments, the active ingredient in PICs is the effort to change the thinking of individual members of the target audi-

4. Weiss and Tschirhart (forthcoming); and Roberts and Maccoby (1985).
5. Salmon (1989).

CARL A. RUDISILL LIBRARY
LENOIR-RHYNE COLLEGE

ence. And this ingredient sets up the possibility for information campaigns to influence the ways citizens understand acts of government and their own role in society.

The use of any policy instrument defines not only a set of activities but also a set of relationships between citizens and government. Such relationships shape opportunities for subsequent political behavior by citizens and citizens' confidence in the efficacy of political participation. Two such relationships are implicit in social science analyses of public information campaigns, as signaled by the language used to describe campaigns. I have called them "public information campaigns," a relatively neutral term. Some researchers use the more pejorative term "propaganda" to describe the identical activity.[6] This label signals awareness of a relationship in which campaigns disempower citizens and induce passivity while enhancing the power and status of government propagandists.[7] Yet other social scientists describe the same activity approvingly, referring to public "education" or "deliberation" to describe active, organized communication from government to citizen.[8] These positive labels signal awareness of a relationship in which government officials seek to enlighten citizens.

In the following sections, I look at the effects of PICs on the relationship between citizens and government. I make use of a collection of 100 examples of campaigns by governments in the United States and around the world.[9] From these examples and other literature, I identify negative and positive consequences for democratic processes of using public information campaigns. These consequences address four underpinnings of democratic participation: the competition of ideas, the integrity of democratic processes, equality of access to information, and the role of the citizen. Negative and positive consequences prove difficult to disentangle, even when looking at individual campaigns. I find that attention to democratic processes has implications for the design and use of information campaigns as policy instruments.

The Dangers of Information Campaigns for Democracy

Public information campaigns can have four important negative consequences for democratic participation. First, campaigns may weaken

6. See Yudof (1983); Ginsberg (1986); or Qualter (1985).
7. Ellul (1965).
8. For example, Reich (1988); Landy, Roberts, and Thomas (1990); and Dryzek (1990).
9. These examples were collected by Weiss and Tschirhart (forthcoming).

and distort the competition of ideas in a free and open marketplace. Such a competition is often seen as a vehicle to ensure freedom of expression and to protect dissent. Domination and deception undermine "communicative rationality" that permits society to learn through discussion and to discover good public policies.[10] Repeated endorsement of particular positions or behavior may have the effect of limiting and restricting debate. If well-financed businesses are powerful enough to dominate channels of communication and influence public attention, well-financed government poses a similar threat. Examples include Singapore's campaign to induce its ethnic Chinese citizens to "Speak Mandarin" rather than local dialects[11] or the U.S. army's campaigns to recruit volunteers for military service.[12] A government campaign can drown out dissent by conveying only one side of a political controversy.

Second, public information campaigns may threaten democratic processes by circularity of democratic control and self-aggrandizement by government agencies. The circularity problem is that government agencies use campaigns to shape public attitudes and values, which in turn shape the public's expectations and demands on government. By creating, at least in part, the public attitudes that are supposed to govern them, the agencies are subverting the process of democratic accountability. An example is a campaign by the California Department of Parks and Recreation to encourage voters to support a bond issue to acquire park land.[13] The aggrandizement problem comes when public information campaigns relentlessly promote the wisdom, beneficence, and value of government programs or agencies. Such campaigns sabotage the public's capacity to hold agencies accountable by manipulating the image of the agency. For example, the campaign featuring Smokey Bear in his forest ranger cap has been an extraordinary success in promoting the U.S. Forest Service and its employees.[14] Both circularity and aggrandizement suppress or deflect popular demands on government that might legitimately emerge in the absence of the information campaigns.

Third, public information campaigns may exacerbate inequalities in access to information between well-educated and poorly educated citizens. By dealing in the currency of information and ideas, information campaigns may be more readily understood and used by those with better

10. Dryzek (1990); and Lindblom (1990).
11. Kuo (1984).
12. Shyles and Hocking (1990).
13. Yudof (1983).
14. McNamara, Kurth, and Hansen (1981); and Morrison (1976).

educational skills.[15] The result of relying on PICs as policy instruments may be that better educated citizens become even more advantaged than poorly educated citizens. This has been a concern in the AIDS campaigns; middle-class gay men have made better use of information from prevention campaigns than less affluent, less educated intravenous drug users and their partners.[16]

Fourth, public information campaigns may constrict the role of citizens by closing off opportunities for choice or autonomy, promoting passivity in political discussion, or denying the legitimacy of the citizens' own understanding of social circumstances. Communication through the mass media can be authoritarian, grounded in assumptions about who is entitled to speak and who is supposed to listen. For example, the "say no" messages of anticocaine campaigns of the mid-1980s were more likely to convey the moral disapproval of government officials than to constitute effective intervention into life decisions of cocaine users or their families.[17] One study concluded that the most significant effect of PICs that use television advertising is their encouragement of political passivity by citizens.[18]

The Value of Information Campaigns for Democracy

If public information campaigns have potentially dangerous consequences for democracy, they also have great potential for constructive consequences. On all of the same dimensions, PICs can enhance the quality of political discussion for individuals and for society, thereby strengthening the democratic process.

First, public information campaigns can improve the richness and fairness of the competition of ideas. When government officials weigh into a public debate, they publicize arguments that may otherwise be submerged by communication from entrenched interests. This counterbalance is especially important when PICs work at cross-purposes with massive commercial advertising. Examples include campaigns against cigarette smoking or campaigns to promote breast feeding over using baby formula.[19] Multimedia government campaigns may also reach a

15. Tichenor, Donohue, and Olien (1970).
16. Fisher and Fisher (1992).
17. Shoemaker (1989).
18. Paletz, Pearson, and Willis (1977).
19. See Flay (1987) on smoking and Hornik (1988) on breast feeding.

wider audience than conventional channels of mass media might otherwise reach, extending public debate throughout the population.

Second, public information campaigns can enrich the possibilities for citizens to hold government officials accountable through democratic participation. Better-informed citizens may participate more knowledgeably and effectively in all democratic processes. Achieving policy results through the spread of information may be less coercive and more respectful of individual rights than achieving the same results with other policy tools, such as taxes or penalties.[20] Information campaigns break down barriers between experts and citizens, demystifying bureaucracy and empowering genuine participation on controversial issues. Some analysts talk about such campaigns as civic education; in the environmental arena most citizens need more information before they can participate in a constructive way.[21] Using PICs, public officials can do their work in ways that enhance public understanding of public policy choices and strengthen democratic processes.

Third, public information campaigns can be effective in informing the least well informed citizens, thereby reducing inequality in access to information. Some researchers have found that campaigns can narrow the information advantage of the highly educated.[22] The highly educated are typically well informed both before and after exposure to PIC messages. But the less well educated may make the greatest gain from exposure to government-sponsored campaigns, especially when campaigns use channels and messages that are well suited to audiences without much prior knowledge of the issues of the campaign. For example, the asbestos awareness campaign succeeded in raising awareness of asbestos hazards among blue-collar workers who were likely to be exposed to asbestos and who were less well informed about asbestos before the campaign than better-educated segments of the population.[23] In family planning, drug abuse, and AIDS prevention, numerous campaigns have addressed precisely those audiences that have not benefited from information widely disseminated by mainstream media.

Fourth, public information campaigns can expand citizens' horizons and imagination. They may treat citizens as partners in addressing collective problems and opportunities and endorse the legitimacy of citizens' understanding of their own circumstances. For example, New York City

20. Weiss (1990).
21. Landy, Roberts, and Thomas (1990).
22. Robinson (1981).
23. Freimuth and Van Nevel (1981).

used a campaign to mobilize parents to pressure landlords into installing safety devices on windows to prevent children from falling.[24] In so doing, city officials did not blame parents for negligence, but instead promoted autonomy and a sense of political efficacy among citizens.

When information campaigns succeed in conveying information and creating the potential for informed deliberation, participation becomes more likely but is not guaranteed. No single policy intervention ever satisfies the requirements for effective participation. Citizens still need institutional structures, supportive political communities, and flexibility to act on what they have learned or decided. However, acts of public policy, such as public information campaigns, contribute to the political environment within which participation takes place. In that sense, they may tilt individuals toward or away from effective involvement in the political process.

The Paradox: Information Campaigns Have Two Faces

Public information campaigns may spin off positive or negative consequences for democratic processes. This presents no problem if government officials could distinguish campaigns with good effects from those with bad ones and engage only in the former. But that is not possible. Nearly all campaigns seem to have both good and bad effects.

Individual campaigns can simultaneously weaken and strengthen the competition of ideas. A campaign by the U.S. government to persuade people to stop smoking cigarettes can enrich the competition of ideas by balancing commercial advertising by the tobacco companies.[25] It also extends health information to a larger share of the affected public than typically has access to such information.[26] But the same campaign can be seen in a less benign light.[27] The campaign embodies the assumption that cigarette smoking is a problem of individual smokers, not of society more broadly. Therefore individual smokers, in their own interest, must summon the discipline to quit. By hammering home the assumption that smoking is an individual problem with an individual solution, the campaign reinforces and perpetuates the tobacco industry's message that

24. Spiegel and Lindaman (1977).
25. Warner (1977).
26. McAlister and others (1989).
27. Wallack (1990).

cigarette smoking is a matter of individual tastes and freedom. Hence it is not an appropriate subject of government regulation or prohibition. Such a campaign can be seen to narrow debate, to rule out structural alternatives for ameliorating health problems, and to divert attention away from policies opposed by business interests. This perspective is not to denigrate antismoking campaigns but to point out that many public information campaigns seem to have positive and negative effects on the competition of ideas.

Campaigns may simultaneously strengthen and threaten democratic values and equal access to information. For example, campaigns promoting household energy conservation educate many people who can benefit from technical advice about household energy consumption and who may not receive credible advice from other sources.[28] The audience for these campaigns is empowered to make more informed judgments about their political positions toward energy as well as about their own household behavior. The same campaigns, however, seem to push forward favorable images of federal and state regulatory agencies and reduce public demand for more aggressive energy policy aimed at energy producers and distributors. The energy conservation campaigns may deliver messages of more value to homeowners than to renters, perhaps reinforcing the belief of lower-income citizens that government is only interested in the needs of the middle class. As a result, rates of participation among the poor will be lower than those of the middle class. The very same campaigns thus may stimulate political participation along some lines while suppressing it along others.

Public information campaigns may strengthen the capacity of individuals to act as responsible citizens while simultaneously constricting opportunities for citizens. Family planning information campaigns may offer parents the efficacy and control to realize their aspirations to limit the size of their families. This benefit seems to expand autonomy and choice, especially for women. But these campaigns may also be coercive in changing social expectations about family size, denying the legitimacy of at least some parents' wishes, and diverting attention away from demands for economic change by focusing on the predicament of individual families.[29] A Nigerian campaign promoting reading and adult literacy, for another example, ignores the value that many Nigerian cultures place

28. Farhar-Pilgrim and Shoemaker (1981); and Hutton (1982).
29. Warwick (1990).

on oral traditions.[30] However, it also opens avenues for self-improvement and self-esteem by those who need encouragement and skills to participate more productively in modern society.

The paradox of simultaneous good and bad effects is highly unsatisfactory. It frustrates generalization. Perhaps the paradox can be unraveled to separate the good from the bad.

One possibility is to consider separately campaigns addressed to high-status versus low-status targets. Helen Ingram and Anne Schneider (chapter 4) suggest that public policies are grounded in social images and assumptions about target groups; policies send messages to targets with implications for political participation. Ingram and Schneider hypothesize that policies addressed to powerful, advantaged target groups are likely to assume voluntary compliance and to build capacity among members of those groups. Public information campaigns, which build capacity and assume voluntary compliance, might thus be focused on high-status groups, who are presumed to be effective decisionmakers. Provide these high-status targets with the right information, and they will make the right decisions, leading to desired policy results. If public information campaigns are indeed disproportionately aimed at powerful groups, then concerns about their consequences for discouraging political participation are less troubling; powerful groups, by definition, have the resources to resist exploitation.

Mary Tschirhart and I coded a set of campaigns into those addressed to the general public, to high-status segments of the public, and to low-status segments of the public.[31] We found that the clear majority (60 percent) are aimed at the general public, a smaller cluster (31 percent) targets relatively low-status groups, and an even smaller cluster (8 percent) is aimed at relatively high-status groups. Campaigns addressed to high-status groups include those dealing with drug abuse, mental illness, and business practices. Campaigns dealing with drug abuse, family planning, pest control, immigration, and parenting address low-status groups. This limited evidence suggests that information campaigns are at least as likely to be directed to low-status or stigmatized target groups as to high-status target groups. The argument is plausible that policy designers use PICs with high-status groups in the belief that these groups are rational citizens who can be persuaded to behave appropriately. But it is also plausible that policy designers use PICS with low-status groups in the

30. Nweke (1987).
31. Weiss and Tschirhart (forthcoming).

belief that these people have information deficits or are easily manipulated by campaigns. The instrument does not inherently embody a message that values or devalues the target.

If individual campaigns do not necessarily send negative messages, the cumulative effect of many campaigns may be a source of concern. Public information campaigns help to set the public agenda, inviting citizens to think about the issues on the minds of government officials.[32] Government officials in a democracy have some responsibility for ensuring that their voice does not drown out all other voices in setting the agenda. This concern may require restraint in the use of public information campaigns, even when a good case can be made for the value of any particular campaign. A parallel to commercial advertising and political advertising may make this point clearer. No individual commercial may be troubling. But the drumbeat of commercial advertising seems to have pervasive cultural effects that promote a consumer orientation.[33] Similarly the aggregate effect of political advertising for candidates may be alienating to voters even when individual ads are inoffensive. In this way, PICs in aggregate may promote system support even when no single campaign seems inappropriate. Some observers find this possibility deeply troubling; others find it not only tolerable but desirable for government to participate in socialization of citizens leading to support for their government.[34]

The paradox remains. To inform, educate, and persuade is, from another point of view, to distract, deceive, and manipulate. Disentangling the positive and negative contributions of public information campaigns to the relationships between government and citizens cannot be done in a way that will survive scrutiny from multiple perspectives. Inevitably, the very mechanism that can produce constructive results for democracy—reliance on conveying ideas to individuals to produce change in social outcomes—enables government officials to distract attention and evade accountability by conveying ideas to individuals that discourage and divert change.

This analysis highlights the relationship between policy and democracy in policy design. Public information campaigns, like other policy instruments, are more than neutral means for achieving ends. Their use raises broader questions about how citizens and governments deal with one another. Whether these questions are ignored or recognized, they

32. Graber (1992).
33. Schudson (1984).
34. Ginsberg (1986); and Kotler and Roberto (1989).

are important and inescapable features of the selection of this policy instrument.

Design Implications: Safeguards against Misuse

One response to the dangers of PICs is to build institutional safeguards against potential abuses of campaigns. In the United States, three important institutional safeguards are in place. One is the fragmentation of authority within the executive branch. Because problems are divided among highly specialized bureaucracies, federal and state governments run public information campaigns that originate in different agency agendas, are shaped by different kinds of professional expertise, and seldom reinforce one another. Another aspect of fragmentation is the difference in perspective between the line agencies and the oversight agencies of the executive branch. The Office of Management and Budget during the Reagan and Bush presidencies actively discouraged the use of public information campaigns and other kinds of publicity activity by federal agencies.[35] When multiple voices speak through campaigns, the dangers of manipulation seem less severe.

A second safeguard comes from the differing interests of the executive, legislative, and judicial branches in public information campaigns. Congressional and judicial oversight of executive activity can ensure that public information campaigns are grounded in the legitimate mission of an agency and the authorized expenditure of tax dollars. Such oversight helps to minimize the opportunities for executive self-aggrandizement and circularity of accountability. Numerous legislative provisions constrain executive agency efforts to inform or propagandize the public.[36] The courts have played a small but crucial role in restricting executive use of information campaigns. The courts may enforce legislative restrictions on executive activity or impose direct limits on government communications. For example, a case decided by the California Supreme Court in 1976, *Stanson v. Mott*, examined promotional materials distributed by the state Department of Parks and Recreation to promote passage of a bond issue to acquire park land.[37] Although the court found the promotion campaign questionable, it remanded the case to a lower court to determine whether the expenditures were properly authorized. Legal

35. Yarwood and Enis (1988).
36. Graber (1992); and Yarwood and Enis (1988).
37. Yudof (1983).

solutions permit courts to call legislative attention to alleged abuses by government agencies.

A final institutional safeguard in the United States is the First Amendment. Citizens have constitutional rights to speak in disagreement with information or arguments proffered by government agencies. Like the other safeguards, it is highly imperfect because few individual citizens have resources that permit effective competition with messages of the U.S. government or other institutions with massive resources.[38] Still, those who hold opposing views have a legal right to express them, using communication media within their means. This protection adds to the capacity of citizens to resist manipulation.

If PICs are creations of legitimate governments working according to their established procedures, then the legitimacy of the government and its procedures are some protection against the misuse of PICs. The more thoroughly the government has institutionalized democratic assumptions, the more likely these institutional arrangements will serve as a check on gross abuse. However, because PICs are by definition creations of government officials, they may seldom strive to enhance democracy and citizenship beyond the status quo.[39]

Design Implications: Enhancing Positive Consequences

To strengthen democratic participation, we must look to conditions that promote positive uses of public information campaigns. Because of the potential of government information campaigns to enrich democratic process and deliberation, encouraging these positive consequences is good in itself and an inoculation against the destructive consequences of more manipulative government campaigns.

One strategy is to raise the ethical awareness of the people who conceive, design, sponsor, and implement information campaigns about the double-edged consequences of effective campaigns. This includes government officials and the private contractors, typically advertising agencies, who often do campaign design and execution. Although the technical activity involved in campaigns is similar to commercial accounts, ethical considerations are somewhat different. Training in universities and in continuing midcareer workshops for public managers and their private

38. Lindblom (1990).
39. Montgomery (1988).

contractors can direct attention to the potential trouble spots in many kinds of information campaigns. Management review of proposals for public information campaigns can also include an ethical component, to remind people to consider such concerns in the initial stages of design.

Several of the issues that might trigger review are the accuracy and completeness of the message, the fit of the message to the needs of the target audience, and the channels used to convey the message. Government campaigns should be held to high standards of accuracy. When campaigns fail to reach these standards, the failure contaminates not only the message at hand but the public institution that sends the message. For example, advertising campaigns to recruit volunteers to join the U.S. army promise prospective soldiers the chance to "be all that you can be." Campaign materials emphasize tangible benefits of military service, especially educational opportunities and job training in specific fields of expertise. One study noted that the active-duty soldiers interviewed "perceive appeals to be false when compared to subsequent personal experience."[40] Soldiers who are not given access to education or training "may feel resentment toward the Army, especially when they see advertisements attempting to attract new recruits by showing the attractive MOSs [military occupational specialties] that they themselves are prohibited from occupying."[41] Misleading advertisements by business may result in disgruntled customers; misleading advertisements by the U.S. army may result in lower morale among recruits and lower rates of reenlistment, with implications for national security.

Accuracy is not the only important criterion for evaluating message content. Messages also need to be informative, that is, they should provide enough information for citizens to act in an informed way. For example, a survey of state AIDS coordinators found an "astonishing" divergence between what the AIDS coordinators thought should be done in an effective AIDS media campaign and what they were actually doing.[42] For example, almost all coordinators thought specific and direct promotion of condom use should be a major element of an effective campaign, but only six of thirty-one included such promotion for fear of censorship by media organizations or public officials. Similar problems arise in campaigns about drug abuse, family planning, and other socially controversial domains. It is hard to justify considerable investment in

40. Shyles and Hocking (1990, p. 379).
41. Shyles and Hocking (1990, p. 382).
42. Bush and Davies (1989, p. 58).

government campaigns when those campaigns fail to assist the most vulnerable segments of the population to improve their lot.

If political implications are considered explicitly, policy designers and citizens may take them into account in designing and evaluating individual information campaigns. Evaluation of individual campaigns can assess whether and how campaign designers have been sensitive to the normative implications of their work: Do the campaign messages acknowledge multiple perspectives on issues? Do campaigns make special efforts to reach citizens with the least capacity to benefit from information? Scoring well on these criteria is no simple matter. The technical demands of mass media communication, especially television, restrict and simplify messages to make them accessible and attention grabbing.[43] And most PICs need mass media to reach their intended audiences. This technical constraint limits the flexibility of PIC designers to respond to normative concerns with more complex or customized messages that mirror the multiple interests at stake in the political process.[44] Nevertheless, some campaigns succeed better than others in striving to communicate with the target audience in a way that promotes informed choice. For example, the McGruff crime prevention campaign broadcast messages that elicited changes among citizens who perceived themselves at high risk of becoming crime victims as well as somewhat different changes among those who saw themselves at little risk.[45] The message content appeared suited to the situations and resources of different social groups. Careful testing and refinement of message content and delivery makes it more likely that vulnerable groups can benefit from nutrition and agricultural campaigns.[46]

A second strategy for enhancing the positive political outcomes of public information campaigns is to build into the campaign provisions for reply, discussion, or debate from the target audience. Perhaps the most common provision is a telephone hotline that people can call to register questions, reactions, and complaints about the campaign or its message. Another option is to encourage people to follow up on the message of the campaign with other people in their social network—such as a physician, technical expert, or teacher—who are likely to continue the discussion and promote active deliberation about the issues of the

43. Iyengar and Kinder (1987).
44. Graber (1992).
45. O'Keefe (1985).
46. Hornik (1988, 1989).

campaign. Some campaigns deliberately foster other arenas for discussion by forming follow-up groups or putting people in touch with local experts or other people facing similar life circumstances. For example, Austria ran a campaign to foster discussion about nuclear power plants with the goal of encouraging questions and debate; the hope was that open discussion would improve the quality of subsequent policy deliberations.[47] By using campaigns not only to deliver a message but to encourage active deliberation, the campaign sponsors make it more likely that the political repercussions of the campaign will expand participation and the sense of involvement and efficacy among citizens.

The legal version of this strategy would be a formal right of reply to public information campaigns by groups with opposing viewpoints. But it is hard to imagine a workable version of this solution. Mark Yudof raises the pertinent questions, "Is every government message to give rise to a right to reply? If not, how do courts distinguish among those that should and those that should not? Which groups should be given such a right, and who decides? What if there are not two positions on a question but a multitude of positions? Need the government pay for such replies, including purchasing time on television and radio?"[48] The appropriate institutional supports for positive approaches to public information campaigns are not legal but administrative—built into the design of the campaign itself.

Although campaigns can be improved through better conception and implementation, the most powerful force for improvement may come from technology. Rapidly improving information technology may drastically change the possibilities for stimulating dialogue and citizen involvement. The potential for shared forums of communication through interactive cable, electronic conferences and bulletin boards, and other uses of computer-mediated communication opens up new vistas for a new generation of public information campaigns. These media create the possibility for customized messages directed to the needs and interests of highly specialized target audiences. They also open up the possibility of campaigns organized around what citizens want to know rather than what government officials want to tell. For example, envision government data bases on chemical risks. Chemical manufacturers, users, and citizens concerned about chemicals in their communities could locate and contribute information useful to them in monitoring health effects of toxic

47. Hirsch and Nowotny (1977).
48. Yudof (1983, p. 293).

and hazardous substances.[49] Future government campaigns may make data available to citizens who extract what they want to know. Providing information through electronic means will not usher in a nirvana of democracy. Those government officials who frame the issues, define the categories, and make the rules for communication will retain control over the value and uses of even highly interactive information exchange. However, the positive consequences of informed citizens, potential for interaction with information providers and other citizens rather than passive receipt of messages, and ongoing provision of up-to-date information may become more common with the spread of technology.

Conclusion

This exploration of the consequences of public information campaigns for democratic participation suggests that such analysis can be done. Although I have looked here at one policy instrument, analysis of other instruments can proceed along similar lines. In evaluating the potential of alternative policy instruments to achieve policy objectives, analysts can anticipate in broad outline the implications for how citizens and government will deal with one another.

Understanding these implications permits adjustments to be made in the policy design stage to mitigate negative consequences and to enhance positive consequences. Some of these adjustments apply to the conduct of the campaigns. Others may involve combinations of public information campaigns with other instruments that compensate for the risks associated with campaigns. Still others involve protections in the broader institutional environment that make government officials less manipulative or make citizens less vulnerable. The practice of policy design can be strengthened by adding explicit consideration of democracy to the evaluation of policy alternatives.

Although devotees of rational analysis may see this consideration as a diversion from the pursuit of efficient, effective alternatives, in the long run it is no diversion at all. The policy design choice to use public information campaigns, or any other instrument, emerges from the give and take of the political process. These policy choices will be only as well informed and thoughtful as those processes permit. The relationships between citizen and government create the context within which government officials learn what to do and how to do it. Policy instruments that

49. Hadden (1989).

promote learning among citizens may create environments that promote learning among government officials too. This look at public information campaigns thus raises in stark form a more general phenomenon. In the use of any policy instrument, political officials launch two interacting processes: the effort to achieve policy objectives and the ongoing reconstruction of relationships that constitute collective governance.

References

Bush, Alan J., and Victoria Davies. 1989. "State Governments' Response to the AIDS Crisis: An Advertising Perspective," *Journal of Public Policy and Marketing* 8: 53-63.

Dryzek, John. 1990. *Discursive Democracy: Politics, Policy, and Political Science.* Cambridge University Press.

Ellul, Jacques. 1965. *Propaganda: The Formation of Men's Attitudes.* Knopf.

Farhar-Pilgrim, Barbara, and F. Floyd Shoemaker. 1981. "Campaigns to Affect Energy Behavior." In *Public Communication Campaigns,* edited by Ronald E. Rice and William Paisley, Jr., 161–80. Beverly Hills: Sage.

Fisher, Jeffrey D., and William A. Fisher. 1992. "Changing AIDS-Risk Behavior." *Psychological Bulletin* 111 (May): 455–74.

Flay, Brian R. 1987. *Selling the Smokeless Society: Fifty-six Evaluated Mass Media Programs and Campaigns Worldwide.* Washington: American Public Health Association.

Freimuth, Vicki S., and J. Paul Van Nevel. 1981. Reaching the Public: The Asbestos Awareness Campaign." *Journal of Communication* 31 (Spring): 155–67.

Ginsberg, Benjamin. 1986. *The Captive Public: How Mass Opinion Promotes State Power.* Basic.

Graber, Doris A. 1992. *Public Sector Communication: How Organizations Manage Information.* Congressional Quarterly.

Hadden, Susan G. 1989. *A Citizen's Right to Know: Risk Communication and Public Policy.* Westview Press.

Hirsch, Helmut, and Helga Nowotny. 1977. "Information and Opposition in Austrian Nuclear Energy Policy." *Minerva* 15(Autumn–Winter): 316–34.

Hornik, Robert C. 1988. *Development Communication: Information, Agriculture, and Nutrition in the Third World.* Longman.

———. 1989. "Channel Effectiveness in Development Communication Programs." In *Public Communication Campaigns,* 2d ed., edited by Ronald E. Rice and Charles K. Atkin, 309–30. Newbury Park, Calif.: Sage.

Hutton, R. Bruce 1982. "Advertising and the Department of Energy's Campaign for Energy Conservation." *Journal of Advertising* 11(2): 27–39.

Iyengar, Shanto, and Donald R. Kinder. 1987. *News That Matters: Television and American Opinion.* University of Chicago Press.

Kotler, Philip, and Eduardo L. Roberto. 1989. *Social Marketing: Strategies for Changing Public Behavior.* Free Press.

Kuo, Eddie C. Y. 1984. "Mass Media and Language Planning: Singapore's 'Speak Mandarin' Campaign." *Journal of Communication* 34 (Spring): 24–35.

Landy, Marc K., Marc J. Roberts, and Stephen R. Thomas. 1990. *The Environmental Protection Agency: Asking the Wrong Questions.* Oxford University Press.

Lindblom, Charles E. 1990. *Inquiry and Change: The Troubled Attempt to Understand and Shape Society.* Yale University Press.

McAlister, Alfred, and others. 1989. "Anti-Smoking Campaigns. Progress in the Application of Social Learning Theory." In *Public Communication Campaigns,* 2d ed., edited by Ronald E. Rice and Charles K. Atkins, 291–308. Beverly Hills: Sage.

McNamara, Eugene F., Troy Kurth, and Donald Hansen. 1981. "Communication Efforts to Prevent Wildfires." In *Public Communication Campaigns,* edited by Ronald E. Rice and William J. Paisley, 143–60. Beverly Hills: Sage.

Majone, Giandomenico. 1989. *Evidence, Argument, and Persuasion in the Policy Process.* Yale University Press.

Montgomery, John D. 1988. *Bureaucrats and People: Grassroots Participation in Third World Development.* Johns Hopkins University Press.

Morrison, Ellen Earnhardt. 1976. *Guardian of the Forest: A History of the Smokey Bear Program.* Vantage Press.

Nweke, Ken M. C. 1987. "Promoting the Reading Habit among the Literate in Nigeria." *The Reading Teacher* 40 (March): 632–38.

O'Keefe, Garrett J. 1985. "Taking a Bite Out of Crime: The Impact of a Public Information Campaign." *Communication Research* 12 (April): 147–78.

Paletz, David L., Roberta Pearson, and Donald Willis. 1977. *Politics in Public Service Advertising on Television.* Praeger.

Qualter, Terence H. 1985. *Opinion Control in the Democracies.* St. Martin's Press.

Reich, Robert B., ed. 1988. *The Power of Public Ideas.* Cambridge, Mass.: Ballinger.

Roberts, Donald F., and Maccoby, Nathan. 1985. "Effects of Mass Communication." In *Handbook of Social Psychology,* 3d ed., edited by Gardner Lindzey and Elliott Aronson, 539–98. Random House.

Robinson, John P. 1981. "Mass Communication and Information Diffusion." In *Reader in Public Opinion and Mass Communication,* 3d ed., edited by Morris Janowitz and Paul M. Hirsch, 348–62. Free Press.

Rogers, Everett M., and J. Douglas Storey. 1987. "Communication Campaigns." In *Handbook of Communication Science,* edited by Charles R. Berger and Steven H. Chaffee, 817–46. Beverly Hills: Sage.

Salamon, Lester M. 1981. "Rethinking Public Management: Third-Party Government and the Changing Forms of Government Action." *Public Policy* 29 (Summer): 255–75.

Salmon, Charles T., ed. 1989. *Information Campaigns: Balancing Social Values and Social Change.* Newbury Park, Calif.: Sage.

Schudson, Michael. 1984. *Advertising, the Uneasy Persuasion: Its Dubious Impact on American Society.* Basic Books.

Shoemaker, Pamela J., ed. 1989. *Communication Campaigns about Drugs: Government, Media, and the Public.* Hillsdale, N.J.: L. Erlbaum Associates.

Shyles, Leonard, and John E. Hocking. 1990. "The Army's 'Be All You Can Be' Campaign." *Armed Forces and Society* 16 (Spring): 369–83.

Spiegel, Charlotte N., and Francis C. Lindaman. 1977. "Children Can't Fly: A Program to Prevent Childhood Morbidity and Mortality from Window Falls." *American Journal of Public Health* 67 (12): 1143–47.

Tichenor, P. J., G. A. Donohue, and C. N. Olien. 1970. "Mass Media Flow and Differential Growth in Knowledge." *Public Opinion Quarterly* 34 (Summer): 159–70.

Wallack, Lawrence. 1990. "Improving Health Promotion: Media Advocacy and Social Marketing Approaches." In *Mass Communication and Public Health: Complexities and Conflicts,* edited by Charles Atkin and Lawrence Wallack, 147–63. Newbury Park, Calif.: Sage.

Warner, Kenneth E. 1977. "The Effects of the Anti-smoking Campaign on Cigarette Consumption." *American Journal of Public Health* 67 (7): 645–50.

Warwick, Donald P. 1990. "The Ethics of Population Control." In *Population Policy: Contemporary Issues,* edited by Godfrey Roberts, 21–37. Praeger.

Weiss, Janet A. 1990. "Ideas and Inducements in Mental Health Policy." *Journal of Policy Analysis and Management* 9 (Spring): 178–200.

Weiss, Janet A., and Mary Tschirhart. Forthcoming. "Using Public Information Campaigns as Policy Instruments." *Journal of Policy Analysis and Management.*

Yarwood, Dean L., and Ben M. Enis. 1988. "Problems in Regulating Federal Executive Branch Publicity and Advertising Programs." *American Review of Public Administration* 18 (March): 29–46.

Yudof, Mark. 1983. *When Government Speaks: Politics, Law, and Government Expression in America.* University of California Press.

6. Citizen Action Programs and Participatory Politics in Tucson

SALLIE A. MARSTON

ON AUGUST 20, 1964, President Lyndon B. Johnson signed into law the Economic Opportunity Act. He stated publicly upon signing it that "on this occasion the American people and our American system are making history. . . . Today for the first time in the history of the human race, a great nation is able to make and is willing to make a commitment to eradicate poverty among its people."[1] The centerpiece of the Economic Opportunity Act (EOA) was Title II-A, the community action programs, which were defined as and intended to be ". . . developed, conducted, and administered with the *maximum feasible participation* of the residents of the areas and members of the group served."[2] Johnson had declared an "unconditional" war on poverty and its social consequences in America, and Congress had empowered him to deploy community action as the chief weapon aimed at its elimination. Yet after only three years, the president effectively abandoned the war on poverty for the war in Viet Nam, and by the early 1970s the post mortems on the Economic Opportunity Office's efforts were being filed. Many commentators, for different reasons, called the war a dismal failure and said the community action programs had done more harm than good or had co-opted the activist poor.[3] A few, like Richard Cole, argued that the war could not be viewed as an absolute loss because the weaponry of community action had significantly reconfigured the citizen-government relationship.[4] He indicated that community action programs (CAPs) had improved the

I would like to thank the late Fred Acosta, Sharon Maxwell, Corky Poster, John McNair, and Sal Baldenegro for sharing their knowledge of the history of citizen participation in Tucson as well as Manuel Herrera, Jr., Rebecca Quintero, Alberto Montano, Maria Black, and Bertha Valenzuela for talking with me about their participation in neighborhood activism.

1. Moynihan (1969, pp. 3–4).
2. P.L. 88-452, sec. 202 (a) (3) (emphasis added).
3. Banfield (1974); Piven and Cloward (1971); and Moynihan (1969).
4. Cole (1974).

delivery of municipal services in some cities and positively affected citizens' attitudes about the accessibility of government.

The OEO effectively ceased funding CAPs approximately two decades ago, and many scholars and politicians regard the war on poverty as a failure equal to the war in Southeast Asia that supplanted it.[5] Yet while poverty has persisted and even increased, the war on poverty programs can be seen to have left a legacy of increased citizen participation in local governing.[6] Interestingly, though the funds for federal community action initiatives have long been discontinued or redirected to different uses through the Community Services Administration, vestiges of the 1960s CAPs persist across the country; some have even evolved into powerful, high-profile, municipally funded agencies. In this chapter I talk about how the community action programs of the 1960s have shaped local politics in the 1980s and 1990s. I use the sprawling metropolitan area of Tucson, Arizona, as an illustrative case.

The Economic Opportunity Act

Lyndon Johnson signed the EOA into law, but John Kennedy conceived the war on poverty in 1963 when he decided that he wanted "a comprehensive, coordinated attack on poverty" as part of his 1964 legislative program.[7] Carefully maintaining his reluctance to confront directly the increasingly volatile civil rights struggle as a racial crisis, Kennedy chose to transform it into a class issue and to promote programs that would alleviate poverty and address, through the back door, the politically difficult demands of black Americans. In short, the poverty programs came to be predicated on the assumption that poverty was equivalent to being black or minority.[8] Thus the issue of civil rights for African Americans could be subsumed into the seemingly more tractable and less politically contentious problem of ameliorating poverty.

With Kennedy's assassination, Johnson inherited the fractious civil rights claims of African Americans and turned to Sargent Shriver to direct drafting of the war on poverty legislation. The bill contained six principal areas of concentration: youth programs, community action programs, special antipoverty programs for rural areas, loans for small businesses

5. See Lemann (1991); contrast Morone (1990) and Browning, Marshall, and Tabb (1984) for more sanguine views.
6. Gittell (1980).
7. Anderson (1975); and Sundquist (1968).
8. Miller and Rein (1969).

not otherwise able to obtain credit, work experience programs, and volunteer service and administration programs. What was perhaps most innovative about the EOA of 1964 was Title II-A, which "encouraged or required the poor themselves to assume an important role both in planning and implementing the war at the local level."[9]

Institutional change was at the heart of the CAP and it had emerged through a number of influences, most importantly Kennedy's Committee on Juvenile Delinquency and Crime, a book coauthored by one of the members of the committee, and the Ford Foundation's Grey Areas Project.[10] The message from these and other sources was that *institutional change* at the *community level* was absolutely essential to the success of an attack on poverty and that such an attack could not be waged without the assent and cooperation of those who suffered from poverty.[11] The focus on institutional change and community context, as well as several political constraints, helped to establish Title II-A—citizen action or participation—as the keystone in the design and implementation of the Economic Opportunity Act.[12]

According to Joseph Kershaw, a model CAP has four principal attributes:

—It "mobilizes and utilizes resources, public and private, of any urban or rural area in an attack on poverty";

—It "provides services assistance, and other activities of sufficient scope and size to give promise of progress toward elimination of poverty or a cause or causes of poverty through developing employment opportunities, improving human performance, motivation, and productivity, or bettering the conditions under which people live, learn, and work";

—It is aimed at "the strengthening of community capabilities for planning and coordinating Federal, State, and other assistance related to the elimination of poverty"; and

—It is to be "developed, conducted, and administered with the maximum feasible participation of the residents of the areas and members of the groups served."[13]

In each jurisdiction the planning, conducting, administering, evaluating, and coordination of the citywide community action programs were to be undertaken by a local Community Action Agency (CAA). Program

9. Kershaw (1970, p. 25).
10. Cloward and Ohlin (1960).
11. Marris and Rein (1967); and Friedman (1977).
12. Peterson and Greenstone (1977).
13. Kershaw (1970, pp. 46–47).

resources were to be allocated among the city's low-income neighborhoods through the CAA, and residents were to elect individuals from
their neighborhoods who would represent them on the CAA board of
directors.[14] Residents were also to be encouraged and trained to participate in the decisionmaking surrounding the design, implementation, and
disbursement of funds for local antipoverty programs.[15] The CAA itself
was originally intended to be a "public or private nonprofit agency (other
than a political party), or a combination thereof." The governing board
of the CAA was to be made up of three categories of representatives:
from private and public agencies (elected officials, members of the board
of education, board members of major private social welfare agencies);
community leaders (religious, business, minority group leaders); and
"residents of the areas and members of the groups to be served" (at least
one member from each of the CAP target neighborhoods elected through
"traditional democratic processes").[16] The 1966 and 1967 amendments
to the act altered the composition of the governing board of the CAA to
the extent that one-third of the board was to be composed of public
officials or their representatives. The amendments were meant to send a
signal to cities and other political jurisdictions that they were expected
to assume financial responsibility for the CAA as federal funding began
to be withdrawn. In early 1969 over 1,000 CAAs were operating in
American cities, and Tucson was one of them.[17]

The War on Poverty in Tucson:
OEO and Model Cities

In 1964, in hopeful anticipation of funding by the OEO, a number
of organizers of Tucson's impoverished Mexican-American and Native-
American communities gathered to begin planning for receipt of funds.[18]

14. Fox (1971).

15. Cahn and Cahn (1971); Gilbert (1970).

16. Office of Economic Opportunity (1965, pp. 16–18).

17. See Kershaw (1970, p. 52). As Morone (1990) points out, the implementation of
the CAA was the most ambiguously conceived component of the war on poverty campaign.
Communities received very little direction on how to proceed with such vagaries as "maximum feasible participation" or how the CAAs were to coordinate with preexisting local
government programs and institutional arrangements. The CAAs thus ended up varying
dramatically from city to city.

18. I am greatly indebted to Sharon Maxwell and to the late Fred Acosta (interview,
March 14, 1991), who were involved at an early stage in citizen participation in Tucson,
for relating to me the city's history with the OEO and model cities. Fred Acosta was, until

Nine inner-city areas, which included Native-American, Mexican-American, and African-American populations, were targeted for community action. When the OEO funds were received in 1966, the poor neighborhoods, most of them Mexican-American, had already made some decisions about fund allocation and the design and composition of the coordinating community action agency, locally called the Committee on Economic Opportunity (CEO). The CEO board was made of equal numbers of business representatives, agency representatives, and citizens and operated independently of city staff and administrative structure. When funds were finally granted, the nine neighborhood councils were quickly convened in each of the target neighborhoods. Council representatives were elected by fellow residents who sent some of their number to the CEO, which also included appointed representatives from the business community and social service agencies. The CEO managed the operation of the various components of the OEO program from budget and management to citizen participation. The neighborhood councils worked singly and together with the CEO to improve services—food and nutrition, education, delinquency counseling—to the neighborhoods.

As OEO funds began to dry up by the end of 1967, community organizers, citizens, and city staff met to plan an application for other federal funds, this time to the model cities program. In 1969 Tucson was selected to be one of the 150 model cities demonstration sites. Like the CAP component of the OEO, the federal model cities program had been designed to demonstrate how city governments and neighborhoods could work together to address social and economic problems. More important, though, model cities was also intended to bring disenfranchised groups into the political process by instructing them about how the political process worked and how they could become more involved in local decisionmaking. Under model cities, six inner-city, "poverty pocket" neighborhoods, approximately six square blocks each, were included in the program. Most were Mexican-American. The nine neighborhoods originally targeted under the OEO were more or less incorporated into these six. A policy board and a model neighborhood council, composed of 80 percent residents and 20 percent city staff, were created.

<hr>

his death in spring 1992, head of the local Job Corps, while Sharon Maxwell is chief administrator of the Citizen Participation Office. Their narratives as well as my own cross checking of newspaper articles, published organizational reports, and interviews with neighborhood activists and advocates, especially John McNair (interview, June 25, 1991), Corky Poster (interview, May 2, 1991), and Salomon Baldenegro (interview, September 20 and October 9, 1991), constitute the foundation for the history that is presented here.

Twelve neighborhood task forces composed of residents were also created. Besides developing model neighborhood plans for land use, the task force addressed neighborhood issues such as economic development, transportation, drug abuse prevention, housing, education, crime and delinquency, recreation, and services to the elderly. The Inner City Neighborhood Council, composed of 80 percent city staff and 20 percent residents, coordinated activities. By 1972, through a federal mandate, the model cities program had expanded beyond the inner city to include another six low-income neighborhoods. The neighborhood-level task forces were enlarged to include representatives from the new areas, and the Expanded Neighborhood Council was created, in tandem with the Inner City Council, and charged with coordinating the activities of the six new neighborhoods. In 1974, when model cities funding was cut off, the federal government's revenue-sharing dollars were used to continue some of the uncompleted neighborhood projects and to keep citizen participation and planning in operation. Lack of funds caused the task forces to be disbanded in 1976, although in 1977 funds from the community development grants were used to finish up several projects and maintain resident participation. Through both the more recent revenue-sharing and the earlier community development phase, the city maintained, to a large degree, the organizational model mandated under model cities.

Between 1975 and 1978, the city began, through its Office of Budget and Research, to study the citizen participation process to assess the value of and need for a permanent city-funded Office of Citizen Participation. The office was established and organized by the city in 1976, but city staff and citizen volunteers and appointees continued to study the possibility of a citizen-designed citizen participation process. Following the advice of a citizen advisory task force, city staff utilized the existing six political wards as planning units, divided them into three subunits of approximately 20,000 residents each, and organized elections for representatives to the Citizen Participation Council, a group that would advise the mayor and council on decisions such as the distribution of community development block grants, capital improvements, and human services monies. In 1980, the citizen-designed participation process, centering on a restructured Office of Citizen Participation, was adopted by the mayor and council, and it is still in operation in 1993.

The history of the Citizen Participation Office (CPO) is one of waxing and waning popular and administrative support, most often depending on citizen activism and its impact on land development projects. As a citizen advocacy agency, it sits uncomfortably within the city's administrative structure, receiving criticism sometimes from residents and sometimes from inside the bureaucracy, depending on which way the political and economic wind is blowing. Economic circumstances in the early 1990s caused operating capacity at the CPO to be at an especially low ebb. However, since their inception in 1966, community action programs have continued to be a viable, sometimes a pivotal, part of Tucson's government structure, and institutionalization has had an undeniably important impact on local politics.

The Neighborhoods and Citizen Activism in Tucson

The war on poverty citizen action programs and their successive incarnations have had at least four enduring effects on citizens' empowerment and Tucson's local political culture. Of these four, perhaps only a single one, the political empowerment of the disenfranchised, can be regarded as an intentional consequence of poverty policy. The other three—the fostering of a participatory tradition in local political culture, the emergence of middle-class, growth-related activism, and the creation of the neighborhood as the contemporary public sphere of participatory democracy—were unintended. The unintended ones have had, I would argue, the most persistent and profound impact on local politics, planning, and policymaking and citizen empowerment.

Political Empowerment of the Disenfranchised

The primary aim of the CAP was to bring previously alienated social groups into the political process by teaching them how to make the political system work for them.[19] In its larger attempt, through citizen participation, to eradicate poverty and permanently improve the political power of the poor, the CAP failed in Tucson as it did elsewhere.[20] Still, the 1970s witnessed an overall increase in the formal political participation of the Mexican-American population, who have employed the framework of citizen action as well as more traditional electoral mecha-

19. Shingles (1975).
20. Haveman (1977); and Lemann (1991).

126   SALLIE A. MARSTON

nisms to press their demands. Evidence of the formal incorporation of
Mexican Americans into the local political system can be traced in individual histories as well as at the group level. Mexican Americans, many
of whom cut their political teeth on the CAP, occupy seats on the city
council and county board of supervisors, are elected to the Arizona state
legislature, and hold influential civil service positions. Mexican Americans have for the past two decades constituted a significant voting bloc,
and the Southside, mostly Mexican-American neighborhoods, is well
organized and active on a range of issues from filing class action lawsuits
over trichloroethlene pollution in the groundwater to petitioning for
improved street lighting and police protection.

Most recently Nicholas Lemann has argued that the political incorporation of the poor and disenfranchised would have occurred anyway
owing to earlier civil rights legislation.[21] As some analysts have shown,
however, the CAPs, and especially the CAAs, were bootcamps for civil
rights advocates, drawing African and Mexican Americans into the political arena and mobilizing them for a more activist political posture—
formal and informal.[22] It is indeed true that neither the war on poverty
nor the citizen action programs eliminated poverty—a deep structural
problem not amenable to superficial solutions. The CAPs did, however,
alter the terrain of local (and state and national) politics by establishing
competing forces to existing political organizations, which became institutionalized opportunities for the poor to participate in the decisions that
affected them. This newly configured political terrain had ramifications
beyond poor neighborhoods.

Currently in Tucson, the CPO helps poor neighborhoods orchestrate
their demands and remain connected to the political process. Yet as
scholars of citizen action correctly point out, their connection to the
system has, in a real sense, depoliticized them by directing their demands
to issues surrounding the distribution of resources and deflecting their
discontent from the larger structural questions of political and economic
organization and production.[23] While the stated objective of drawing the
disenfranchised into the political process has been a mitigated success,
the three unintended policy consequences of the CAP and the institutionalization of a Citizen Participation Office in Tucson have been far less
equivocal.

21. Lemann (1991).
22. Browning, Marshall, and Tabb (1984).
23. Young (1990); Castells (1983); and Katznelson (1981).

The Citizen Participation Office and the Participatory Ideal

Since the implementation of the first CAP in Tucson in 1966, citizen activism has grown largely through the support of the CPO.[24] Neighborhood and community groups who register with the CPO can expect to receive support for the printing and mailing of newsletters and other neighborhood literature. CPO staff members are also charged with maintaining communication between citizen groups and city government; coordinating "town halls" on community issues; and instructing, educating, and providing technical assistance to citizen groups so they may participate in government decisionmaking or present objections to plans and policies proposed by city government.[25] In 1992 more than 150 neighborhood associations and coalitions were registered with the CPO. In metropolitan Pima County, outside the legal boundaries of the city, while no agency exists to facilitate the organizing of neighborhoods, more than 100 of them have organized independently of government assistance often for the purpose of preparing a neighborhood or area plan (as mandated by the state of Arizona's Urban Management Act). Once organized, many of these associations remain active in order to address land use changes that occur frequently in the undeveloped areas beyond the city limits. Though currently reduced to a small staff of four, down from its heyday of nineteen staff members in 1975, the CPO still provides critical services and, perhaps even more important, by its presence is an official touchstone of the participatory ideal in local political culture. During the past several years of shrinking budgets, justification for continued funding of the CPO has been challenged by city bureaucrats as well as private development interests. Each time the challenge is made public, city neighborhoods and influential neighborhood leaders fight back and save it from elimination. For neighborhoods, the CPO is the symbol and facilitator that gives them access to the local decisionmaking processes. The CPO not only gives residents administrative support but also offers them timely access to information and guarantees their presence on important and influential advisory committees and task forces.

24. The description of the present state of neighborhood activism in Tucson is distilled from a work in progress. See Marston (forthcoming). Information on the activism of Southside Mexican-American neighborhoods comes from interviews with resident activists, including Bertha Valenzuela (June 5, 1991), Manuel Herrera Jr. (June 12, 1991), Rebecca Quintero (June 13, 1991), and Alberto Montano and Maria Black (June 18, 1991).
25. City of Tucson (1980).

In a city where a great deal of capital is generated for land development, citizen participation is often regarded by both developers and local government as a costly obstacle to economic growth. The CPO enables citizens to influence the growth process, and not just on election days.

The Enfranchised Participate

Interestingly, the war on poverty programs of the late 1960s had the ripple effect of encouraging middle-class Anglos to participate more directly in local government actions. A 1990 metropolitanwide survey of neighborhood activists in the city found that the typical activist is a long-time Tucsonan, is Anglo and middle class, has a college education, and works in a professional occupation.[26] As the "growth machine" began to accelerate in the late 1960s and early 1970s, this group saw itself becoming increasingly powerless to alter the developments that were directly affecting its property values and quality of life.[27] In the CPO, the institution that the CAP had initiated and model cities had institutionalized, middle-class Tucsonans found a residentially based participatory model and a city agency that would also facilitate their access to decisionmaking. These middle-class neighborhoods, often drawing in poorer neighborhoods for general moral and sometimes specific issue support, have been extremely successful in having their demands considered through the formation of policies that manifest themselves as changes to the city charter. One of these is the neighborhood protection initiative, which was pushed by neighborhoods in the 1985 election and added to the city charter in 1986. It requires "voter approval of controlled access highways and grade separated interchanges." The notification requirement passed and entered into the city charter in 1984 requires that the CPO "mail projected and final agendas of Mayor and Council meetings to neighborhood representatives" two weeks before the meeting is to occur. It also requires the CPO to "notify appropriate neighborhood associations within a one-mile radius of a proposed large or high intensity development (including industrial, business, and residential uses) by distributing information provided by the Planning Department."[28]

26. Marston (1991).
27. Molotch (1976).
28. This information includes historic district/plan reviews, neighborhood plans/inventories, annexations, zoning, code revisions, rezoning applications, zoning examiner meetings, community design review committee meetings/public hearings, citizen advisory planning committee meetings/public hearings, and so forth (Mayor and Council Policy Manual Policy 510-04).

Middle-class neighborhoods in the city and the county from time to time form coalitions for various purposes. These coalitions are usually proactive and, along with some of the high-profile activists, are among the most influential constituencies in the city and county. The coalitions, such as the Neighborhood Coalition of Greater Tucson (NCGT), which is functionally a political action committee, have successfully promoted political candidates sensitive to neighborhood issues, pushed for policies that ensure citizen control over large-scale transportation changes, provided a measure of protection for the area's architectural and environmental resources, and made the city council and the county board of supervisors aware of the interests of neighborhood groups. A former president of the NCGT has suggested that the emergence of middle-class, neighborhood-based activism is evidence of the failure of local officials and local government bureaucracies to represent citizen concerns adequately. He states that the widespread system of neighborhood associations and coalitions in Tucson "parallels the formal government system" and argues that this "underground government is building up because the existing government cannot represent the average citizen."[29]

Electoral victories have also been one of the success stories of middle-class-dominated neighborhood activism in the city and county over the last decade. In 1987 neighborhood candidates, endorsed by the NCGT and running on a neighborhood platform, won the mayoral and several council seats despite a high-profile oppositional campaign by the Southern Arizona Homebuilders Association, which plastered billboards across the city with the worried query, "Does your job depend on growth?" In the 1989 elections, two more neighborhood candidates were added to the city council. Neighborhoods have also had some success at halting or creating crippling delays for private development proposals through ballot propositions and demonstrations before city council meetings. In a practice exhibited across the country and particularly in western cities as different as Los Angeles, San Antonio, and San Francisco, middle-class Tucsonans who, two decades ago, would have invoked the ballot box to articulate their political choices and concerns, increasingly use methods of direct democracy and their neighborhoods as territorial organizing bases.[30]

29. Quotations are based on interviews with Tucson activists in 1988. They are part of a study described in more detail in Marston and Meadows (1988).
30. For examples from other sunbelt cities, see Davis (1990); Plotkin (1987); and Mollenkopf (1983).

The Neighborhood as Public Sphere

By targeting the neighborhood as the crucible for the enfranchisement of the poor, a direct legacy of the CAPs has been the strengthening of the neighborhood as the predominant public sphere of popular political life in Tucson. Accelerated by suburbanization and more recent urban restructuring, especially the increasing segregation of production, commerce, and residence, middle-class Tucsonans have used CAP tactics and the organizational base of the neighborhood to wage their own growth-related battles. One result has been that for the poor and the middle class, the neighborhood has become a public service delivery unit as well as the venue for civic discourse, opinion formation, and political action.[31]

Consistent with republican constructions about the importance of the public sphere to the health and smooth functioning of a liberal democracy, the neighborhood is a space of face-to-face interaction where the critical activity of public talk—discussions about the functioning of the political economy—may be readily entered. One of the obvious advantages of the neighborhood as public sphere is that neighborhoods are spaces to which almost everyone has access—everyone lives somewhere, although the homeless are notable exceptions. Another is that in the neighborhood, public and private converge and the personal is often most clearly political. Thus, for example, in San Francisco the private issue of sexual preference was politicized in large part through neighborhood organizing.[32]

Unfortunately, the neighborhood as public sphere is also a limited social construction. Not all neighborhoods, for instance, are safe public spaces, nor are all neighborhoods accessible to all people. As a result, the neighborhood as a public space is impoverished because class, race, and ethnic residential segregation dangerously restrict the range and depth of discussion. As Iris M. Young argues, a public space is "a place accessible to anyone, where anyone can participate and witness . . . [and] in entering the public one always risks encounter with those who are different,

---

31. I do not mean to imply that the CAPs are solely responsible for constructing the neighborhood as a new public sphere. Certainly, earlier private and public agents, such as the settlement workers and political machines, which had organized their undertakings at the neighborhood level, helped to engender a kind of neighborhood politics. What is unusual about the case in Tucson as well as in other American cities is how citizen action programs helped to shape the middle-class activism that has used the neighborhood as a competing political institution. See Davis (1990).

32. Castells (1983).

those who identify with different groups and have different opinions or different forms of life."[33]

Furthermore, neighborhood demands tend to revolve around a rather narrowly constructed critique of the inequalities of public resource distribution. In Tucson, neighborhood complaints and demands center on changes in land use and inadequate delivery of public services such as police protection. There is no public talk about the social relations that produce and reproduce urban landscapes and public resource distributions, the market system that drives them, or the bureaucracy that operationalizes them. In short, the public sphere of the Tucson neighborhood often invokes a participatory ideal that is built around a narrow range of issues and mostly balkanized constituencies. Consequently, the contemporary construction of the neighborhood as the space for public discourse is both an advance and a retreat on the original liberal ideal, which was predicated on the exclusive participation of white, middle-class, property-owning males.[34] It is an advance in that new groups have been encouraged to enter into public discourse and a retreat in that the sphere of discussion has been sharply circumscribed.

The Battle for Citizen Participation

Paul Peterson and David Greenstone have argued that because the CAPs were in essence aimed at attacking political poverty, their success or failure needs to be assessed first by examining the shape and extent of the citizen participation they engendered and second by assessing their impacts on political processes and institutions. The critical question about citizen participation is whether CAPs fostered *substantive representation*, that is, "the extent to which the formal representatives acquired sufficient power to alter government policies so as to benefit large numbers of constituents."[35] Undoubtedly, in Tucson, Mexican Americans have been well integrated into the political mainstream, from holding elected offices to using direct democracy tactics to press their demands.

Certainly, one of the successes and intended effects of the community action programs of the 1960s is that the CPO has enhanced the capacity of citizens, poor or otherwise, to participate directly in some of the

33. Young (1990, p. 240).
34. See Habermas (1989) for an extended discussion of the liberal notion of the public sphere.
35. Peterson and Greenstone (1977), p. 257.

planning and decisionmaking that affects the quality of their lives and their futures. The institutionalization of citizen participation has changed the way that the local government operates—not as a monolithic and impenetrable bureaucracy but through the interaction of informal neighborhood units with the formal political apparatus.[36] While some critics have argued that civil rights legislation is chiefly responsible for the integration of the poor into the political process, CAPs surely hastened their political incorporation.

What is more interesting than the debates about the shortcomings of the community action programs is the unexpected outcomes of their implementation (an important point that Susan Gonzales Baker addresses in relation to the Immigration Reform and Control Act in chapter 7). I believe the CAP helped to bring about the wholesale transformation of the political terrain in Tucson. First, the participatory ideal has gained widespread currency. Maintained by the city's Office of Citizen Participation, neighborhood activism is well established and often effective. During the past twenty-five years, through the critical support of the CPO, neighborhood groups have agitated for the implementation of policies that have gained them timely access to information as well as a measure of control over the pace, location, and direction of growth and development in the city.

Second, the neighborhood organizing model advanced through CAP initiatives in poor neighborhoods in Tucson has been captured by middle-class citizens who have used it to rally their neighbors around issues of growth and the quality of life. During the 1980s these middle-class neighborhoods have become an impressive, often formidable, force in local politics. Third, in this morphologically sprawling and suburbanized metropolis of nearly three-quarters of a million people, the neighborhood has become the most effective space of civic life. While this innovation can be a positive force for participatory democracy, it has also been a force invoked to debate rather parochial issues. Furthermore, more often than not, the neighborhood is an exclusionary and demographically homogenous space and thus limits the potential for a full range of debate. In short, the neighborhood as a new public sphere circumscribes the ideal of a true open forum where anyone can speak and anyone can listen. The implications of a limited forum are clear in Tucson, where the issues are most often constructed around a contentious middle-class ideal of a controlled growth that relegates necessary but unwanted land uses to areas

36. Kotler (1977, pp. 281–83).

where there is the least resistance, that is, poor, unorganized neighbor-hoods. Thus, while a greater number of citizens have gained direct access to the local political system and many of the critical decisions that affect their lives, their gain has been at the expense of other citizens who do not have the time, resources, security, or confidence to rally their neigh-bors and articulate their needs. Ultimately everyone loses in such an unbalanced political context, as the 1992 riots in Los Angeles amply demonstrate.

While the discussion has focused exclusively on Tucson, I should point out that this city is not unique in possessing a capacity-building office like the CPO and a politically engaged citizenry operating from a neigh-borhood base. Miami, Cleveland, Dayton, and Seattle, to name just a few cities, operate neighborhood offices promoting citizen participation, many of them with roots stretching back to the OEO initiatives.[37] Across the country there is evidence that neighborhoods have become the focal point for citizens organizing to seek greater access to government. For example, a recent publication by the Kettering Foundation found that while many citizens feel alienated from the formal political process—as evidenced by decreasing voter participation rates—they have not aban-doned political activity entirely but have turned to the public life of their neighborhoods where they feel they can make a difference.[38] This dra-matic transformation of local politics suggests that although the war on poverty was lost more than twenty-five years ago, its central campaign, the citizen action program, has dramatically altered the political geog-raphy of American life. The contours of this new political landscape are now in evidence, and while the implications for contemporary citizenship are being clearly felt, they are only vaguely understood.

37. For more information on these cities see Hallman (1977); Sharp (1986); and Berry, Portney, and Thomson (1993).
38. Kettering Foundation; and chapter 11 in this volume.

References

Anderson, James E. 1975. "Administrative Politics and the War on Poverty." In *Analyzing Poverty Policy*, edited by Dorothy Buckton James, 75–88. Lexington, Mass.: D.C. Heath.
Banfield, Edward C. 1974. *The Unheavenly City Revisited*. Little, Brown.
Berry, Jeffrey M., Kent E. Portney, and Ken Thomson. 1993. *The Rebirth of Urban Democracy*. Brookings.
Browning, Rufus P., Dale Rogers Marshall, and David H. Tabb. 1984. *Protest*

Is Not Enough: The Struggle of Blacks and Hispanics for Equality in Urban Politics. University of California Press.

Cahn, Edgar S., and Jean Camper Cahn. 1971. "Maximum Feasible Participation: A General Overview." In *Citizen Participation: Effecting Community Change*, edited by Edgar S. Cahn and Barry A. Passett, 9–68. Praeger.

Castells, Manuel. 1983. *The City and the Grassroots: A Cross-Cultural Theory of Urban Social Movements.* University of California Press.

City of Tucson. 1980. Administrative Directive, 1.06-22.

Cloward, Richard A., and Lloyd E. Ohlin. 1960. *Delinquency and Opportunity: A Theory of Delinquent Gangs.* Free Press.

Cole, Richard L. 1974. *Citizen Participation and the Urban Policy Process.* Lexington, Mass.: Lexington Books.

Davis, Mike. 1990. *City of Quartz: Excavating the Future in Los Angeles.* Verso.

Fox, Daniel M. 1971. "Federal Standards and Regulations for Participation." In *Citizen Participation: Effecting Community Change*, edited by Edgar S. Cahn and Barry A. Passett, 129–43. Praeger.

Friedman, Lawrence M. 1977. "The Social and Political Context of the War on Poverty: An Overview." In *A Decade of Federal Antipoverty Programs: Achievements, Failures, and Lessons*, edited by Robert H. Haveman, 21–47. Academic Press.

Gilbert, Neil. 1970. *Clients or Constituents: Community Action in the War on Poverty.* San Francisco: Jossey-Bass.

Gittell, Marilyn. 1980. *Limits to Citizen Participation: The Decline of Community Organizations.* Beverly Hills: Sage.

Habermas, Jürgen. 1989. *The Structural Transformation of the Public Sphere: An Inquiry into a Category of Bourgeois Society.* MIT Press.

Hallman, Howard W. 1977. *The Organization and Operation of Neighborhood Councils: A Practical Guide.* Praeger.

Haveman, Robert H. 1977. "Introduction: Poverty and Social Policy in the 1960s and 1970s—An Overview and Some Speculations." In *A Decade of Federal Antipoverty Programs: Achievements, Failures, and Lessons*, edited by Robert H. Haveman, 1–20. Academic Press.

Katznelson, Ira. 1981. *City Trenches: Urban Politics and the Patterning of Class in the United States.* Pantheon Books.

Kershaw, Joseph A. 1970. *Government against Poverty.* Brookings.

Kettering Foundation, 1991. *Citizens and Politics: The View from Main Street America.* A report prepared by the Harwood Group, Bethesda, Maryland. Dayton: Kettering.

Kotler, Melton. 1977. "Discussions." In *A Decade of Federal Antipoverty Programs: Achievements, Failures, and Lessons*, edited by Robert H. Haveman, 281–83. Academic Press.

Lemann, Nicholas. 1991. *The Promised Land: The Great Black Migration and How It Changed America.* Alfred A. Knopf.

Marris, Peter, and Martin Rein. 1967. *Dilemmas of Social Reform, Poverty and Community Action in the United States.* Atherton Press.

Marston, Sallie A. 1991. "Neighborhood and Politics: Activism and Activists in Tucson, 1966–1991." Paper presented in the Udall Center Fellows Lecture Series, March.
————. Forthcoming. *The People and the Public Sphere: Neighborhood and Participatory Politics in Tucson.* University of Arizona Press.
Marston, Sallie A., and R. Meadows. 1988. "Citizens in Conflict: Neighborhood Politics and Urban Growth in Tucson." Department of Geography and Regional Development. Discussion Paper 88-6. University of Arizona.
Miller, S. M., and Martin Rein. 1969. "Participation, Poverty, and Administration." *Public Administration Review* 29 (January–February): 15–24.
Mollenkopf, John H. 1983. *The Contested City.* Princeton University Press.
Molotch, Harvey. 1976. "The City as a Growth Machine: Toward a Political Economy of Place." *American Journal of Sociology* 82 (September): 309–30.
Morone, James A. 1990. *The Democratic Wish: Popular Participation and the Limits of American Government.* Basic Books.
Moynihan, Daniel P. 1969. *Maximum Feasible Misunderstanding: Community Action in the War on Poverty.* Free Press.
Office of Economic Opportunity. 1965. *Community Action Program Guide.* Washington.
Peterson, Paul E., and J. David Greenstone. 1977. "Racial Change and Citizen Participation: The Mobilization of Low-income Communities through Community Action." In *A Decade of Federal Antipoverty Programs: Achievements, Failures, and Lessons,* edited by Robert H. Haveman, 241–78. Academic Press.
Piven, Frances Fox, and Richard A. Cloward. 1971. *Regulating the Poor: The Function of Public Welfare.* Pantheon Books.
Plotkin, Sidney. 1987. *Keep Out: The Struggle for Land Use Control.* University of California Press.
Sharp, Elaine B. 1986. *Citizen Demand-Making in the Urban Context.* University of Alabama Press.
Shingles, Richard D. 1975. "Problems of Policy Evaluation: The Case of Community Action." In *Analyzing Poverty Policy,* edited by Dorothy Buckton James, 125–44. Lexington, Mass.: D.C. Heath.
Sundquist, James L. 1968. *Politics and Policy: The Eisenhower, Kennedy, and Johnson Years.* Brookings.
Young, Iris Marion. 1990. *Justice and the Politics of Difference.* Princeton University Press.

7. Immigration Reform: The Empowerment of a New Constituency

SUSAN GONZALEZ BAKER

$\mathbf{W}$ITH THE Immigration Reform and Control Act (IRCA) in 1986, Congress reaffirmed Ambrose Bierce's trenchant characterization of amnesty as "the state's magnanimity toward those offenders whom it would be too expensive to punish."[1] In an attempt to regain control over a faltering immigration system, IRCA created a one-time-only legalization (or amnesty) program. As a result 1.7 million undocumented immigrants ultimately petitioned to legalize their status. The U.S. legalization program was the largest ever mounted in the world.[2]

Few programs in immigration history created more conflict during design and field implementation than did IRCA amnesty. Legalization of undocumented immigrants already in the United States was a grudging concession for many lawmakers—a trade-off for new monies and new policy tools that allowed the Immigration and Naturalization Service (INS) to beef up its law enforcement activities.[3] The primary emphasis during IRCA's legislative journey was on regaining control of U.S. borders by hiring more Border Patrol agents and expanding INS authority to prosecute U.S. employers who hired undocumented immigrants. "Cleaning the slate" of undocumented immigrants already in the United States through a corollary legalization program survived the final IRCA vote by the narrowest of margins.

---

1. Bierce (1911).

2. An additional 1.3 million undocumented immigrants applied for legal immigration status under a separate program targeting alien farm workers. For an overview of this program, see generally Baker (1990).

3. According to the U.S. Senate Judiciary Committee (1985), "the United States is unlikely to obtain as much enforcement for its dollar if the INS attempts to locate and deport those who have become well settled in this country, rather than to prevent new illegal entry or visa abuse." Along with legalization, IRCA provided the INS with the authority to enforce civil and criminal penalties against U.S. employers who hired undocumented immigrants. IRCA also authorized new resources for border control operations to be carried out by the U.S. Border Patrol.

Resistance to legalization centered on its image as a reward to law-breakers—immigrants who circumvented the visa preference system and entered the United States without documents. Supporters saw legalization as a necessary, humane response to past immigration policy failures. Both images, however, portrayed the target population as rather passive recipients of the new benefit. Lawmakers portrayed undocumented immigrants as clients needing services (the dependents identified by Helen Ingram and Anne Schneider in chapter 4) or as lawbreakers deserving punishment (the deviants in the Schneider and Ingram typology).

This view of undocumented immigrants as disaffiliated recipients of a benefit grudgingly conferred had predictable implications for program parameters. A decidedly cautious welcome was extended to these immigrants by the INS. Yet immigrants and their advocates succeeded in expanding the scope of the program dramatically during implementation. This paper examines how amnesty evolved from a tightly rationed benefits program with narrow policy goals to a more expansive, inclusive model for conferring immigration benefits, targeting a wide variety of would-be immigrants. One key set of policy actors during program implementation—immigrant advocacy groups and community-based organizations—was central in facilitating the transition for the target group from "deviant" to "dependent" to "contender," with important implications for future immigration policy (see chapter 4).

The Social Construction of the Amnesty Program

Undocumented immigrants, while entitled to the basic civil rights accorded all persons in the United States, enjoy few significant political rights (they cannot vote) and few social rights, although they are entitled to some emergency social services and to public education for their children. Before examining the legalization program, one must examine what legalization means for the target population. Why might undocumented immigrants avail themselves of this benefit?

The Legalization Benefit

Congress restricted the legalization benefit to those immigrants with "firm equities" in the United States. Legalization was available only to those immigrants who had been residing unlawfully in the United States for more than five years. This sector of the population, lawmakers felt, had the most legitimate claim to formal membership in U.S. communities. Floor speeches during IRCA debate resounded with the claims that legalization would bring aliens "out of the shadows" and afford them the opportunities for full social and economic participation.[4]

To some extent, this assumption was true. In the wake of new IRCA employment restrictions, legalization was the only way for the undocumented population to maintain its economic foothold. Achieving legal permanent resident status would provide these immigrants with the potential for economic security they lacked otherwise. And it was just such economic logic that drove immigrants to take advantage of the program. Applicants for legalization cited fear of job loss as their primary reason for seeking the benefit.[5]

But the next step—from legal resident to citizen—means more than the right to work in the United States. It represents a more dramatic break with the country of origin—an important consideration for Mexican immigrants, who maintain strong linkages to their home communities. Indeed, legal Mexican immigrants, historically, have had comparatively low rates of U.S. naturalization. Still, citizenship has practical benefits ranging from enhanced access to social programs to liberal terms under which additional visa petitions can be filed for family members.[6]

With these countervailing pressures, attention to the context in which undocumented immigrants participated in legalization can aid in predicting how far they will go in reconstructing their identities as potential U.S. citizens. If street-level bureaucracies made legalization an arduous process, one would expect diminished incentive for further bureaucratic contact (for example, later applications for citizenship).[7] To the extent that basic social rights—for example, authorization to work—are all that undocumented immigrants seek, again one would expect slight incentive for eventual citizenship.

On the other hand, if the target population experienced legalization as an opportunity to effect proactive change on its own behalf, future interaction with state authority might be enhanced (see chapters 4 and 6). To the extent that aspirations for this immigrant cohort include the

4. Baker (1990).
5. Hagan and Baker (forthcoming).
6. While permanent resident aliens can file petitions to bring immediate family members to the United States, these visa slots are subject to annual ceilings. U.S. citizens, however, have unrestricted rights to bring immediate relatives into the country.
7. Lipsky (1980).

acquisition of political rights and the exercise of civil rights, one would expect the transition to citizenship to be viewed as valuable. Thus I examine the latent messages about membership and inclusion embedded in INS implementation decisions about legalization.

Initially, the INS adopted strict readings of congressional intent in defining the target population for legalization. By statute, legalization was available to all undocumented immigrants residing in the United States before January 1, 1982, who were not excludable on any of the grounds spelled out for other legal immigrants.[8] Additionally, these undocumented immigrants had to have maintained a "continuous physical presence" from the date of IRCA enactment (November 6, 1986) to the date of their applications. The INS promulgated regulations fleshing out these statutory guidelines, and these regulations typically embodied a narrow view of eligibility. Those initially barred from legalization included foreign students and visitors who illegally overstayed their visas, undocumented immigrants who had returned to their countries of origin for brief periods during the early 1980s, applicants who had received certain types of public assistance, and applicants whose documentary evidence of eligibility was affidavits from friends, family, and employers attesting that the applicant had been in the United States during the requisite periods.

Program revisions during implementation altered this guarded opening stance dramatically. The point is that the initial INS construction of the target population emphasized tightly rationing the legalization benefit. The INS exercised discretion by keeping a tight limit on those petitioners whose claims lay at the margins of congressional intent.

Two factors account for this cautious opening posture. First, tight rationing might be expected in any unprecedented program such as legalization, which offers a most valuable benefit to a population whose size could only be estimated in rough terms. Indeed, rationing benefits through eligibility regulations is a hallmark of street-level attempts to control workload.[9] Second, given the conflicting program objectives—an effort to "clean the slate" of undocumented immigrants without seeming to reward lawbreakers—and INS opposition to a legalization program, it is not surprising that the long-standing INS orientation toward undoc-

---

8. These grounds, thirty-three in all, included such characteristics as participation in Nazi persecution activities, communicable disease, "sexual deviance," and likelihood of becoming a "public charge." Public charge would become a source of controversy and, ultimately, litigation in the IRCA legalization program.

9. Lipsky (1980).

umented immigrants as a target group to be enforced against, rather than served, took precedence in implementation decisions.[10] Thus tight reins were established by the INS around the legalization benefit. The next task would be to design a service delivery system enabling those who did qualify for the benefit to have their petitions heard. Again, in designing such a system, congressional mandates would be filtered through implementation choices made by the INS.

The Amnesty Model of Benefits Conferral

Immigration policy employs tools for enforcing the law (arrest, incarceration, and deportation) and tools for conferring benefits (formal petition, administrative review, and adjudication) in its handling of immigrants. Historically, the INS orientation toward undocumented immigrants has been one in which law enforcement tools predominated. Undocumented immigrants living in the United States represented the failures of the INS to enforce immigration law. Thus one challenge for Congress in legalization would be to bring the tools of benefits conferral to bear on a population toward whom the lead implementing agency maintained a long-standing adversarial relationship.

The amnesty model provided a structure in which these adversaries could come together. The amnesty concept absolved undocumented immigrants and the INS of their real and perceived trespasses against each other. It offered a new orientation toward the target population: one in which success could be measured not by keeping out but rather by bringing in as many undocumented immigrants as possible. It suggested a new orientation toward the INS: one in which a feared agent of the state became a service bureaucracy offering a valuable benefit. These shifts in focus were pronounced departures from business as usual in the immigration realm. Framing the amnesty program as an extraordinary, one-time-only effort served to motivate targets and to motivate the INS to implement the program generously.[11]

Although eligibility standards were strict, the initial INS plan for delivering legalization services reflected a new approach to service. For

10. Baker (1990).
11. Cleaning the slate would be no small feat. The Census Bureau estimated in 1980 that the resident undocumented population numbered some 3 million to 6 million, half of whom were of Mexican origin (Warren and Passel, 1987). Furthermore, demographers estimated that 100,000 to 300,000 new undocumented immigrants entered the United States annually throughout the 1980s (Woodrow, Passel, and Warren, 1987).

several years before IRCA's passage, new trends had emerged, though slowly, in INS management and adjudications. The watchwords were "centralize and standardize." Implementing a major program like legalization gave the INS an opportunity to test the limits of this approach.

These limits became clear when INS Central Office officials proposed that legalization be run entirely from Washington, with the thirty-three INS districts serving only as front-line processors of applications to be adjudicated in the Central Office. The four INS regional commissioners and thirty-three district directors, who had long operated with great autonomy, balked at conceding such a high-profile program. As an alternative, an implementation plan emerged that gave street-level bureaucrats a more prominent position.

Under this "hierarchical review" model, intake for temporary resident alien (TRA) status (referred to as Phase I) would take place in a local legalization office under the direct authority of an INS district. Local INS adjudicators would review documentation and conduct interviews. All applicants received a work authorization card valid while their applications were being processed.

Final adjudication would take place in one of four Regional Processing Facilities (RPFs), where a legalization examiner reviewed both the paper file and the recommendation of approval or denial from the local adjudicator.[12] No interviews took place at the RPF, in keeping with its role as a quiet, centralized location for the review of documentary evidence. Successful TRAs were instructed to return to the local office to trade their work authorization card for their TRA card.

When the TRA period expired, clients received applications for permanent resident alien (PRA) status in the mail (referred to as legalization Phase II). RPF examiners reviewed the applications and scheduled a Phase II interview at a local legalization office. At the local interview, TRAs demonstrated their fulfillment of an English and civics requirement and could then receive the permanent resident alien card (commonly known as the green card).

This procedure—local interview and regional adjudication in Phase I, followed by regional scheduling and local English and civics interview in Phase II—remained largely unchanged throughout the legalization project. However, what went on within this formal framework varied dramatically across sites and over time, as the political interests influencing

12. Regional Processing Facilities were located in Burlington, Vermont (Eastern Region); Dallas, Texas (Southern Region); Lincoln, Nebraska (Northern Region); and Laguna Niguel, California (Western Region).

legalization shifted with the acquisition of field experience. One of the most important shifts took place in the INS relationship with its traditional adversaries and new legalization implementation partners—the immigrant advocacy community.

The Role of Advocacy Groups in Legalization

To facilitate the new orientation toward undocumented immigrants, Congress brought a third party into the INS-immigrant relationship. IRCA required the INS to confer Qualified Designated Entity (QDE) status upon immigrant advocacy groups and community organizations interested in participating in legalization. The QDEs would accept legalization applications and forward them to the INS for decisions. Thus the QDEs could serve as a buffer between the INS and the immigrants, mitigating the "fear factor" that Congress surmised might chill applicants from coming forward.

The QDEs echoed the logic of the community action programs of the war on poverty in that they were mechanisms whereby local-level, streetwise political actors could ensure that program implementation accurately reflected the needs of the target group. Congress assumed that the target group would be so wary of the INS as to compromise legalization objectives. Like community action program organizations of the past, QDEs would bring an immediate legitimacy to this new benefits program from the target's perspective. And like the community action program participants, QDEs would ultimately challenge the very institutions that had provided them with their foothold on the policy process (see chapter 6).

The INS eventually granted QDE status to 977 organizations and individuals, including such long-standing immigrant service groups as Catholic Social Services; such unlikely bedfellows as the United Farm Workers and the California Farm Bureau (the trade group of California growers); and such entrepreneurial interests as the Private Immigration Agency, Incorporated—a for-profit "notary public" service that opened branch offices in Latino immigrant communities around the country.

Steven R. Smith (chapter 9) notes that risks are attached to the creation of formal linkages between government service bureaucracies and private advocacy organizations. Subcontracts between government and advocacy groups for the delivery of public benefits can alter the orientation of advocates, often aligning them more closely with their government counterparts, fostering dependency on state resources, and ultimately circumscribing the range of services available to the public. In short, Smith charges that contracting with the state runs counter to the advocacy function of nonprofit and community-based organizations, resulting in a cooptation of these agencies and a homogenizing of social services.

Indeed, for many nonprofits, the INS-QDE relationship was an uneasy one. The INS viewed the QDE as a preprocessor of applications and, thus, a workload safety valve, not as a lobbying agent on behalf of immigrant petitions. In keeping with this vision, the INS issued few regulations governing QDE activities, virtually assuming that QDEs would engage in value-neutral, bureaucratic processing of applicants' paperwork.

The view from the advocacy community was quite different. Those QDEs with long histories of immigrant advocacy—Catholic Social Services, the League of United Latin American Citizens, and Traveler's and Immigrant Aid, for example—viewed themselves as immigrant advocates, not as moneymakers, intermediaries, or functionaries of the INS. For them, QDE status was a foot in the door, a chance to have access to the legalization process from the inside and to expand its scope from that vantage point. With these mindsets in opposition at the earliest points of implementation, the ensuing conflicts in the field came as little surprise to IRCA observers, although their implications would not be clear until the program's end.

In sum, the legislative and regulatory histories of IRCA legalization illustrate a heavy emphasis on restrictive eligibility standards and local discretion in service delivery, reflecting the traditional social construction of the target population as deviants toward whom benefits were to be conferred only as a matter of last resort (chapter 4). During the 1986 legislative debate about the passage of IRCA, immigrant advocates devoted most of their attention to killing the entire IRCA package. Failing that, they tried to stave off assaults on legalization within that package. With little effective opposition, the INS promulgated tight eligibility standards, preserved significant district and regional autonomy in the decisionmaking process, and relegated the role of the QDE to that of paperwork intermediary. In full implementation, however, each of these opening positions would relax in the wake of a dramatic change in political influences.

A View from the Field

In order to understand how legalization evolved into a more generous benefits program than originally intended, it is necessary to get a firsthand look at the legalization process in the field. Any effort to capture the street-level dynamics of program implementation requires both a clear understanding of formal procedure and a more detailed understanding of the many informal activities that give the program its distinctive character.

Data and Methods

The analyses in this paper rely on field data collected in a nationwide assessment of IRCA implementation. These data, collected collaboratively by researchers from the Urban Institute and the Rand Corporation, include semistructured field interviews and firsthand observational data gathered in eight key sites over two years. The sites were Los Angeles, San Jose, El Paso, San Antonio, Houston, Chicago, New York City, and Miami.

The Urban Institute–Rand implementation study teams conducted two waves of field work, one in late 1988 and another in early 1989. Research team members interviewed several categories of respondents in each site, including personnel in INS district offices and the border patrol, QDE and voluntary organization staff, private immigration attorneys, local and state officials in health, education, and welfare offices, local media, immigration researchers, employers, union officials, and trade association representatives. State agency staff members were also interviewed, as were INS personnel at the four Regional Offices and Regional Processing Facilities. Key informants in Washington, D.C., included INS Central Office officials, directors of national immigration advocacy groups, and members of Congress and their staffs. In total, the study teams conducted 484 field interviews. These interviews were supplemented with field observations in which researchers monitored the activities of local and regional applicants and adjudicators. The research strategy produced a longitudinal, multisite, multilevel database that would allow for comparisons of implementation activities across cities and over time.

Having set a decidedly cautious tone in its regulations, the INS opened the doors to 107 local legalization offices on May 5, 1987. Our research objective was to examine three aspects of legalization as implemented in the field: putting eligibility standards into operation, adhering to the amnesty model for service delivery, and negotiating with the advocacy group partners in implementation, the QDEs.

Eligibility Standards in the Field

Given the tightly defined eligibility standards at the outset, researchers were interested in whether or not many immigrants would come forward, and if they did, what their chances were of filing successful petitions. Would the "bounded generosity" reflected in the INS regulations play itself out in the field? Or would standards relax over time, and if so, why? Eligibility for legalization required much more than a simple attestation by an undocumented immigrant; it required a considerable paper trail. IRCA demanded credible documentary evidence of identity, continuous U.S. residence, and financial responsibility. Two interests guided the assessment of legalization eligibility: the wish to identify any variation in the treatment of evidence across key sites or over the yearlong life of Phase I legalization, and the attempt to account for this variation by identifying the major influences on INS actions throughout implementation.

Treatment of evidence. Respondents in nearly every site identified two countervailing trends in local Phase I implementation: an overall relaxation of documentary requirements and a gradual restriction of cases based solely on affidavits as evidence.

The earliest legalization applicants filed their petitions with copious supporting evidence. It was not unusual, INS staff claimed, to see applicants in the first weeks of the program coming forth with shoeboxes filled with rent receipts, paycheck stubs, and other evidence demonstrating their continuous U.S. residence. Over time, local INS adjudicators and QDEs became more comfortable with fewer pieces of documentation supporting a petition. As one QDE respondent in Houston noted, "Anything with the date '1981' in your file, and your interview was over. You were in." Local INS adjudicators in Los Angeles reported accepting "two to three documents to cover each year" including "postmarked envelopes mailed to the applicant (showing a U.S. address), date-stamped photographs . . . birthday cards." Adjudicators attributed this shift to two factors: increasing confidence that the fraud level was minimal, and financial incentives to encourage program participation.

In a real sense, the early applicants produced the shift toward lighter documentary requirements by providing such careful paper trails to adjudicators. Adjudicators commented frequently on the high quality of records provided by the earliest cohorts of applicants in the summer of 1987. Unfortunately, these applicants trickled into the offices slowly, prompting concerns by the INS Central Office that the legalization program would lose money, since national program start-up costs were to be recouped with applicant fees. With a high quality of early applications and a financial incentive to encourage higher application rates, the INS consistently relaxed its paper demands.

However, despite this general easing, adjudicators expressed a decidedly negative opinion toward one type of evidence, the affidavit. Recognizing the catch-22 qualities inherent in asking "undocumented" immigrants to produce documents proving eligibility, IRCA allowed petitioners to use affidavits, or sworn statements from landlords, employers, and so on, to fulfill the identity, residence, and financial responsibility requirements. However, both adjudicators and immigrant advocates reported that a stricter scrutiny was applied to affidavit-only cases. A San Jose legalization office worker reported requiring "more than affidavits" because "people lied about how long (the applicant) had been in the United States." This suspicion seemed to affect female applicants disproportionately. As a Houston attorney noted, "We put together a special packet for the live-in maids, because they were going to be the ones with the biggest documentation problems . . . All these women had were affidavits. . . . There are thousands and thousands of these women in Houston."

In sum, while documentary requirements eased in response to administrative and financial incentives, the INS continued to exert some indirect gate-keeping efforts through their critical assessment of affidavit evidence—evidence that was, in the regulations, equivalent to other types of documentation. This disparate treatment prompted class-action lawsuits in two INS regions and a precedent decision from the INS Legalization Appeals Unit in which an affidavit case denial was reversed through a revised interpretation of the documentary standard. Thereafter, affidavit-based cases were to be decided using the criteria outlined in this precedent decision.[13]

Litigation as a key implementation influence. The case of affidavit-only petitions highlights another field observation on legalization eligibility: the gradual increase in the influence over INS standard setting wielded by litigation and threats of litigation. Throughout legalization, it became abundantly clear that eligibility standards were subject to a variety of interpretations. With no direct policy precedent, the INS cut eligibility standards from whole cloth, and these standards would be challenged repeatedly in the courts.

Field respondents in the advocacy community across all sites reported that they had soon recognized the importance of legal challenge to INS-authored standards. Even a slight expansion in eligibility held enormous significance for the target population. Subtle interpretive shadings might

13. For a full reading of the precedent decision, see U.S. Department of Justice (1989).

mean the difference between bare survival on the margins of U.S. society and an eventual opportunity for full U.S. citizenship.

In a sense, INS officials recognized this same potential and reacted to it by attempting to manage target population size through the drafting of strict eligibility standards. Yet, by the close of Phase I in May 1988, every INS region was operating under some court-mandated revision altering eligibility standards and providing an extension of the program on behalf of class members. Although the INS eventually conceded many points, it fought court-mandated extensions. In the late months of Phase I—the summer of 1988—front-line program staff and Central Office officials alike reported an eagerness to "put closure" on this temporary, one-time-only program. Nevertheless, court-mandated extensions prevailed, resulting in new lines forming at local legalization offices well into 1990, as applicants who had become eligible through long-awaited court decisions reinitiated the application process. Plaintiffs in successful actions against the INS included immigrants represented by the League of United Latin American Citizens, Catholic Charities, United Farm Workers, Haitian Refugee Center of Miami, and Ayuda, Inc., of Washington, D.C.—all of whom, ironically, also served as partners in implementation through their status as QDEs.

In an effort to stave off the backlogs and bad publicity generated by repeated court losses, the INS largely abandoned the strategy of fighting each eligibility or procedural issue in court and instead attempted to anticipate points of contention and draft regulations closer to the middle of the continuum for eligibility. These affirmative revisions to legalization were clearest in the procedural changes adopted in Phase II legalization, the transition to permanent resident status.

The Amnesty Model in the Field

Along with interviews, the study teams had the opportunity to observe program activities firsthand around the country. A qualitative shift in the tone and nature of the typical interaction between the INS and immigrants took place between Phase I and Phase II. Whereas a guarded posture characterized Phase I, Phase II reflected a more open posture toward the target population. The amnesty ideal envisioned by Congress did not take hold until well into the second phase of the program.

In formal terms, the transition from a guarded Phase I to a more open Phase II could not have been more obvious. In Phase II, eligibility standards were amended significantly during the writing of regulations, in response to advocacy group suggestions. Many of these points had been the basis of Phase I class action litigation. Advocates in Houston recognized a distinct change in the tenor of their relations with INS officials in their communities, as the following quotations illustrate:

> The thing that's been positive is that some of the legalization office people are now over at the district headquarters, and they're a lot easier to deal with. (Immigrant service agency director)
> The INS didn't want us coming along on interviews with immigrants at first. But they came to respect us and we ended up with a good working relationship. They would meet with us and with other QDEs on a monthly basis. I think the adjudicators could have been better trained. They had too much discretion. But they worked hard and I sympathized with them. (Church group/QDE)

Indeed, the INS interpretations of statutory language were more expansive in Phase II. For example, immigrants could meet the Phase II English and civics requirement by passing an English and civics examination given at the time of the Phase II interview, or by demonstrating enrollment in an INS-approved course of English and civics study for a given number of hours. The INS set the "course of study" requirement at forty hours of attendance in a sixty-hour course—a lower level of obligation than many advocacy groups anticipated. The INS provided English and civics exemptions for very young, elderly, physically disabled, and developmentally disabled immigrants. Going one step further, the western INS region, which covered the 950,000 California applicants, developed several versions of the English and civics test—including one version that could be administered by videotape and previewed several times before the actual test.

More important, the tone of the Phase II interview itself evinced little of the applicants' caution and the adjudicators' suspicion typical in Phase I. Rather, adjudicators reported taking pride in seeing applicants through to the final stage of the legalization process. A typical Phase II interview lasted no more than ten minutes. An applicant demonstrating little English proficiency would be asked simple questions—names of U.S. presidents, for example—while one with advanced English skills might be asked to identify the three branches of government or to provide the number of amendments to the U.S. Constitution. The reading and writing components of the test, particularly the writing component, were cited by local adjudicators as more difficult for applicants than the civics questions. If any Phase II test component proved too difficult, adjudicators could accept certificates indicating that the applicant had been enrolled in a local English and civics class or reschedule the applicant for a second test and give him or her instructions to seek out a Phase II class.

Finding those Phase II classes often proved more difficult for applicants than INS officials realized. Even where classes were available, appropriate adult education instructors were in short supply. As one Houston school administrator noted, "There are not enough bilingual or adult education teachers to go around. Eighty-five percent of our (legalization) students are preliterate or Level One (literacy). We had to make our teachers understand that some of these students may not even have experience holding a pencil, much less speaking, reading, and writing English."

Such observations were echoed in Chicago, where an educator noted, "The first way you learn a language is 'listening comprehension.' That's demonstrating progress. We had a hard time convincing the INS what a low [literacy] level these people are at to begin with." As a result of complaints from advocates, the Chicago INS district issued clarifying instructions to its local offices emphasizing the voluntary nature of the test when an applicant also possessed a certificate from an INS-approved course provider.

With a legalizing population composed largely of limited-English-proficiency immigrants, these "enrollment certificates" proved crucial to the successful adjustment of many applicants. Nearly half of the successful Phase II applicants thus far have fulfilled their requirements through the presentation of such a certificate.[14] Indeed, a Houston civic leader characterized Phase II legalization as "the biggest Hispanic adult education program ever mounted in Houston." Coupled with affirmative changes in Phase II procedures (and even more recent extensions of the Phase II application period in the 1990 Immigration Act), these educational resources offer an opportunity for this cohort of legal immigrants to enhance their human capital. However, whether this opportunity will be realized depends not only on the actions of immigrants, but also on the capacity of local educational systems to sustain their instructional efforts and on the capacity of immigrant advocates to place and to keep immigrant education on the public education agenda. Indeed, just such an expanded role for immigrant advocates emerges from the field data as one of the most significant political legacies of IRCA.

14. Baker (1990).

The Emergence of Immigrant Advocacy
in the Field

The importance of immigrant advocacy as an influence on the implementation process through litigation has already been highlighted. However, field experiences illustrate a more localized, and perhaps more significant, transformation in the advocacy community as a result of legalization.

Advocacy community involvement was a constant in Phase I legalization implementation. However, some variation in the nature of the advocacy group role did exist. Variation across sites came in the tenor of relations between advocates and the local INS office. Variation over time manifested itself as an increasing integration of advocacy groups into coalitions that formed around IRCA issues but soon expanded their mandates to broader immigration and immigrant policy agendas.

The local INS and advocates as allies and adversaries. Los Angeles provides an example of a more cooperative relationship between the INS and local advocates, particularly those advocates affiliated with the Catholic church. Catholic service organization respondents met on a weekly basis with INS officials during Phase I and cited joint public appearances by the INS regional commissioner and the Los Angeles archbishop as factors encouraging applications in the Latino immigrant communities.

In other sites, advocacy groups served as legalization monitors, challenging the INS to provide better services. In Houston, local groups reached into the statute itself to support their monitoring efforts. Section 111(c) of IRCA allows for "the establishment of appropriate local community task forces to improve the working relationship between the Service (the INS) and local community groups." Citing this statutory language, Houston advocacy groups convened a community task force and called INS officials before their board to answer legalization questions for the public.

In San Antonio, the INS-advocacy relationship was adversarial, as reported by both INS and advocacy respondents. Advocates reported that past conflicts with the INS district director on such issues as political asylum for Central Americans adversely affected legalization. INS officials refused to meet with community groups whose leaders included sanctuary activists, with whom the district had clashed repeatedly. This tension extended to the relationship between the INS and city government, as evidenced by the remarks of one elected city official, "During the first few months [of legalization], the best advice I could give people was not to go to [the INS]. We were afraid that these people would literally be turning themselves in. . . . I never did send people directly to [the INS]."

Such INS-advocacy relationships parallel the ultimate performance of the various sites in legalization turnout. Turnout was heaviest in absolute terms and matched preimplementation turnout estimates most closely in those sites where INS-advocate relationships were cooperative or, at the very least, were characterized by a healthy respect and an effort to communicate. For instance, Houston, Chicago, and Los Angeles accounted for nearly 80 percent of the 1 million applications filed in the eight study sites.[15]

The wide variation in INS-advocacy relationships illustrates the tendency of street-level bureaucrats to exercise discretion in program implementation, discretion that ultimately becomes public policy.[16] The INS, with its long-standing policy of decentralized decisionmaking, in which district directors wielded great authority relative to the Central Office, was prone to inconsistent program implementation across sites. In several sites, advocates capitalized on the ability of the INS to exercise discretion by obtaining closer working relationships with the agency than had ever been achieved previously. In these sites, program turnout improved and fewer implementation controversies emerged. In a sense, rather than the INS coopting advocates, as Steven Smith's work might anticipate, advocates were able, in key sites like Los Angeles, Houston, and Chicago, to reconstruct the legalization program in an image closer to their political interests.

The expanded community role of the immigrant organization. Legalization changed the relations between the INS and advocacy groups. It also changed relations between advocacy groups and the immigrant community, which may prove more significant for immigrants newly settled in U.S. communities.

Conventional wisdom at the close of Phase I held that QDEs and other advocates were not especially important in legalization. Fully 82 percent of the applicant pool filed directly with the INS, implying that these applicants bypassed their QDE intermediaries altogether. However, the field data belie this portrayal in several ways.

First, QDEs supplemented local publicity and outreach efforts, espe-

15. Baker (1990).
16. Lipsky (1980).

cially on behalf of smaller immigrant constituencies. Most of the national INS-sponsored legalization publicity came late in the program and disproportionately targeted Latinos. Local QDEs serving the Haitian community in Miami, the Polish community in Chicago, and the Asian communities of Los Angeles, for example, produced and distributed their own materials in the first months of the program. These materials included pamphlets, posters, public service announcements, and even comic books in the immigrant languages, providing accessible information on legalization procedures.

Second, QDEs were important sources of preliminary information on program procedures. Although most applicants ultimately filed their petitions with the INS, the application process actually began, typically, with a visit to a QDE, where immigrants asked questions and received reassurance before taking their first steps toward applying. The costs of this preliminary information and assistance were not reimbursable to the QDE, and such contacts went unrecorded in the INS reporting system. Thus the formal processing of 18 percent of the legalization applicants by QDEs understates their contact with the target population and their financial and organizational commitment to that population.

Finally, as noted earlier, QDEs disproportionately adopted the "hard cases" among legalization applicants. The composition of QDE cases was typically skewed toward applicants with the thorniest eligibility issues. QDEs became the key local source of assistance for legalization appeals, often picking up the pieces after failed efforts by applicants to construct their petitions with the costly help of *notarios publicos*, or notaries who set up for-profit legalization offices in most Latino immigrant communities. As *notarios* closed down at the end of Phase I, and as private immigration attorneys returned to their non-IRCA caseloads, legalization appeals fell to QDEs and volunteer lawyer associations in most of the sites.

Aside from their largely unsung role in the legalization program, advocacy groups retain a final legacy from the IRCA experiment. Legalization proved a catalyst for immigrant advocacy groups to coalesce and to use their expanded resources to address broader immigration policy issues. For instance, the Houston community legalization task force soon turned its attention to a wide range of immigration issues, including city police participation in INS raids on employers, detention issues affecting immigrants awaiting deportation, the treatment of undocumented immigrant children by the INS in the Rio Grande valley, and the alleged targeting of minority businesses for employer sanctions violations in the

Houston area. Indeed, the task force succeeded in securing a policy state-ment of noncooperation with INS enforcement activities from the Hous-ton chief of police. In San Antonio, an advocacy coalition organized around legalization set up a hotline for the reporting of Border Patrol human rights violations and published a multilingual pamphlet on im-migrant rights during detention by the INS. Some QDEs in each site expanded their immigrant services to include education services extend-ing beyond the forty hours of instruction required for Phase II legaliza-tion. Even construction labor unions, many with long histories of oppo-sition to immigrant labor, joined immigration service group coalitions in an effort to organize immigrant workers. In short, legalization provided an immigration policy agenda from which new and broader political agendas continue to emerge.

The Implications of Legalization for Immigration Policy and Citizenship

Having reviewed the legalization program in its design and implemen-tation phases, I can now reflect on its significance for the policy com-munity and for the target population. The legalization experience con-firms some important observations about public policy as experienced by local-level political actors (that is, target groups and street-level bureau-crats) and about citizen empowerment, but it also raises some questions that bear further examination.

Michael Lipsky's observations about street-level bureaucrats and their preoccupation with service rationing are borne out by my analysis.[17] Legalization officials expended great energy erecting boundaries around the program's scope by restricting eligibility in the regulatory process. As Lipsky's theory predicts, the rationales for these boundaries had more to do with the interests of street-level bureaucrats in managing program operations than they did with serving congressional intent or the needs of undocumented immigrants.

Similarly, Lipsky's observation that target populations are not impor-tant reference groups for street-level bureaucrats can be observed in the field data. During Phase I, INS personnel showed few concerns about client satisfaction. Indeed, the prevailing social construction of undocu-mented immigrants as "deviants" gave street-level bureaucrats an ideo-logical basis for their guarded posture.

17. Lipsky (1980).

So deeply entrenched was the view of this target population as one to be enforced against, rather than served, that an amnesty service delivery model—a complete break with INS precedent—was deemed necessary by Congress to achieve IRCA's objectives for legalizing undocumented immigrants. Over time, this unprecedented policy tool facilitated ideological and behavioral shifts by the INS and the target group. Amnesty as a policy tool has now affected immigrants in other ways. The amnesty idea—a temporary application period for a new immigration benefit—was recently extended to the provision of safe haven for certain Central American undocumented immigrants through the 1990 Immigration Act. Similarly, those spouses and children of IRCA-legalized aliens who did not themselves qualify for adjustment under IRCA, but who have also lived in the United States, are now eligible for work authorization and temporary legal status until an IRCA-legalized family member can file an immigrant visa petition on their behalf. In short, legalization spawned a new effort to design and implement benefits that fill existing gaps in immigration law, rather than relying repeatedly on the law enforcement tools of the past.

Indeed, IRCA's provisions for legalization may well have proved more successful than its provisions for law enforcement. As planned, legalization adjusted the status of a significant share of the undocumented population, bringing immigrants' de facto settlement in the United States under the control of public policy. Recent analyses estimate that the legalization program adjusted the status of approximately two-thirds of the target undocumented population. Legalized immigrants are more rationally incorporated into tax systems, public health systems, education systems, and local economies than are their undocumented counterparts. The new IRCA enforcement tools, however, have thus far generated only modest reductions in the flow of undocumented immigrants across the southern U.S. border.[18]

Still, portrayals of legalization as the onset of an abandonment of enforcement-based immigration policy are certainly too sanguine. Public service systems have yet to feel the full effect of these 1.7 million newly legalized immigrants and their families, since these immigrants' use of public assistance is proscribed by statute for five years after legalization. As states and localities feel the full pressure of delivering services to new constituencies in the mid-1990s, cries for relief may include calls for a return to strict immigration policy.

18. Bean, Edmonston, and Passel (1990).

Debates by policymakers over restrictive immigration policy, however, will be played out upon a political landscape forever changed by the legalization experience. IRCA illustrates how political influences can shift from the design to the implementation stage of policy development. Most of the political action in IRCA's design focused on efforts to ration the legalization benefit. However, one concession to inclusionary policy interests—the incorporation of advocacy groups into the *implementation* of the program as QDEs—proved far more significant than planners anticipated. With access to INS planning information, statutory authority to participate in local program activities, and an immediate common objective transcending their varied constituencies, advocacy organizations transformed their role as legalization intermediary initially envisioned by the INS and emerged from the program as more powerful actors in immigrant social and political issues at the local and the federal levels. This phenomenon constitutes a departure from the view of public-private partnerships offered by Steven Smith (chapter 9), in that private-sector advocates did not dilute their advocacy positions simply by virtue of their formal position in a public program. The question becomes, why not?

Smith notes that contractual relationships between advocacy groups and government agencies can lead to a weakening of the advocacy role and a bifurcation of social rights, in which the neediest citizens are served by the state through quasi-private intermediaries while elites purchase their social goods—education, police protection, health—from the private sector. Under these circumstances, the link between the public provision of social goods and an inclusive form of citizenship encompassing all members of society may be threatened. Cooptation of innovative private service providers is an ever-present threat.

Yet in the case of legalization, advocates expanded their client-centered mandates. How?

Unlike most contracting relationships, the QDEs were not constrained heavily by regulations governing their participation in the program. In the race to implement legalization, the INS relegated the QDEs to their manifest objective—serving as a buffer between frightened immigrants and INS adjudicators—and allowed them wide latitude in working toward that goal. The QDEs quickly recognized that such latitude might allow them to expand their influence over the legalization process through the mechanisms described earlier—counseling immigrants, forming coalitions to hold the INS accountable for implementation decisions, and, if all else failed, suing their public-sector implementation partner into compliance with their vision of congressional intent. Capitalizing on those opportunities, the QDEs edged themselves from the margins to the center of implementation.

The QDEs were better equipped than the INS to embark upon legalization ideologically and organizationally. Amnesty required the INS to reorient itself toward the target population and to reinvent itself for the target population. No such metamorphosis was necessary for the QDEs, saving street-level QDE service providers the time and energy necessary to change their attitudes and their client-processing procedures. One might argue that ideological and behavioral shifts were necessary by the QDEs in their relationship to the INS, but that would only be true if the QDEs accepted the role defined for them by statute and regulation, which they did not. Legalization fit well within the QDE framework of service to community; and, as the scope of the legalization program expanded, it offered a launching point for broader provision of services to a newly empowered constituency.

The unique position of this new constituency relative to the state suggests another reason advocates avoided the co-optation trap. Smith's examples of public-private partnership center on the conferral of social benefits: education, health care, income support. Immigration benefits constitute a different sort of benefit. Immigration benefits confer political citizenship: fundamental rights of residence, family formation, and political participation. In the future, provision of social services to immigrants through private entities such as QDEs may well reflect the processes of co-optation Smith identifies. The public-private conferral of basic political benefits, however, may not be susceptible to the same interorganizational dynamics as that of providing social services. Building a public-private partnership implies that pulling indigenous organizations into state efforts to expand political membership—through the implementation of voting reform, for example—might facilitate the success of intended reform. One need only look at the linkages between voting reform efforts and local churches and community groups in the civil rights era for evidence of such integrity in public-private partnerships. In short, public-private partnerships can build the capacity for citizen empowerment when political rights are at stake.

But how far will this capacity building take the target population in this case? Lipsky's work suggests that the context in which targets seek benefits determines how likely they are to perceive public goods as accessible and appropriate and how likely they are to continue seeking such benefits.[19] If legalization was perceived by targets as an accessible, appropriate program, one would expect their continued contact with the state to be enhanced. They might naturalize in greater numbers than previous cohorts. They might avail themselves of public social services more readily.

At present, statutory timelines preclude answering these questions definitively. IRCA-legalized aliens are only now becoming eligible to naturalize and to apply for social services. Yet preliminary evidence suggests that immigrants have no great desire to deal with the immigration bureaucracy again to seek full citizenship. Rather, legalization seems to have linked immigrants more closely to their countries of origin by giving them the opportunity to travel freely across international borders.[20] Ironically, IRCA, with all its restrictionist rhetoric, may have strengthened international ties rather than severing them.

The analysis in this research suggests that if legalized immigrants shift their orientation, moving toward full membership in the host community through full citizenship, they will do so because current trends will lead to better immigration policymaking in the fuure. That is, an advocacy community that can counsel its constituency on the benefits of citizenship and deal with the state from a position of power will be necessary. Should the expanded scope of immigrant advocacy groups into education, social work, and other areas lead them to adopt the features of contracting agencies outlined by Smith, prospects for political advocacy on behalf of immigrant constituents may well be jeopardized. The critical lesson of the IRCA amnesty program is that such pitfalls need not ensnare private linkages to state policy implementation. When given leeway to preserve their advocacy and monitoring functions in conferring a benefit truly appropriate to target needs, private organizations can maintain their integrity in partnership with the state and may well foster a climate in which policy initiatives can effectively promote positive social change.

19. Lipsky (1980).
20. Hagan and Baker (forthcoming).

References

Baker, Susan Gonzalez. 1990. *The Cautious Welcome: The Legalization Programs of the Immigration Reform and Control Act.* Washington: Urban Institute Press.
Bean, Frank D., Barry Edmonston, and Jeffrey S. Passel. 1990. *Undocumented Migration to the United States.* Washington: Urban Institute Press.
Bierce, Ambrose. 1911. *The Devil's Dictionary.* New York: Neale.
Hagan, Jacqueline, and Susan Gonzalez Baker. Forthcoming. "Implementing the U.S. Legalization Program: The Influence of Immigrant Communities and Local Agencies on Immigration Policy Reform." *International Migration Review.*
Lipsky, Michael. 1980. *Street-Level Bureaucracy: Dilemmas of the Individual in Public Services.* New York: Russell Sage.
U.S. Department of Justice. Legalization Appeals Unit. 1989. *Matter of E.M.* Interim Decision 3113 (decided by the commissioner, May 24).
U.S. Senate. Committee on the Judiciary. 1985. *Immigration Reform and Control Act of 1985.* Report 99-132. 99 Cong. 1 sess.
Warren, Robert, and Jeffrey S. Passel. 1987. "A Count of the Uncountable: Estimates of Undocumented Aliens Counted in the 1980 United States Census." *Demography* 24 (August): 375–93.
Woodrow, Karen, Jeffrey S. Passel, and Robert Warren. 1987. "Preliminary Estimates of Undocumented Immigration to the United States, 1980–1986: Analysis of the June 1986 Current Population Survey." Proceedings of the Social Statistics Section of the American Statistical Association (August).

Part Three
Public Policy for Empowering Citizens

THE AUTHORS IN THIS section advocate and illustrate policy analysis that represents an advance from most of that performed in the past. The pioneers of policy analysis, frequently trained in economics, organizational theory, and public administration, concentrated on the extent and efficiency with which policy goals were achieved. As the field of policy analysis matured and other social scientists contributed their perspective, criteria for policy success and failure became more complex and sophisticated. It is now recognized that many public problems are not and cannot be solved by policy and many goals formerly espoused are unattainable. The objectives of policy are often unclear and were often framed to gain political support rather than to legislate achievable targets. Consequently, contemporary policy analysts tend to apply multiple measures of policy effects and to consider in their evaluations the contexts in which institutions work. R. Kenneth Godwin, Steven Rathgeb Smith, and H. Brinton Milward and Keith G. Provan place squarely on the agenda of public policy scholars the additional question of whether policies empower citizens.

Citizens may gain capacity and power in different ways, and for Godwin the ability of citizens to exercise choice and control over their lives is critical. Godwin takes as a starting point the portrayal by Helen Ingram and Anne Schneider of dependent target groups as persistently disadvantaged by the social construction embodied in policy. Further, paternalistic policies directed toward such groups place severe limits on meaningful choices. Citizen empowerment for Godwin is like consumer sovereignty. People are economically liberated to pursue their welfare through markets. Empowering policies mean limiting government, and, through vouchers and other mechanisms, providing the poor with

greater economic power to serve their wants and change their
social constructions. Godwin analyzes family-planning policies in
less industrialized countries and educational policies in the United
States to illustrate how policies can increase the access to services
and enhance the welfare of dependent populations.

Smith gives citizen empowerment a broader meaning than
Godwin and comes to very different conclusions about how much
privatization serves democracy. While Godwin focuses on individuals' freedom of choice to gain goods and services, Smith considers the political role of groups and the effect of privatizing
policies, such as contracting, on nonprofit organizations. Expansion in government contracting with nonprofit organizations for
the provision of services tends to destabilize these agencies, he
notes, and make them overly dependent on public sources of
funds. Further, contracting may undermine the role of nonprofit
organizations as alternatives to government and market organizations, constrain agency leadership, and complicate the task of
public accountability for the expenditure of public funds.

Smith, like Godwin, urges that analysts look beyond ideology
or theory in predicting the effect of privatizing policies on citizenship and instead evaluate the empirical evidence of policies operating in particular contexts. The consequences of contracting
governmental services to private organizations in the United
States is different from the European experience with corporatist
policies. In Europe organizations have monopolies in their areas
of service and are less politically vulnerable. Citizenship in a
mixed system of public and private welfare is becoming more
complex, and Smith counsels policy analysts to be sensitive to
how policy changes are changing the organizations through which
citizens participate in the system.

Like Smith, Milward and Provan examine the implications for
citizenship and public policy of the restructuring of public service
delivery. They focus on the privatization of mental health policy
through the contracting of services to private organizations. They
call attention to the fragmentation of services and the difficulties
encountered by public officials in maintaining adequate accountability for the expenditure of public funds by these contract organizations. Milward and Provan view the mental health case as a
good illustration of a larger phenomenon, which they call "the
hollow state." To them, the public sector is increasingly delegating responsibility for service delivery to private entities, leaving
public organizations with a hollow core. They worry that this

trend in public management will result in a deterioration in the quality of public services received by the citizenry.

Whether citizens were empowered by the policy design changes Smith and Milward and Provan studied is questionable. The consumer power Godwin believes will flow from transferring the provision of some public goods to private hands certainly did not accrue for the mental health patients who are the focus of the chapter by Milward and Provan. The scarcity and rationing in the underfunded field of mental health transformed providers into gatekeepers who do little or nothing to promote services. By not producing sufficient treatment to minimally meet the need, mental health policy reinforces the message to the mentally ill that they are not important to society. Further, when the state becomes hollow because it has turned its functions over to private entities, citizens are not able to hold the government accountable for policy even if they are inclined to mobilize and act.

8. Using Market-Based Incentives to Empower the Poor

R. KENNETH GODWIN

I BELIEVE THAT THE economic marketplace *can* be the most empowering institution for people who normally are not participants in the political process and whom public policies treat as deserving but helpless. In taking this perspective, I seem to be at odds with most of the other authors in this volume, as their works generally discuss how to structure the political sphere to empower citizens. I hope to show, however, that the market approach is not the opposite of empowerment policies; rather, appropriately structured markets offer the best hope for long-term policy success in delivering services to previously powerless people and developing their capacities as citizens.

Discussions of when the government should intervene to overcome market failures and when the market should intercede to rectify government failures are laden with the problem, "I believe it, therefore I see it." Persons who usually support governmental intervention to resolve problems created by imperfect markets will often compare the perfect government implementation of policy with an existing market system that is obviously flawed. Similarly, those who normally oppose government intervention and believe that government actions rarely solve problems but usually benefit advantaged populations will compare a flawed government policy with an ideally structured market with clear and enforceable property rights and low information and transaction costs. In either comparison the contest between the government and the market is similar to a contest between two singers in which after the first performs, the prize is given immediately to the other because there were flaws in the first one's performance.[1] Because both the market and the government have flaws, policy comparisons must be based on the extent of those flaws, the likelihood of correcting them, and who is

---

1. This analogy is not original and I wish I remember where I first heard it. Unfortunately, I do not.

163

harmed by various alternatives. Policies that create and use markets can encourage the most fundamental aspects of a free society: free speech, meaningful choices, control of self, enhanced opportunity, and community. Markets can also destroy people and rob them of their dignity. If we wish to empower citizens, then we must determine when the market is likely to have deleterious effects and when it is likely to have beneficial effects.

Helen Ingram and Anne Schneider (chapter 4 in this volume) classify policies according to the characteristics of the populations who must change their behavior if a policy is to succeed. They categorize populations into four types: advantaged, contender, dependent, or deviant. Ingram and Schneider argue that prevailing social constructions lead the general public and policymakers to see dependents as inferior and incapable people. Slave owners justified their policies by contending that "African Americans were incapable of taking care of themselves." Banks justified economic discrimination against women because "they couldn't handle money." The Bureau of Indian Affairs justifies its paternalistic policies concerning Native Americans because "they are incapable of making complex choices." One of the worst aspects of social constructions of dependent populations and the policies they engender is that the objects of these policies (African Americans, women, Native Americans) internalize the messages that the policies send them and, in fact, become less capable. In this chapter I look at two dependent populations, rural women in less industrialized countries and inner-city parents in the United States. Each of these populations has all the characteristics that Ingram and Schneider identify with dependents, and in each case the social construction surrounding these people has led to policies that deny them control over their lives and the lives of their families.

I shall argue that changing from paternalistic policies to policies that create markets would help these two populations substantially. In accepting the challenge to empower dependents, I propose placing the power of choice in the hands of dependents rather than in those of governmental officials or governmentally provided experts. In making this argument I shall identify those aspects of markets that are necessary if the market is to empower the people rather than exploit them.

If one accepts Ingram and Schneider's arguments that the prevailing social construction surrounding a target population results in predictable and persistent policy patterns and that these patterns will continue to help the advantaged and harm the dependent, then it does not make sense to expand government activity in a way that might give dependents more political power. This is because such policies, if they are to succeed, necessitate changing the entire social construction that surrounds dependents, require that politicians ignore the political costs and benefits to them of their policy actions, and demand that dependents remain politically active over the long term.[2] The most logical strategy to empower dependents is to reduce government's power over them. If dependents have sufficient economic power, they can force the society to view them as clients to be served rather than objects to be treated, managed, or administered. The critical issue concerns *when* using markets rather than attempting to change an entire social construction is more likely to empower dependents. The answer depends on whether it is possible to construct a competitive market with low information costs that provides dependents with sufficient economic power.

The Argument

Adam Smith and John Stuart Mill made clear two great principles of economics. In *The Wealth of Nations*, Smith showed the benefits of the market as a mechanism for improving the welfare of those who participate in it. Persons who freely enter into trades expect to improve their welfare position, otherwise they would not make the trade. For example, if a buyer purchases a book, the buyer believes that the book is worth more to him or her than alternative uses of the money. At the same time, however, a completely "free" market, one that does not include transfers of income and opportunity from the more fortunate to the less fortunate in society, is more severe than most people would prefer. In response to this problem, John Stuart Mill showed in *Principles of Political Economy* that, within broad limits, society can choose to redistribute wealth without harming the efficiency and choice advantages of the free market. In short, the market makes possible free choice for those who have money; society, through redistribution of wealth, makes those choices available to a broader population without destroying the advantages that a capitalist system has for increasing productivity and providing choices.[3]

2. Sallie Marston (chapter 6) shows the difficulty of this last solution even when the government subsidizes such participation.
3. This insight by Mill is generally forgotten by those who advocate the beauty of an unfettered market. The key to Mill's argument is that efficiency applies only to production and the movement of capital to the production of goods and services that have the highest value to consumers. But each distribution of income has a different efficiency. For example,

The market makes no pretense of being just; it is not a place where benefits necessarily go to the "deserving." In the absence of governmental restraints, persons of great wealth have far too much power over persons who are poor. This inequality of power destroys what most people envision when they speak of democratic government. The obvious, but rarely used, solution to this problem is to provide enough money to all so that they can make meaningful choices. Schneider and Ingram suggest why governments rarely use such a straightforward approach. Policymakers view the politically powerless but deserving (a set of individuals that overlaps extensively with the set of persons who are poor) as incapable of making "correct" choices. For this reason, governmental policies tend to be paternalistic and place control over these persons' choices in the hands of governmental officials or other experts. The message implicit in such policies is that dependent populations are poor, helpless, needy people who are unable to do things for themselves.

There are, of course, flaws in the neoclassical models of market behavior. For the purposes of this chapter, the greatest of these is that if a market is to work efficiently, transaction and information costs must approximate zero. In neoclassical market models, competition and the feedback it provides must produce information to market participants at a price that approximates zero so that they may make choices that maximize their utility.[4] Government intervention is frequently justified on the grounds that transaction costs often are too high and information too costly for the market to work efficiently. Proponents of governmentally provided goods and services to dependents further contend that these individuals are not in a position to make good choices or that they are unable to make good choices. Because of this condition, society must rely on experts to make choices for these people.

---

consider two distributions of income and see how this would affect demand and supply but not efficiency. First, imagine a society of one hundred families in which the two wealthiest receive $1 million a year and the other ninety-eight families receive only $10,000 a year. In this situation, the demand for automobiles will be two luxury cars. No one else can afford a car. Now imagine a society in which the two wealthiest persons each receive $100,000 and the remaining members of society receive $28,368.37. The total wealth of the society is the same—$2,980,000. But the demand for cars changes drastically. The two wealthiest families will probably buy very good cars, but not luxury cars, and the remaining families have sufficient money to buy a subcompact. Now the efficient production of cars will be two very good cars and ninety-eight small cars. In each case the market would be efficient as long as it produced the cars demanded at the lowest possible cost.

4. North (1990).

The Market and Merit Goods

A growing body of literature in more and less industrialized countries advocates the greater use of fees and the privatization of governmentally provided services. Richard Rose points out that "three-quarters of public spending in the average advanced industrial nation today is allocated to programmes that *are marketable but not marketed*, that is, private benefits."[5] In the less industrialized countries governments have enacted policies that, if fully funded, would provide social services equal to or greater than those found in more industrialized countries. However, the consequences of using pricing and other market incentives are different for the two sets of countries. In more industrialized countries the debate concerns the efficiency of provision and the message that using the market to allocate merit goods makes about the obligations of a community to its members.[6] In less industrialized countries the issue is not whether the existing provision is efficient, though it usually is not, but whether large sectors of the population who, by law, should receive services will receive them in the absence of revenues from fees collected for the services.[7]

In most countries, the government is the principal provider of education. To promote the use of this service and to acknowledge its characteristics as merit goods, governments offer education at little or no cost to consumers. In less industrialized countries this policy has led to demand that far exceeds supply.[8] This excess demand has led many people to argue that government should charge user fees to raise additional revenues so that it can expand service provision.[9] Proponents of fees contend that offering a service for a price gives important information about what consumers will pay for, even if the charges are only a fraction of the cost of providing the service.[10] Proponents of user fees further argue that fees would increase equality of provision in the less industrialized countries. Equality would increase because the beneficiaries of public services tend to live in urban areas and to be relatively well-off while the costs of these programs fall disproportionately on the rural poor.[11]

5. Rose (1989, p. 266). (Emphasis in the original.)
6. Walzer (1983).
7. Roth (1987).
8. Gertler and Glewwe (1989); and Roth (1987).
9. Akin, Birdsall, and de Ferranti (1987); Birdsall (1983); Jimenez (1987); Thobani (1983); and Psacharopoulous, Tan, and Jimenez (1986).
10. Rose (1989, p. 274).
11. Griffin (1989).

Opponents of fees for merit goods contend that services such as education and health care should be available without charge to all sectors of the population. By keeping something outside the realm of the market, the society proclaims its special value.[12] Opponents further contend that raising fees will reduce educational and health attainment among the poor and thus exacerbate inequality. Other critics believe that the provision of free services leads to greater social cohesion. Bleddyn Davies writes, "Social services are not merely 'utilitarian instruments of welfare' but also 'agents of altruistic opportunities.' Social policy provides and extends opportunities for altruism in opposition to the possessive egoism of the market place."[13]

Coupled with this argument is the belief that if lower-income persons must subject themselves to a means test, their self-esteem is lowered and a sense of powerlessness is reinforced. Thus, if the service is not free, egoism replaces altruism. If the service is free only to some individuals, they will become damaged psychologically, because the social construction that they are inferior will be reinforced.

I believe that some of the above arguments are untrue, others are only partially correct, and that the failure to use markets destroys social values that most people rank more highly than the above-mentioned rationales for avoiding the market. The examples I use to illustrate the argument are family-planning policy in less industrialized countries and educational policy in the United States. By taking one policy from the less industrialized countries (LICs) and one from the more industrialized countries (MICs) I hope to show the differences between the two situations and to show that, despite these differences, the arguments for empowering dependent populations by making them consumers are valid in many circumstances.

Family-Planning Services in Less Industrialized Countries

Between 1963 and 1977, sixty-two LICs adopted policies to reduce fertility rates and to provide family-planning services. This rapid adoption of population policies reflected a consensus among LIC elites that reducing fertility rates would improve individual living conditions and spur economic development. Partially as a result of these policies, fertility

12. Kelman (1981); and Klees (1984).
13. Davies (1980, p. 133).

rates in Asia and Latin America dropped by 26 percent and 23 percent, respectively, between 1965 and 1980.[14] Although these policies have been generally successful, fertility rates have remained high in rural areas and continue well above the goals set by LIC governments. This high fertility continues even though a substantial unmet demand for contraceptives exists.[15]

The adoption of fertility reduction policies by LICs shows that elites in these countries see reduced fertility as a desirable national goal. To achieve this goal, however, individuals—in LICs this generally means females—must act to reduce the probabilities of pregnancy and birth. The elite decision that fertility reduction is a governmental priority and the external economies resulting from individual consumption clearly qualify contraception as a merit good.[16] As such, it falls into the same category of such governmentally supplied goods as immunization, control of vector-borne diseases, and primary school education.

Without doubt, LICs undersupply all of the above-listed services, that is, the marginal value of an additional unit of any of the above services is worth more than its marginal cost. Studies of the social impacts of fertility reduction indicate that the social benefits are much greater than the costs of these programs.[17] Although the merit good characteristics of contraception lead most countries to subsidize family-planning services, contraception clearly is a private good—it is rival and exclusive. While many of the benefits of reduced fertility accrue to the society, the greatest benefits go to the woman whose pregnancy is averted or aborted and to her family. For example, more than 50 percent of all live births in rural Ecuador occur without anyone other than a family member present, and less than 25 percent of these women receive postpartum medical care.[18] Infant and maternal mortality are high. Infection, anemia, and disease are common results of pregnancy and childbearing. Such circumstances strongly encourage women to use effective, reliable contraception. The problem is that contraceptives are unavailable.

A comparison of family-planning delivery systems can test the validity of the efficiency and equity arguments about the use of the market to

14. Mauldin and Lapham (1985, p. 37).
15. Bulatao and Lee (1983); Caldwell (1983); and Jones (1984).
16. I define merit goods as those providing external economies to society and deemed by a ruling group to be appropriate for government subsidies or subject to government control. This definition follows that of Musgrave (1969); and Judge (1978).
17. Wheeler (1985).
18. Florez (1990).

assist the delivery of a merit good. Currently, some countries charge fees while others do not, and some countries have decentralized delivery of services while others plan and coordinate delivery in the hierarchical, centralized manner that Schneider and Ingram say is typical for programs designed to help dependent populations.

Given the high social and individual utility of contraception in LICs, why is it so undersupplied in rural areas? Three factors contribute to this situation: the hierarchical, centralized character of most family-planning programs; the passive nature of family-planning delivery; and the politically powerless position of most rural populations, which has led to a strong delivery bias in favor of urban areas. Among the greatest difficulties facing program implementation of any type in the LICs is the inability of central governments to coordinate their programs and to deliver materials and services, especially health care and related programs, in a timely fashion. The *World Development Report* concluded that central governments' decisions on the allocation of key inputs into health-care programs often does not match the institution's needs or the community's preferences, but central administrators have neither the financial power nor the incentive to change them and they lack critical information on what inputs are needed.[19]

Barbara Herz argues that a second factor leading to the undersupply of family planning is the passive nature of its delivery.[20] Most LICs deliver public family-planning services through public health clinics and hospitals. This arrangement has the advantages of using the existing health-care infrastructure and of increasing the probability that centers can introduce effective contraceptive methods to women who come in for prenatal and postpartum care. The disadvantages are the system's domination by medical doctors, its concentration in urban areas, its passive approach to recruiting new contraceptive users, and the fact that in rural areas and among urban poor, neither prenatal nor postpartum care is usually available. Herz describes the approach of most family-planning clinics: "Services are usually provided through urban clinics where supervision of service providers is easier. . . . Usually, only a few methods— the least controversial ones—are offered. . . . Advertising or 'informational' efforts are quite limited; clinics offer services to those who come and ask and are thus quite passive."[21]

This passive approach presents a serious obstacle to contraceptive use,

19. World Bank (1988, p. 135).
20. Herz (1984).
21. Herz (1984, p. 50).

especially continued use. Effective family planning depends heavily on minimizing the private costs to potential users of the service. These costs include obtaining knowledge of contraceptive sources and techniques and the time needed to travel to a source. For example, custodians in hospitals, who have near-zero costs for knowledge and travel, are much more likely to practice contraception than custodians in factories. Studies in numerous LICs have found that the use of modern contraceptives increases monotonically with a decrease in travel time.[22] Unless outreach workers come to them, rural women are less likely to know about alternative types of contraceptives or where to obtain them.[23] The costs of coming to urban areas and of finding a contraceptive source can also be prohibitive.

The passive nature of the public health structure limits its ability to recruit. Public health clinics operate on the basis that if people want a service, they will come. The public health worker receives her salary whether or not she has clients. In contrast, a system providing incentives to employees based on the number of contraceptive acceptors or one allowing the provider to charge and profit from the fees she collects creates a situation where, unless there are acceptors, there is no income.

Proponents of incentives and fees argue that their use should encourage an active orientation among providers of services, encouraging the provider to discover those proximate factors that turn potential acceptors into actual acceptors. These influences are often location specific and relate to daily concerns and behaviors of the target populations.[24] Diverse variables such as religion, family structure, occupation, and attitudes and norms associated with injections, pills, and body manipulation may be important determinants of whether a woman will choose contraception and the type of contraception that she will use. User charges provide useful information about which family-planning services clients value most and may allow service providers to adapt their products to local conditions and to receive immediate feedback on strategies and products that work best.

The third factor that greatly inhibits effective service provision to rural women is the politically powerless position of rural populations. Because the governmental health system provides contraceptives, the characteristics of that system strongly affect contraceptive availability. Numerous studies show that government-subsidized health care in developing coun-

22. Judge (1978).
23. Boulier (1985).
24. Salmen (1987); and Sheehan (1976).

tries has a strong urban bias and emphasizes curative rather than preventive care.[25] The World Bank estimates that the average health-sector subsidy to urban households in Colombia, Indonesia, and Malaysia is up to five times that given to rural households.[26] Even in supposedly rural-oriented China, per capita health expenditures are roughly three times greater for urban areas than for rural areas.[27]

The poverty, low educational attainment, and geographic dispersal of rural populations make it difficult for them to organize into a political force that can successfully pressure governments into providing services. In some LICs, the model of economic development that elites pursue exploits the rural sector in order to invest in capital equipment and infrastructure in urban areas.[28] The demand by a powerless population for merit goods in this situation has a low priority compared with demands from more politically powerful urban populations.

In summary, the condition of rural women in LICs makes them the "ideal" dependent population. The Ingram and Schneider model accurately predicts policies related to this group. For a long time the need of women for family-planning services was dismissed as a problem that was too private for public action. Even after the governments in the LICs recognized the merit good characteristics of family-planning services, medical doctors and other experts determined which women could have access to what contraceptive services. The essentially passive nature of the clinic-based system did not respond to the real-life circumstances of the women needing the service and therefore did not overcome the barriers to contraceptive use by rural women. Finally, because rural women are so powerless politically, the priority of providing them with adequate services was too low for the government to address their problems. How might market-based tools overcome these problems?

Alternative Approaches to Rural Provision: Experiences in Four Countries

To illustrate the arguments for more decentralized and market-oriented systems, I compare family-planning delivery in four countries: Peru, Ecuador, Colombia, and Indonesia.[29] Peru and Ecuador are examples of

25. Akin and others (1985); Jimenez (1987); Maxwell (1981); and Meerman (1979).
26. World Bank (1988, p. 135).
27. Griffin (1989, p. 38).
28. Hirschman (1986).
29. The author has worked with the delivery programs in the three Andean coun-

centralized, public programs that use neither provider incentives nor user fees. Colombia's delivery system is centralized in its public sector but relies heavily on a decentralized private sector to provide most family-planning services. Indonesia uses a highly decentralized public delivery system that maximizes information and feedback by employing limited economic incentives to service providers, user fees, and government-subsidized private delivery. In 1976 the four countries were roughly comparable in total fertility, ranging from 5.0 to 5.6. By 1988, however, the differences among the four countries were striking. The total fertility rates in the rural areas of Indonesia and Colombia had dropped substantially (to 3.6 and 4.2, respectively), while in Peru and Ecuador the respective rates remained at 5.2 and 5.0.[30]

Do the differences in fertility rates in the four countries occur because of the characteristics of their family-planning and health-care delivery systems, or do they reflect other factors? Although it is always possible that unmeasured variables account for the variation in observed fertility rates, most possible alternative explanations can be ruled out. Past studies of fertility decline have found that fertility drops as general economic development increases and that the single variable with the greatest negative impact on birth rates is female education. To determine if either of these factors was instrumental in the greater declines in Indonesia and Colombia than in Peru and Ecuador, I regressed fertility rates and fertility declines onto income, urbanization, infant mortality, and female education in ninety-three LICs. Using the results of this analysis, I then computed the expected total fertility rate and the expected fertility decline. The actual total fertility rates of Indonesia and Colombia are 21.6 percent and 17.3 percent below the levels that socioeconomic development and female education would predict; the rates of Peru and Ecuador are 2.0 percent and 8.3 percent above the predicted score. The differences in the predicted and actual declines in fertility rates in the four countries are even more dramatic. The actual declines in fertility rates from 1970 to 1985 are 96.6 percent and 44.8 percent *greater* than predicted in Indonesia and Colombia; the declines in Peru and Ecuador are 40.6 percent

---

tries. Information on the Indonesian program comes from interviews with USAID officials and contract employees in Indonesia and from the studies of Boulier (1985); Maraviglia (1990); Rohde and Hendrata (1982); and Warwick (1982).

30. The 1976 rates for Peru, Colombia, and Indonesia are from World Fertility Survey (1984). For Ecuador, the rate is estimated from the 1982 rate estimated from 1978 USAID Demographic and Health Surveys. The 1988 rates for all four countries are estimated from USAID Demographic and Health Surveys in these countries.

and 63.7 percent *less* than predicted.[31] What accounts for these striking differences? I believe that a large part of the answer is found in the structure of the service delivery systems in the four countries.

Peru typifies the information and management problems that centralized, hierarchical delivery systems present. The United States Agency for International Development (USAID) and the government of Peru decided to expand the country's family-planning services by using rural health-care clinics. USAID-Peru hired a Washington-based consulting firm to design a logistical system for managing contraceptive deliveries to health-care centers. Using survey data on current contraceptive use and desired family size, the firm developed an elaborate computer program to estimate the quantity and mix of contraceptives that would be needed monthly to meet the demand in each area. This program, however, has been ineffective because it does not accurately predict contraceptive needs.

Peru, like many LICs, legislates that new medical doctors spend a period of time in rural clinics to repay the country for its investment in their medical education. In actuality, these doctors rarely leave the cities. Rural clinics, which official records show to be staffed, are not. The Ministry of Health privately estimates that fewer than one clinic in ten operates in the manner prescribed by law and reported in national budgets.[32] Where the clinics do operate according to plan, the demand for modern contraceptives is greatly underestimated because a reliable supply of contraceptives creates a greater demand. For example, when supplies of oral contraceptives are not dependable, the likelihood of their use is small. If, however, a woman knows that she will have consistent access to oral contraceptives, she is more likely to practice contraception and to pursue activities that do not include additional children in the near future.

Ecuador presents a similar example of rural health-care delivery. As is true in Peru, government documents show Ecuador as having rural health-care clinics in all provinces, districts, and large villages. Depending on size, either a newly minted M.D. or a licensed nurse staffs these clinics. All medical care and medicines, including contraceptives, are free. In reality, most rural clinics rarely open, and most women do not have a reliable contraceptive supply. Consequently, rural women in Ecuador

31. Because aggregate data on countries are not available for rural areas only, the equations are for the entire country.

32. The figures reported for clinic staffing in Peru and Ecuador come from the author's interviews in Peru in December 1988 and in Ecuador in July 1989. See also Florez (1990).

rarely use effective contraceptives until they go to private clinics in the cities to be sterilized.[33]

Ecuador has a second public supplier of contraceptives, the social security system. This system provides free health care for employees of the government and of large companies in rural areas. Because these employees are relatively better off and because most live in concentrations large enough to support a health clinic, the social security system should be able to provide effective family-planning services. Unfortunately for these employees, the orientation of the health-care system is curative rather than preventive and is dominated by male doctors who do not support contraceptive and sterilization programs. As a result, family planning has a uniformly low position in the hierarchy of services.[34]

Colombia differs from its Andean neighbors in two significant ways. First, the Colombian public health-care system charges for services. Although this fee depends on income, all patients pay something toward their medical care. In 1985 the average charge for an outpatient visit was thirty-six cents, excluding the cost of medicines. While this amount is small, it is sufficient to maintain staffing by nurse practitioners. Second, Colombia decided in 1970 to allow the commercial distribution of oral contraceptives and injections by pharmacies. PROFAMILIA, the International Planned Parenthood Federation affiliate in Colombia, buys contraceptives in bulk and then resells them at heavily subsidized rates to pharmacies, private doctors, and the government's social security system. By 1986, although overall contraceptive prevalence had increased to 65 percent among married women, the Ministry of Health's clinics and hospitals were providing contraceptives to less than 20 percent of contraceptive users. The dominant supply system consisted largely of private clinics, health-care workers, and small drug stores (boticas). The Colombian government allows boticas to distribute pills and injections as well as barrier methods, and the boticas are the major source of these methods.[35]

As is true in almost all LICs, when compared with urban areas, the rural areas of Colombia have lower contraceptive prevalence rates. But, unlike Peru and Ecuador, in Colombia rural clinics are almost always staffed. The staffing, except in larger villages, is usually by nurse practi-

33. Female sterilization is the most widely used method of contraception in Ecuador. The median age of the women undergoing this operation is thirty-three. Florez (1990).
34. Godwin, McGreevey, and Charo (1990).
35. Merrick (1990, pp. 150–52).

tioners, but there is a staff, and revenues from the clinics pay the staff's salaries. Because of PROFAMILIA's active participation in the sale of contraceptives, their dependable supply in rural areas is more likely.[36] This is particularly true of the social security facilities that serve populations similar to those in the Ecuadorian program but charge fees and sell contraceptives heavily subsidized by PROFAMILIA. Even Colombia, however, has not overcome the largest barrier to higher contraceptive use in rural areas: the passive nature of a clinic-based program.

Indonesia provides an excellent case study of how a governmentally sponsored decentralized delivery system can work. The government established the National Family Planning Coordinating Body (BKKBN) to implement the national family-planning policy. The BKKBN hired 7,000 field workers, principally village leaders and local midwives, who then recruited contraceptive acceptors by making house-to-house visits, forming "Acceptors Clubs," and using credit unions to promote family planning.[37] Local Islamic leaders who accepted the program were asked to remind the faithful that the Koran requires two years of breast feeding of new infants.[38]

The Indonesian program is unique in several ways. First, it uses existing village authorities, local midwives, and Islamic religious leaders as workers in the program.[39] Second, during its initial two years, the project offered incentives to workers for each new acceptor. Third, the program quickly branched out to include preventive health care, nutrition, village beautification, and entertainment. Finally, the BKKBN worked to "demystify" medical technology and to turn nutritional management and family planning over to the people of the village. In this decentralized, village-level delivery, family-planning workers made a portion of their income from the sale of their products, and they made decisions on program administration, resupply, and record keeping. Because their incomes depended on their sales, providers had a strong incentive to recruit new acceptors and to keep previous acceptors satisfied with services.[40]

---

36. Two difficulties for the Colombian program have been the government takeover of part of the private family-planning distribution network and a 1984 attack by the Catholic church on the government for allowing sterilization. These events reduced the availability of sterilization.

37. Warwick (1990).

38. Rohde and Hendrata (1982).

39. For example, the World Fertility Survey in Indonesia found that village headmen supplied 22 percent of the contraceptives used by rural women. See Jones (1984, p. 62).

40. The private sale of publicly purchased contraceptives has never been officially authorized by the government. Nonetheless, evaluations of the Indonesian program esti-

Even in public health clinics, the Indonesian government subsidizes private delivery of contraceptives and relies on the market to assist in their distribution. Only 6 percent of Indonesia's health-care providers are employed full time in the private sector. Most of the rest work "full time" in the public sector. The Indonesian government allows many of these employees to use clinic facilities after hours to provide services for fees. Because these hours are often more convenient and involve less waiting time, services provided in this way are in great demand. Nydia Maraviglia found that most medical doctors make more money from their after-hours practice than from their public employment.[41]

By the standards of program impact and efficiency, Indonesia's program clearly ranks as the most effective and efficient. Indonesia is the only country of the four to reach equality of service in rural and urban areas. In 1988 contraceptive prevalence was 46 percent among women in rural areas and 54 percent in urban areas.[42] Once controls for education are made, comparably educated rural women have higher rates of prevalence than urban women. Indonesia also has the lowest public costs per contraceptive user, three dollars a year, despite the rural nature of the coverage and the use of incentives to contraceptive providers. Colombia, although behind Indonesia in the decline in fertility rates and in current contraceptive prevalence in rural areas, ranks second in these categories and in the cost-per-acceptor category; it spends four dollars per acceptor a year. The costs in Peru and Ecuador are five and fifteen dollars, respectively.[43]

The Ethics of Markets for Merit Goods

The prime argument against fees for health and education is that they are merit goods and, as such, should be available without charge to all sectors of the population. Governments make the same arguments for family planning. The 1974 World Population Conference in Bucharest

---

mate that approximately 20 percent of the contraceptives purchased for public delivery are sold privately. Recently, the government hired a U.S. firm to develop a logistics system that would reduce this "leakage" by delivering contraceptives to providers based on their reported public sales. In the author's view, this action is a major error and will hurt the rural delivery system.

41. Maraviglia (1990).

42. Maraviglia (1990, tables 1–7).

43. The costs in Ecuador are high because voluntary sterilization is the dominant form of contraception among rural women.

adopted the Plan of Action that recognized as a basic human right the ability to choose freely and responsibly the number and spacing of children. More important, the risks of childbearing are so great in the rural areas of less industrialized countries that a woman's right to choose whether and when she will become pregnant is certainly a fundamental health-care right.

To what extent do fees and decentralization increase or decrease this right? As pointed out in the introduction, while primary education, health care, and access to family planning are merit goods, they are also goods that individuals consume privately and that have utility to them. Thus the total utility of these goods is the sum of individual utility plus the utility to society that the external economies of individual consumption create. To the extent that these goods are available at a cost lower than or equal to the amount individuals are willing to pay, everyone in society benefits. Consumers benefit because they are receiving the good or service, and the society benefits because of the external economies.

From my perspective, the women in rural Colombia and Indonesia who have access to family planning and pre- and postpartum care, even if they must pay a small fee for this care, clearly are better off than the women of Peru and Ecuador who are condemned to pregnancy in high-risk situations with little, if any, pregnancy-related health care. To argue that this care should be free misses the point. Only because the care is not free is it delivered. To achieve the access and contraceptive prevalence that Indonesia has achieved, the government had to make it in the interest of service providers to seek out and convince—sell if you will—potential acceptors that they should become actual acceptors.[44]

Did the use of the private sector or fee-for-service provision of family planning diminish equality in Colombia or Indonesia? No. In both countries, the government subsidizes the provision of the service, and rural and urban areas have far more equal access than they do in Peru and Ecuador. Furthermore, the decentralization of family planning and the use of a village-based delivery system in Indonesia made possible the later

44. It could be argued that incentives to providers would be better than fees charged to acceptors. There are two difficulties with this proposal. First, the cost to the government is greater and, therefore, services are less likely. Second, experience with incentives to providers has shown that they convince acceptors to choose only those methods for which the government pays high incentives rather than the most appropriate method for the acceptor. This experience reinforces the importance of policies that give consumers the choices rather than policies that place choices in the hands of providers.

provision of immunization, child nutrition, and other health-related programs that the government subsidizes heavily.

Is there sufficient excess demand for contraception in countries such as Peru and Ecuador to reduce fertility rates if contraceptives were available, even with a fee? The World Fertility Survey found that the level of unmet contraceptive need was approximately 50 percent in Peru and 30 percent in Ecuador. This figure was likely to be much higher in rural areas.[45] Certainly there is no a priori reason to expect that the response to a fee-based system would be different in these countries than in Colombia. The three countries have similar levels of female education, income, and urbanization, and they have a similar cultural background.

The final argument against fees is that charges for merit goods reduce social cohesion. Interestingly, recent changes in the Indonesian program contest this hypothesis. In 1988 Indonesia introduced the strategy of *KB Mandiri*, a term that combines self-reliance and community obligation. The concept of *KB Mandiri* is linked to the long-standing Javanese tradition of *Gotong-Royong*, the individual's responsibility to act for the social good. In the context of family-planning services this idea means that those who can afford to purchase the service should do so in order that those who cannot afford it can receive the service without charge.[46] This approach enables the relatively better off to provide anonymous transfers to those who are less well off. Indonesian officials believe that this approach increases social cohesion through the participation of all in producing the social good of a lower fertility rate. The government increases the symbolic meaning of purchases through the marketing of the Blue Circle brand of contraceptives—a symbol designed to show the connections among all members of the society. Although it is too early to evaluate the effectiveness of the *KB Mandiri*–Blue Circle efforts, the program suggests that governments can foster social cohesion in more ways than by using governmental coercion to make social transfers. Perhaps by stressing the obligation of individuals to contribute voluntarily, the Indonesian plan is ethically superior to its alternative.

45. The World Fertility Survey defined "unmet need" as the percentage of fecund women who respond that they want no more children but are not using an efficient contraceptive. World Fertility Survey (1984, pp. 53–54). A more conservative definition of unmet demand is the percentage of women who fit the above category and who indicate that they would use contraception if it were readily available. These percentages are 17.2 percent for Ecuador and 21.4 percent for Peru. World Fertility Survey (1984, p. 54).

46. Maraviglia (1990, p. 33).

To summarize, a comparison of countries that use market mechanisms and those that do not indicates that fees and the information about demand they provide greatly increase the provision of merit goods, help to overcome the powerless situation of rural women, and save lives. The use of fees is not the only factor involved, however. By making it in an individual's economic self-interest to determine the type of goods rural women desire and to meet those desires, the market can help overcome the policy bias toward the more powerful in society. In the end, the cost to the government is less expensive as consumers pay a portion of the costs of goods that communitarians argue should be beyond the market. However, the most important question from my perspective is, "If you were a rural woman in an LIC, would you prefer the delivery systems of Colombia or Indonesia or would you prefer those of Ecuador or Peru?" I believe that most people would choose a delivery system with fees and profits rather than no delivery at all. In the LICs, this is the choice.

Education in the United States

How applicable are the above findings to other policy situations? I believe that the arguments for creating markets and using them as empowerment tools are compelling in all countries *if* policies can create a market where information and transaction costs are low and equity considerations receive priority. The areas most amenable to such policies are those that deal with the provision of services characterized by private consumption with positive externalities and recognized as merit goods by the political authorities.[47] Perhaps the classic case of such a good is primary and secondary education.

Most readers probably will agree that the public schools in the United States are not effectively educating the poor, especially the inner-city poor. In part, this problem occurs because of insufficient funding. However, the problems of public schools for the poor and working-class populations go well beyond finance. In a hotly debated book, John Chubb and Terry Moe analyzed the records of more than 8,000 public and private secondary schools and found that, after controlling for the socioeconomic status and previous educational attainment of students as well as resources, size, and curriculum, students in private schools did significantly better on tests that measured the gains in their skills over a two-

47. Godwin (1992).

year period.[48] Chubb and Moe argued that these gains occurred because private schools are intrinsically more likely to adapt to meet the needs of various sets of consumers of educational services. Although the methods and conclusions of Chubb and Moe have been criticized,[49] clearly thousands of parents spend millions of dollars to send their children to private schools to obtain what the parents believe is a superior education.

In 1992 President Bush reintroduced the idea of providing educational vouchers worth $1,000 to low- and middle-income families who could use them to send their children to private schools or to schools in other public school districts. The idea of educational vouchers is an old one compared with other educational reforms. Adam Smith discusses the idea briefly in *The Wealth of Nations*, and Thomas Paine made the first formal policy proposal in the United States in *The Rights of Man*. Milton Friedman renewed the idea. More recently John Coons and Stephen Sugarman proposed a voucher system that would provide much greater assistance to low-income, physically or mentally challenged, and other high-risk or high-cost students.[50] Coons and Sugarman contend that large vouchers for these groups would lead private schools to recruit these students and to respond to their needs. This process would bring about racial and economic integration, empower low-income parents, and improve the education of high-risk students.

Another argument for vouchers for public and private schools is that they would significantly increase the freedom of speech for the least advantaged sectors of society. Coons has written that raising children in accordance with the parents' values is the most important form of free speech most people will ever experience. A society that truly cherishes freedom of expression would ensure that all families could choose a public school or a private school that supports their values.[51] In the United States education is provided in a way that allows children of the wealthy to exercise this free speech, but denies the poor this opportunity. Upper-middle-class and wealthy families cluster in chosen government enclaves or send their children to private schools; middle-class and poor families get whatever school goes with the price of their residence. This system constitutes welfare for the economically advantaged and entails far more financial exclusivity than any other public service such as li-

48. Chubb and Moe (1990).
49. Witte (1991).
50. Friedman (1955); and Coons and Sugarman (1978, 1992).
51. Coons (1992).

braries, pools, highways, or even hospitals.[52] For the poor, decisions about how and where their children will be educated are made by computer, geography, counselors, or teachers.

As one would expect when a service deals with dependents, the denial of choice to low-income and working-class parents creates costs for them and their children. Parents learn that society does not trust them to make good choices for their children and does not take seriously their desires for their children's education. Current policy tells them that strangers are better judges than they are of what education is most suitable for their children. The children learn that the relationships they have with their parents are subordinate to the commands of strangers.

Proponents of a voucher system contend that such a program would change educational service delivery dramatically. Vouchers would allow parents to choose what type of school their children will attend and what values their children will receive. Shifting authority to the parents would show that the society trusts the parents, respects the rights of children, and believes in the sanctity of the family. A voucher system that provided higher vouchers for low-income, physically and mentally challenged students, and other high-risk groups would do more to integrate schools than all the efforts, or lack thereof, since *Brown* v. *Board of Education*.[53]

Despite the possible benefits that proponents of vouchers herald and the inability of public schools to effectively educate the inner-city poor or to achieve racial, ethnic, or economic integration, voucher systems have rarely become policy instruments. In the late 1960s and early 1970s the Office of Economic Opportunity (OEO) attempted to implement a voucher experiment for the poor. The experiment never took place because the OEO was unable to obtain enabling legislation from any state legislature. In 1984 Judge Russell Clark ruled in *Jenkins* v. *State* that Kansas City, Missouri, did not meet the federal requirements for integration. He ordered the creation of magnet schools in the inner city, mandated increased spending on inner-city schools, and required the school district to give vouchers to inner-city parents of minority children who wanted to attend school districts in the suburbs. The suburban school districts, however, refused to participate. When fifty private schools in the Kansas City area offered racially integrated places to these same children at an average cost one-third that of the Kansas City public

52. Coons (1992, p. 16).
53. Sugarman (1991).

schools, the state refused this offer. The parents of the African-American students unsuccessfully sued to obtain vouchers for use in private schools. In 1992 President Clinton in his acceptance speech at the Democratic National Convention stated that the only school choice would be choice among public schools.

Given the overwhelming evidence of the failure of inner-city public schools and of integration programs, why have voucher programs been so rare and so limited? I would argue that the major reason is that the clients of these schools are dependents. Current policies and their justifications fit precisely the predictions of the Ingram and Schneider model described in chapter 4. Further, the current system benefits the largest organized interests in education: public school teachers and administrators.

To illustrate the antichoice position I ask the reader to stop briefly and consider the reasons that he or she may have for opposing a voucher system and then to determine the extent to which those reasons mirror those of the educational experts. To illustrate the justifications for opposing vouchers to private schools I use the writings of Henry Levin, the director of the Center for Educational Research at Stanford and a leading proponent of school reform. I choose Levin because he is a strong supporter of special programs for low-income and high-risk students, has a respected research record in educational reform, is one of the most respected administrators in public education, and is not a spokesperson for the public school teachers or any other organized interest. If any expert from the education establishment justly can claim to be an advocate for the dependent populations in education, Levin can.[54]

Levin summarizes the provoucher arguments by placing them into three categories.[55] First, families should have the right to choose the type of education they want for their children. Just as parents have the right to raise their children with particular orientations and values, they should have the right to select schools that transmit and reinforce those values. Second, families should be able to choose the school that best fits the educational needs of their children. For example, a parent might choose a school that specializes in bilingual education, a particular pedagogical approach, or a special curriculum. Third, a choice program that empowered parents would force schools to become more efficient and more responsive to the demands of students and parents.

54. See, for example, Levin (1986).
55. Levin (1989).

184   R. KENNETH GODWIN

Levin argues that while these private values are all good and important, society has an overriding interest in ensuring that the educational
system transmits values that the state has chosen. Levin writes:

There are few who would limit the purposes of schooling to only
those aspects that enhance private lives and that should be matters of
family or student choice. It is widely recognized that democratic and
capitalist societies must rely heavily upon their schools to provide an
education that will preserve and support the fundamental political,
social, and economic institutions that . . . make it possible to change
those societies in a democratic fashion. Beyond the fulfillment of private needs, schools must provide students with a common set of values
and knowledge to create citizens who can function democratically.
They must contribute to equality of social, economic, and political
opportunities among persons drawn from different racial and social
class origins. . . .
    To a large extent these requirements suggest that all students be
exposed to a common educational experience that *cannot be left to
the vagaries of individual or family choice.*[56]

Here one sees the first element justifying policies that are aimed at
dependent populations but do not respond to their preferences: the target
population is unable to make the choices that are in the best interests of
society. Levin contends that all schools must meet the minimum educational objectives of literacy in science, technology, and mathematics,
knowledge of music and arts, and familiarity with the philosophical and
institutional bases for the U.S. economy. Equally important, students
must receive education in democratic values, and schools "must produce
graduates with the commitment and skills to defend the Nation."[57] However, a system that allows nonwealthy parents to choose schools according to their own cultural, academic, social, political, ethnic, racial, and
religious values "must necessarily create a divisive system of education
rather than one that converges on a common educational experience."[58]
It would be unrealistic, Levin contends, to expect Catholic schools to
expose students to both sides of the abortion issue, evangelical schools
to offer a disinterested comparison of creation and evolution, or leftist
schools to give a balanced presentation of capitalism.

56. Levin (1989, pp. 6–7). (Emphasis added.)
57. Levin (1989, p. 7).
58. Levin (1989, p. 33).

Levin claims that dependent populations are unable to make the best choices for their children. He argues that education is a "complex service that can not be easily summarized" and that "this challenge is particularly severe for the least-advantaged families such as those where parents are poorly educated, do not speak English, and who tend to move frequently because of marginality of housing markets."[59] Levin further argues that working-class families will choose schools that emphasize conformity and obedience to rules while upper-middle-class parents will choose schools that stress greater freedom of choice and the development beyond basic skills in conceptual thinking, science, art, and communications. These upper-middle-class attributes are "functional in contributing to professional and managerial development such as the ability to consider alternative production techniques, products, marketing strategies, and personnel . . . and to . . . supervise others."[60] Therefore different social classes will choose different types of schools, thus maintaining class segregation.

There are other reasons that school vouchers might not be good policy. Among those cited frequently are that only the families who are educationally and economically advantaged participate sufficiently in their children's education, and only these families will choose the private schools. The exodus of these students will harm those who remain behind. Opponents believe that vouchers will increase rather than decrease racial and socioeconomic segregation because families will be allowed to keep their children in a segregated environment. Finally, some opponents of vouchers contend that for-profit schools will exploit families who do not have sufficient knowledge about education to make good choices.[61]

59. Levin (1989, p. 20).
60. Levin (1989, pp. 38, 39).
61. See Brogan (1991); and Raywid (1992). Two difficulties facing proponents of educational choice for low- and middle-income parents that have substantial persuasiveness to this author are the issues of separation of church and state and the issue of using voucher-funded schools to support segregation practices. Advocates of the complete separation of church and state oppose using public monies to support religious education. Why should they pay to support religious teachings? This is a reasonable concern and there is no adequate answer to those who place the total separation of church and state above the competing values that vouchers to private schools might achieve. Although public vouchers that families can use in sectarian schools will undoubtedly be challenged in the courts, it is likely that such vouchers would be ruled constitutional. Current federal assistance to students in church-related colleges and universities such as Notre Dame or Baylor indicates that the provision of assistance, so long as it goes to the families and not directly to the schools, is constitutional. But "constitutional" and "right" are not the same. The other set of private schools that poses a serious problem for many are those schools that originated

My purpose is not to argue that Levin and other opponents of vouchers for private schools are incorrect in their hypotheses but to demonstrate how remarkably well the Ingram and Schneider model of the power of social constructions on policy predicts those arguments. Ingram and Schneider argue that the tools that society uses to keep dependent populations in their place are symbolic speech, the appeal to expertise, and authoritarian implementation. In denying the opportunity of inner-city poor to choose schools that they believe are most appropriate, policy-makers tell the poor that there is a need for "a common core of democratic values," that "educators know better than they what is best for their children," and that children must learn the "appropriate values" at school because they may not be learning them in the home. A poor child must attend the school that society dictates. Despite the evidence that inner-city public schools are failing, publicly financed private school voucher programs have been kept off the political agenda and are a prototypic "nondecision." Certainly Peter Bachrach and Morton Baratz would not be surprised that the combination of a powerful social construction that supports a set of vested interests would prevent testing whether the hypotheses of the voucher proponents or those of voucher opponents are more correct.[62]

While the *official* public school curriculum may contain Levin's ideals of integration and tolerance, minimum literacy in science, technology, mathematics, and the arts, and the philosophical bases of democratic values, the reality in most large cities is nothing like this dream. Most public schools exhibit exactly the harms that Levin fears: a divisive system of education based on economic and racial segregation rather than one that converges on a common educational experience. Forty years after *Brown* v. *Board of Education*, the schools of Topeka, Kansas, remain segregated racially and economically.

In chapter 2 in this volume, Marc Landy makes two other arguments against educational vouchers. First, because parents are "stuck" in a certain school district, they have strong incentives to exercise their political skills to make it better. Second, public school boards and parent-teacher organizations offer excellent deliberative forums for determining what common principles should be transmitted by the schools and how they should be transmitted. These arguments deal directly with citizen

---

largely for the purpose of avoiding integration. Clearly the public sector must require that schools that receive vouchers have an open admissions system with respect to race, ethnicity, and religion.

62. Bachrach and Baratz (1970).

empowerment and offer an alternative view of how dependent populations might control the education of their children. The issues are whether keeping low-income people "stuck" in their current school empowers them more than allowing them to become choosers among alternative values and educational opportunities, and whether a voucher system would eliminate school boards and parent-teacher organizations or would make these bodies more responsive to parental input.

To the extent that Landy's arguments deal with dependent populations, I believe they fail logically and empirically. First, to empower citizens means to give them choices and greater control over their lives. To keep parents stuck in their present situation against their wills is an illogical and distorted use of the term "empowerment." The argument that because parents are denied choice they will change their children's schools fails empirically. Parents have had these incentives for a long time, but the incentive structure has not protected them or their children. Either the incentives are not great enough, the free-rider problem is too great, or the dependent parents have learned that educational experts do not listen to them and do not care what they think.

Justifying the denial of choice to parents on the grounds that such denial would deprive them and the community of participatory opportunities also fails both logical and empirical tests. The initiation of a voucher program will not eliminate public schools. School boards will still exist, most parents probably will continue to send their children to public schools, and the Parent-Teachers Association will not die. Australia currently provides voucher programs for low-income children. Despite this program, most low-income children remain in the public schools.[63] There is little reason to believe that the U.S. experience would differ so greatly that public schools would disappear. In short, vouchers would not lead to a loss of deliberative forums. More important, the students who use the exit option give critical information to school boards about who is leaving the public system and why they are leaving. When school districts lose revenue because parents and children are choosing to exit, the districts are given a powerful incentive to respond to the voices of those who remain and to attempt to reclaim those who have exited.

A twenty-five-mile trip from my house to the inner-city schools of Dallas finds little heterogeneity, especially in income. What one does find is a little education and a lot of danger. I doubt seriously if the circum-

63. James (1991).

stances differ in Los Angeles, Detroit, New York, Washington, Miami, Cleveland, or San Jose. The belief in the common educational core and tolerance of diversity extolled by those who fear ideological or racial intolerance in private schools fades rapidly in the face of violence, and attempts to prevent these forces from reaching the wealthy suburban schools are made by drawing school district lines that prevent integration. A majority of whites may believe that public schools are taking the necessary steps to promote racial tolerance, but only 33 percent of African Americans agree.[64] The public's message to inner-city poor is that, while the public school system cares little about teaching their children, it will prevent their escape from a degrading and demoralizing situation.

Of course the failure to see the faults with one's own proposals is not restricted to opponents of vouchers. Voucher proponents often feel that simply citing the current failures of the public school system justifies adopting a market system without regard to ensuring that such a system has the necessary low information and transaction costs to allow the market to work efficiently and to empower dependents. Certainly Levin is correct that information about the effectiveness of schools is complex and not easily obtained. If policymakers fail to structure the market so that consumers can obtain the necessary information, adopting a voucher plan will not help families who have been trained by the political system to feel unable to make such choices. Before the state enacts a voucher system it must examine how to create a market that not only provides economic resources to dependent populations but also reduces information and transaction costs sufficiently to allow them to make the choices they would like to make. To date, however, publicly funded public school and private school voucher programs have reduced rather than increased the information and feedback that could lead to an efficient market and an empowered citizenry.

Empirical Data on School Choice

The main difficulty in assessing the arguments for and against vouchers is the almost total absence of empirical data. The only public voucher program that pays the full costs of private schools is in Milwaukee, Wisconsin, a program that began in the fall of 1990. The only large-scale public choice program that has been systematically evaluated is the Minnesota program that allows interdistrict choices among public schools

64. Elam, Rose, and Gallup (1992, p. 50).

and includes special programs for both advanced and high-risk students.[65] Findings from the Milwaukee program are limited because families can use vouchers only in nonsectarian schools (over 80 percent of private school attendance nationally is in religiously affiliated schools), the number of students using the voucher program cannot exceed 1 percent of the public school enrollment, recipients of the voucher must be poor, and the majority of a private school's students must not be voucher students. The findings of the Minnesota program are limited because of its public-choice-only nature and because although school districts cannot refuse to allow students to leave their districts and to pay the expenses of these students, districts can refuse to accept students from other districts so long as they refuse all such students.[66] This provision allows suburban schools to reject inner-city students so long as they reject all out-of-district students. Despite the limitations of the Milwaukee and Minnesota programs, it is possible to examine how consistent the results of these experiments are with the hopes of voucher proponents or with the fears of opponents. The implications of these findings for structuring educational markets can also be studied.

Among the more surprising findings from the Milwaukee program is that the students who use the vouchers are poorer than the remaining eligible students. The mean income of choosing families was $10,700 while the mean income of nonchoosing families who were sufficiently poor to qualify for the vouchers was $12,130. Voucher students were significantly more likely to come from single-parent families, to be African Americans, and to have had more academic and behavioral problems at their prior schools than the control group of low-income students.[67] Thus concerns about the better students leaving the public schools and thereby harming the education of the remaining children find no support in the Milwaukee experiment. However, the average education of the

---

65. Adelman (1992); and Rubenstein, Hamar, and Adelman (1992). The most famous public school choice program is that of East Harlem, New York City. Although school records show that after the initiation of the school choice program student test scores climbed, drop-out rates decreased, parental involvement increased, vandalism decreased, and student attendance increased, the district did not keep track of student attrition and the migration into the district of more qualified students. These flaws cast doubt on the magnitude of any improvements attributed to the program. See Clune (1990); and David L. Kirp, "What School Choice Really Means," *Atlantic Monthly*, November 1992, pp. 119–20. Another brief experiment in public school choice occurred in Alum Rock School District in California. This experiment, lasting from 1972 to 1976, operated special programs in minischools within regular schools. See Bridge and Blackman (1978).

66. Rubenstein, Hamar, and Adelman (1992).

67. Witte and Rigdon (1992).

mothers of voucher children is higher than that of the mothers of non-voucher children with similar incomes, suggesting that more educated parents, even if they are poor, are more likely to know about choice programs and to take advantage of them.

Early results of the Minnesota public choice experiment indicate that few families choose vouchers. Only 1 percent of students took advantage of interdistrict choice. Among this group, the Minnesota results support the expectations that more educated and higher-status parents have better knowledge of programs and are more likely to use them. Similarly, there is migration from poorer school districts to wealthier ones. However, the evaluators of the Minnesota experiment found that less well-educated and poorer families were "fairly well represented."[68] As expected, parents named academic quality, learning atmosphere, and the presence of educational services as the most important reasons for moving children from one district to another. For minorities and for families in which both parents worked, the proximity of a school to home, day-care facilities at schools, and the proximity of the school to the parent's job location also were important factors leading to a change of school.[69]

An important finding of the Minnesota experiment is the variation in how different sets of choosing families found out about the choice program and how few families in Minnesota are aware of their options. That knowledge is especially related to the objective of creating an efficient market that empowers dependent populations. Despite the political conflict that the program engendered and extensive efforts by the media and school principals to make families aware of their options, most Minnesota parents knew little about the choice programs. Interviews with more educated parents found that these families discovered the program through information from school principals and the media. Interviews with low-income and minority families found that they were largely unfamiliar with the program and its options. Those who did know of the program relied much more heavily on word-of-mouth sources such as friends or relatives.[70] A key reason for the low awareness of the Minnesota program was the state law that prohibited districts from advertising their schools or recruiting students from other districts. In this way, the

68. Rubenstein, Hamar, and Adelman (1992, p. v). The researchers could not determine economic bias because census data indicating the actual incidence of various income groups were not yet available.

69. Rubenstein, Hamar, and Adelman (1992, p. 30).

70. Rubenstein, Hamar, and Adelman (1992).

state increased substantially the information costs to potential consumers and created an important structural barrier to an efficient market. Not surprisingly, this barrier had the greatest impact on less educated parents.

Private Efforts to Create Educational Choice

Within hours of President Bush's announcement proposing $1,000 vouchers for low- and middle-income parents, experts claiming to understand the situation of the poor and to represent their interests argued that the program would be a cruel joke because $1,000 did not come close to covering the actual costs of education, and the poor could not afford the additional funds necessary to send their children to private schools. Therefore only upper-middle-class persons could take advantage of the proposed program. Although doubtlessly a larger voucher would be more empowering to poor families and true equality of opportunity in education and equity in free speech would require that vouchers pay close to the full cost of private schools, those who argued that the poor would not take advantage of the vouchers were empirically incorrect. Thousands of poor families already enroll their children in private schools. Even small scholarships to children in poor families stimulates tremendously their use of private schools.

In the fall of 1992, Indianapolis and San Antonio initiated private scholarship programs that provide $750 or 50 percent of private school tuition, whichever is less, to children who qualify for the federal school lunch program. In San Antonio the program was announced in the major daily newspaper and on the radio and television. Furthermore, private schools actively recruited students. The response to the program was immediate, more than 2,300 applications from poor families. The experience in Indianapolis was similar. While it is too soon to know how much the families who applied for scholarships differ from those who did not, the San Antonio and Indianapolis experiments indicate that allowing private schools to compete for students helps poor and minority families learn about their options. The San Antonio and Indianapolis experiments strongly suggest that the inner-city poor see current public education as inferior and unacceptable, that poor families are willing to pay a large share of their total income so that their children can escape public schools, and that many of these families are confident that they can make the choice of what schools are good for their children and what schools are not.

A Proposal for an Educational Market

I have argued throughout this chapter that a market can empower dependent populations only if information and transaction costs are low and those who design the market include equity considerations. What would such a market look like in education? Fortunately, Coons and Sugarman developed a proposal that meets these criteria.[71] Briefly, their proposal would initiate a scholarship program that would have both public and private scholarship schools. During the first years of the program, only the children from the poorest 20 percent of families would be eligible for publicly financed scholarships to private schools. Scholarships would equal the full tuition of the private schools or up to 90 percent of the current average cost of educating a student in the public schools. Later, all students would receive scholarships, but private schools that accepted scholarship students would give preference for 20 percent of their spaces to children from the poorest 20 percent of the population. The only state regulations on private schools would be those existing before the scholarship program (and the 20 percent preference requirement) and the conditions that no school discriminate on the basis of race, color, religion, national origin, or gender; teach hatred of any group on the basis of such characteristics; deliberately provide false or misleading information to consumers; or use the income from the scholarships for purposes other than education.[72]

Why do Coons and Sugarman have a two-stage process? For two reasons. First, they want to advantage the poorest children and make them the targets of recruiters from private schools. This action would reduce information costs to those families that lack experience with taking responsibility for selecting a school. Coons and Sugarman believe that the information problem of these families is overstated if school choice generally is available to the poor. Welfare agencies, churches, and community organizations will assist families by offering information on schools and helping to interpret the information that the schools pro-

71. Coons and Sugarman (1992).
72. See Coons and Sugarman (1992, p. 11). The reasons for keeping regulations to a minimum are to facilitate diversity in schools and to protect free speech. Experience in Australia and elsewhere indicates that publicly funded organizations that take over services previously provided by governments quickly tend to resemble governmental organizations they replaced. See Steven Smith (chapter 9 in this volume); Kemerer, Hairston, and Lauerman (1992); and John F. Miller, "Opting Out: Conservatives against Choice," *New Republic*, November 30, 1992, pp. 12–13.

vide.[73] Second, a two-stage introduction to the scholarship program allows public schools time to prepare for the full-scale scholarship program and to learn from the first stage. Once scholarships become available to the entire population, the requirement of preference for low-income children maintains their access to information and their priority status. Private schools would have an incentive to develop a pool of applicants larger than 20 percent so that they could have greater control over which students they admit.

Why would the Coons and Sugarman proposals be preferable to the Minnesota public choice program, the Milwaukee private voucher program, and the San Antonio and Indianapolis scholarship programs? Because Coons and Sugarman have improved the likelihood that dependent populations are desired clients, the information costs to them are low, there are no structural barriers to getting information, and the proposed scholarships are of sufficient size to empower the poor. At the same time, the Coons and Sugarman proposal does not create new regulations for private schools, allows schools to advertise their special nature such as an emphasis on music, science, or African-American traditions, and prevents the use of public scholarship money for the furtherance of racial and economic segregation and intolerance.

Summary

People who supported minimum incomes and negative income taxes in the 1960s and 1970s made essentially the same argument that I have made here: if the problem is that people do not have sufficient income to purchase merit goods, then a direct transfer of income is the solution that least demeans the dependent population, most reduces their dependence, and most efficiently allocates resources. Furthermore, I argue that in the absence of making a sufficiently large income transfer to dependent populations so that they are no longer dependent—a solution that has proven politically unacceptable—alternative policy solutions are to subsidize a merit good so that the person or firm marketing it can make a profit while those who desire the good can afford to purchase it, or to use a voucher system for the good and ensure that the market has low information and transaction costs. Consumers of merit goods must have sufficient purchasing power to require that those who provide the service do so in the mix and form that the consumers demand. That is empowerment.

73. Coons and Sugarman (1992, p. 29).

Although I have argued that market mechanisms are equally applicable in both more and less industrialized countries, the obstacles to implementing market solutions differ in the two sets of countries. Less industrialized countries can use markets to expand the coverage of merit goods. They can do this by charging user fees that are high enough to ensure service delivery and effective information to consumers while subsidizing the goods sufficiently to allow those who need the goods to purchase them. More industrialized countries face a different problem. Because MICs already provide these goods in some form, current providers have a vested interest in preventing consumer sovereignty and citizen empowerment. As the providers have the greater political power, changes that favor consumers' wishes will find an entrenched and powerful opposition buttressed by a prevailing social construction that demeans the abilities of the dependent consumers. The goal of those who wish to empower dependents must be to assist them in overcoming these interests, even if the enemy we meet is ourselves.

References

Adelman, Nancy E. 1992. *Minnesota's Educational Options for At-Risk Youth: Urban Alternative Schools and Area Learning Centers.* Washington: Policy Studies Associates.
Akin, John S., Nancy Birdsall, and David M. de Ferranti. 1987. *Financing Health Services in Developing Countries: An Agenda for Reform.* Washington: World Bank.
Akin, John S., and others. 1985. *The Demand for Primary Health Services in the Third World.* Totowa, N.J.: Rowman and Allanheld.
Bachrach, Peter, and Morton S. Baratz. 1970. *Power and Poverty: Theory and Practice.* New York: Oxford University Press.
Birdsall, Nancy. 1983. "Strategies for Analyzing Effects of User Charges in the Social Sectors." PNN Technical Note 87-4. Washington: World Bank.
———, ed. 1985. *The Effects of Family Planning Programs on Fertility in the Developing World.* Washington: World Bank.
Boulier, Brian L. 1985. "Family Planning Programs and Contraceptive Availability: Their Effects on Contraceptive Use and Fertility." In *The Effects of Family Planning Programs on Fertility in the Developing World,* edited by Nancy Birdsall, 41–115. Washington: World Bank.
Bridge, R. Gary, and Julie Blackman. 1978. *Family Choice in Schooling.* vol. 4. *A Study of Alternatives in American Education.* Report No. R-2170/4-NIE. Santa Monica: Rand Corportation.
Brogan, Bernard R. 1991. "The Choice Movement: A Consideration of the Issues." *Educational Considerations* 19 (Fall): 3–11.

Bulatao, Rodolfo A., and Ronald D. Lee. 1983. "A Framework for the Study of Fertility Determinants." In *Determinants of Fertility in Developing Countries: A Summary of Knowledge, Part A*, edited by Rodolfo A. Bulatao and Ronald D. Lee, 1–11. Washington: National Academy Press.

Caldwell, John C. 1983. "Direct Economic Costs and Benefits of Children." In *Determinants of Fertility in Developing Countries: A Summary of Knowledge, Part A*, edited by Rodolfo A. Bulatao and Ronald D. Lee, 390–97. Washington: National Academy Press.

Chubb, John E., and Terry M. Moe. 1990. *Politics, Markets, and America's Schools*. Brookings.

Clune, William H. 1990. "Educational Governance and Student Achievement." In *Choice and Control in American Education*, vol. 2: *The Practice of Choice, Decentralization and School Restructuring*, edited by William H. Clune and John F. Witte, 391–423. New York: Falmer Press.

Coons, John E. 1992. "School Choice as Simple Justice." *First Things* (April): 15–22.

Coons, John E., and Stephen D. Sugarman. 1978. *Education by Choice: The Case for Family Control*. Berkeley: University of California Press.

———. 1992. *Scholarships for Children*. Berkeley: University of California, Institute of Governmental Studies Press.

Davies, Bleddyn. 1980. "Policy Options for Charges and Means Tests." In *Pricing the Social Services*, edited by Ken Judge, 132–53. London: Macmillan.

Elam, Stanley M., Lowell C. Rose, and Alec M. Gallup. 1992. "The 24th Annual Gallup/Phi Delta Kappa Poll of the Public's Attitudes toward the Public Schools." *Phi Delta Kappan* 74 (September): 41–53.

Florez, Dario Mejia. 1990. *Poplacion y Planificacion Familiar de Ecuador*. Analysis Technico #007. Quito, Ecuador: Dual and Associates.

Friedman, Milton. 1955. "The Role of Government in Education." In *Economics and the Public Interest*, edited by Robert A. Solo, 123–44. Rutgers University Press.

Gertler, Paul, and Paul Glewwe. 1989. *The Willingness to Pay for Education in Developing Countries: Evidence from Rural Peru*. Washington: World Bank.

Godwin, R. Kenneth. 1992. "Charges for Merit Goods: Third World Family Planning." *Journal of Public Policy* 11 (October–December): 415–29.

Godwin, R. Kenneth, William Paul McGreevey, and Alta Charo. 1990. *Options for Population Policy: Midterm Evaluation*. Population Technical Assistance Project No. 89-048-099. Arlington, Va.: Dual and Associates.

Griffin, Charles C. 1989. "Strengthening Health Services in Developing Countries through the Private Sector." Discussion Paper No. 4, International Finance Corporation. Washington: World Bank.

Herz, Barbara K. 1984. *Official Development Assistance for Population Activities: A Review*. Washington: World Bank.

Hirschman, Albert O. 1986. *Rival Views of Market Society and Other Recent Essays*. Viking.

James, Estelle. 1991. "Private Education and Redistributive Subsidies in Australia." In *Privatization and Its Alternatives*, edited by William T. Gormley, Jr., 79–112. University of Wisconsin Press.

Jimenez, Emmanuel. 1987. *Pricing Policy in the Social Sectors: Cost Recovery for Education and Health in Developing Countries*. Johns Hopkins University Press.

Jones, Elise F. 1984. "The Availability of Contraceptive Services." *World Fertility Survey Comparative Studies*, No. 37. Voorburg, Netherlands: International Statistical Institute.

Judge, Ken. 1978. *Rationing Social Services: A Study of Resource Allocation and the Personal Social Services*. London: Heinemann Educational.

Kelman, Steven. 1981. *What Price Incentives? Economists and the Environment*. Boston: Auburn House.

Kemerer, Frank R., Joe B. Hairston, and Keith Lauerman. 1992. "Vouchers and Private School Autonomy." *Journal of Law and Education* 21 (Fall): 601–28.

Klees, Steven J. 1984. "The Need for a Political Economy of Educational Finance: A Response to Thobani." *Comparative Education Review* 28 (August): 424–40.

Levin, Henry M. 1986. *Educational Reform for Disadvantaged Students: An Emerging Crisis*. Washington: National Educational Association.

———. 1989. "The Theory of Choice Applied to Education." Paper No. 89-CERAS-10. Stanford, Calif.: Stanford University School of Education.

Maraviglia, Nydia. 1990. *Indonesia: Family Planning Perspectives in the 1990s*. Washington: World Bank.

Mauldin, W. Parker, and Robert J. Lapham. 1985. "Measuring Family Planning Program Effort in LDCs: 1962 and 1982." In *The Effects of Family Planning Programs on Fertility in the Developing World*, edited by Nancy Birdsall, 1–40. Washington: World Bank.

Maxwell, Robert J. 1981. *Health and Wealth: An International Study of Health-Care Spending*. Lexington Books.

Meerman, Jacob. 1979. *Public Expenditure in Malaysia: Who Benefits and Why*. Oxford University Press.

Merrick, Thomas W. 1990. "The Evolution and Impact of Policies on Fertility and Family Planning." In *Population Policy: Contemporary Issues*, edited by Godfrey Roberts, 147–66. Praeger.

Musgrave, Richard A. 1969. "Cost-Benefit Analysis and the Theory of Public Finance." *Journal of Economic Literature* 7 (September): 797–806.

North, Douglass C. 1990. *Institutions, Institutional Change and Economic Performance*. Cambridge: Cambridge University Press.

Psacharopoulous, George, Jee-Peng Tan, and Emmanuel Jimenez. 1986. *Financing Education in Developing Countries: An Exploration of Policy Options*. Washington: World Bank.

Raywid, Mary Anne. 1992. "Choice Orientations, Discussions, and Prospects." *Educational Policy* 6 (June): 105–22.

Rohde, Jon E., and Lukas Hendrata. 1982. "Development from Below: Transformation of Village-Based Nutrition Projects to a National Family Nutrition

Program in Indonesia." In *Nutrition Policy Implementation: Issues and Experience*, edited by Nevin S. Scrimshaw and Mitchel B. Wallerstein, 209–30. Plenum.

Rose, Richard. 1989. "Charges as Contested Signals." *Journal of Public Policy* 9 (July–September): 261–86.

Roth, Gabriel. 1987. *The Private Provision of Public Services in Developing Countries*. Oxford University Press.

Rubenstein, Michael C., Rosalind Hamar, and Nancy E. Adelman. 1992. *Minnesota's Open Enrollment Option*. Washington: Policy Studies Associates.

Salmen, Lawrence F. 1987. *Listen to the People: Participant-Observer Evaluation of Development Projects*. New York: Oxford University Press.

Sheehan, Susan. 1976. *A Welfare Mother*. New American Library.

Sugarman, Stephen D. 1991. "Using Private Schools to Promote Public Values." *The University of Chicago Legal Forum* 1991: 171–210.

Thobani, Mateen. 1983. "Charging User Fees for Social Services: The Case of Education in Malawi." World Bank Staff Working Paper No. 572. Washington: World Bank.

Walzer, Michael. 1983. *Spheres of Justice: A Defense of Pluralism and Equality*. Basic Books.

Warwick, Donald P. 1982. *Bitter Pills: Population Policies and their Implementation in Eight Developing Countries*. Cambridge University Press.

———. 1990. "The Ethics of Population Control." In *Population Policy: Contemporary Issues*, edited by Godfrey Roberts, 21–37. Praeger.

Wheeler, David. 1985. "Female Education, Family Planning, Income and Population: A Long-Run Econometric Simulation Model." In *The Effects of Family Planning Programs on Fertility in the Developing World*, edited by Nancy Birdsall, 116–206. Washington: World Bank.

Witte, John. 1991. "Market versus State-Centered Approaches to American Education: Does Either Make Much Sense?" Presented at the annual meeting of the American Political Science Association.

Witte, John F., and Mark E. Rigdon. 1992. "Private School Choice: The Milwaukee Low-Income Voucher Experiment." Presented at the annual meeting of the American Political Science Association.

World Bank. 1988. *World Development Report, 1988*. Oxford University Press.

World Fertility Survey. 1984. *World Fertility Survey: Major Findings and Implications*. Voorburg, Netherlands: International Statistical Institute.

9. The New Politics of Contracting: Citizenship and the Nonprofit Role

STEVEN RATHGEB SMITH

THROUGHOUT THE INDUSTRIALIZED world, privatization of the welfare state has become increasingly common. Privatization may entail selling state industries, government contracting with private, nonprofit, and for-profit organizations, providing vouchers for public education and health care, encouraging voluntarism, or increasing or setting fees for health and social services. In the United States one of the most prevalent privatization practices is for government to contract with nonprofit service organizations. Starting with the war on poverty programs of the 1960s, such contracting has grown to be a central form of public service delivery to people in need.[1] In many states, it is the primary way of delivering services such as mental health care and programs for developmentally disabled children and adults, delinquent youth, and abused children and women. And the American response to AIDS, homelessness, and hunger in the 1980s and 1990s has also largely been through nonprofit organizations funded by government.

Because contracting is often justified by policymakers as a way to improve the efficiency of service delivery, most of the research on it has understandably focused on efficiency.[2] Does contracting save money? Can it improve the targeting of services on the people most in need of them? This chapter, however, examines an equally important concern: the impact on citizenship of government contracting with nonprofit organizations. Contracting with nonprofit agencies has profound effects on citizenship and the relationship between citizens and their government.

I am indebted to Joel Handler, Helen Ingram, Marc Landy, and Michael Lipsky, two anonymous referees, and participants in the conference for comments on earlier versions of this chapter. Partial support for revisions was provided by the Center for the Study of Philanthropy and Voluntarism, Sanford Institute of Public Policy, Duke University.

1. Benton, Feild, and Millar (1978); McMurty, Netting, and Kettner (1991); and Gronbjerg (1993).

2. Savas (1979); Gurin and Friedman (1980); and Schlesinger, Dorwart, and Pulice (1986).

Public services link citizens with the state, and citizen attitudes toward government are shaped by their interaction with public service organizations. Contracting represents a mixed form in which delivery of services is by private, nonprofit organizations and the responsibility for services remains in the hands of government. This mixed form affects the politics of public services, the role of nonprofit organizations in the political process, and citizen participation in the nonprofit organizations.

The conclusions of this chapter are based on data developed from case studies of thirty nonprofit service agencies focusing on their relationship to government and their involvement in politics of social welfare services. I also used research on federal funding of service programs for victims of crime and national data on trends in government funding of nonprofit agencies.

Citizenship in the Mixed Economy of Welfare

Citizenship is a focus of contemporary discussions of the welfare state. American liberals and the political left worry that cutbacks in government social programs will reduce access to needed services. Conservatives argue that a smaller government and larger role for community organizations and business in meeting social needs will lead to better services, more efficiency, and greater citizen responsibility. But these arguments do not reflect the complex, shifting responsibilities of government, nonprofit, and for-profit organizations and people's growing demand for more control over the delivery of public services.

In a classic essay, British sociologist T. H. Marshall argued that the transition of society from the Middle Ages to modern industrial world redefined citizenship.[3] Citizenship, he wrote, now requires that people be able to participate fully in the political, social, and economic life of society. In medieval society, only the wealthy could be full citizens. The development of the market economy and industrialization brought demands that citizenship be extended to the rest of society. Three types of rights were established: civil, political, and social. Civil rights such as freedom of speech, religion, and assembly are protections against the state. Political rights include the right to vote and the secret ballot. Social rights are government-protected minimum standards of health and welfare, including health and unemployment insurance, public pensions, and social services. Marshall argued that the establishment of these rights

3. Marshall (1964).

followed a progression from civil to political to social, with the last primarily a product of the twentieth century.

To Marshall and many other scholars, adequate social rights necessitated the "socialization of distribution."[4] Private charity was inconsistent, unreliable, and parochial; thus the state had to assume responsibility by establishing a bureaucracy of professionals who would provide social services and income maintenance as entitlements rather than gifts. In this socialization of distribution supported through taxation, every person ideally would have the opportunity for full citizenship, would be guaranteed basic minimum services, and would be insured against the risk that illness, disability, unemployment, or other unforeseen events would produce a loss of status, class, or citizenship.

Implicit in Marshall's schema was a certain relationship between individuals and the market, community, and government. When people depend on market services, they usually have to pay for them. Voluntary organizations dependent on private charity such as family service agencies and the American Red Cross also frequently impose fees and provide only short-term relief for persons in distress or need. The democratization of social rights severed dependency on the market or private charity.

In most countries of Western Europe and North America, social rights have been ensured through government provision of income maintenance and social welfare programs. The British National Health Service was a model for Marshall but is also a vivid example of an entirely public system designed to ensure everyone a minimum standard of health care. The Netherlands and Germany expanded their social rights through extensive funding of nonprofit agencies and strict regulation of their services. Germany's system of hospitals and social service organizations is largely nonprofit, but the funding is primarily from the quasi-public sickness and pension funds. Germans are taxed to pay for these services, but they pay nothing directly if they are ill or need counseling. Compared with Germany and most other European countries, the United States has been considered a laggard by many because it has done far less to break the dependence of individuals on market and community provision of services.[5]

Gosta Esping-Andersen has built on Marshall's ideas by linking dif-

4. Walzer (1988, p. 13).
5. Wilensky and Lebeaux (1965, pp. xii–xxv) observed that America was a "reluctant welfare state" because it had done less than other industrialized countries to develop government-protected social rights. They argued that this status might eventually change under the impact of economic growth and industrialization.

ferences in welfare state regimes with the extent of social rights.[6] He contends that despite many differences among the social policies of the advanced industrial countries, three basic types of welfare states exist: social democratic, conservative, and liberal. The social democratic regimes such as Sweden's have extensive social rights that do not primarily depend on whether or how much a person works. The conservative regimes such as Germany's also have many social rights, but they are less extensive and more dependent on a person's work status. The liberal regimes of Great Britain and the United States have the fewest government-guaranteed social rights, and the opportunity for social benefits is strongly linked to a person's work situation. It is also in the liberal regimes that private charity and voluntary organizations are the most important in providing services. Citizenship would be strongest in the social democratic countries and weakest in the liberal regimes.

A contrasting conception of citizenship comes from Alexis de Tocqueville, who viewed the state with suspicion and considered voluntary organizations and their capacity for citizen participation as a vital source of citizenship and citizen empowerment.[7] He put greater reliance on civil and political rights and less on government-guaranteed social rights because he saw government as a potentially oppressive force that could easily curtail individual freedoms. His perspective is shared by Peter Berger, Richard John Neuhaus, Nathan Glazer, and other scholars. Berger and Neuhaus, for example, suggest that mediating institutions such as voluntary associations, churches, neighborhoods, and the family are important in providing social services and protecting freedom. They link citizenship with civil and political rights rather than social rights.[8] Similarly, Glazer contends that government efforts to guarantee social rights and provide extensive social programs can lead to ineffectiveness, inefficiency, excessive professionalization, and bureaucratization.[9]

Another critique of government-guaranteed social rights and implicitly of Marshall's perspective on citizenship is that public bureaucracies often deny rather than promote full citizenship through arbitrary, inequitable, and dehumanizing service provision.[10] Public services may also encourage political passivity that can lead to decreasing citizen participation in politics and society. Andrew Polsky and Claus Offe consider voluntary

6. Esping-Andersen (1990).
7. Tocqueville (1956, pp. 198–209).
8. Berger and Neuhaus (1977).
9. Glazer (1988).
10. Lipsky (1980); Handler (1990); and Polsky (1991).

organizations as vehicles of citizen empowerment to overcome the problems of public bureaucracies.[11] They also argue that voluntary organizations can provide opportunities for political participation for underrepresented groups, including blacks, women, and environmentalists.

Such critiques as these fueled the growth of government contracting with nonprofit agencies in the 1960s and 1970s. An important strategy of the war on poverty was the use of community organizations governed by local citizens to spend public funds to provide needed social services.[12]

Yet the critiques do not address the increasingly blurred boundaries between voluntary organizations and government that are caused by public funding and regulation. What happens to citizenship, citizen participation, and empowerment as public funding of voluntary organizations grows more common? What is the impact of contracting on the public social agenda? Contracting is crucial to our understanding of welfare state development because of the extensive scale on which it is carried out and because it mixes political and social rights as put forth by Marshall. One reason we value voluntary organizations is that they represent citizens' concerns in political matters. Contracting enlists these organizations in the service of public social objectives. How this affects the political role of nonprofit organizations is crucial to evaluating the impact of contracting on citizenship.

The Growth of Contracting

The current use of contracting reflects in part the sharp expansion in the 1960s and 1970s of federal funding for social welfare services. Federal expenditures as a percentage of all social service expenditures rose from 38.9 percent in 1965 to 64.6 percent in 1980.[13] This funding was channeled to nonprofit service agencies in three ways. Federal agencies such as the Department of Health, Education and Welfare provided funding to state governments that it then distributed to nonprofit agencies, such as child and family service organizations, residential care programs for children, and halfway houses. Federal agencies such as the National Institute of Mental Health (NIMH) and the Law Enforcement Assistance Administration provided research and demonstration funds directly to an array of nonprofit social welfare agencies including battered women shelters, rape crisis centers, community mental health centers, and com-

11. Polsky (1991); and Offe and Heinze (1992).
12. Marris and Rein (1982); and Peterson and Greenstone (1979).
13. Bixby (1991, p. 13).

munity action agencies. Finally, federal agencies directly contracted with local service providers. NIMH, for example, created a nationwide network of community mental health centers (CMHCs) by directly funding local nonprofit providers and in some cases creating new nonprofit organizations that would be designated CMHCs. In addition, federal spending spurred state and local governments to appropriate their own funds for contracted services.

This increase in government funding, combined with the political and social changes of the 1960s and 1970s, altered the landscape of nonprofit service organizations. Nonprofit agencies can be divided into three categories: traditional, government-sponsored, and new community-based organizations. The traditional agencies, such as family service agencies, child guidance clinics, orphanages, and settlement houses, which often date to the 1800s and early 1900s, dominated social services provided by nonprofit agencies until the 1960s. Typically, they relied on private fees, contributions from the United Way and individuals, and in some cases investment income from their endowments.

The government-sponsored agencies are voluntary service organizations founded in response to government funding initiatives. Usually, the organizations have only a brief existence before they begin receiving government funds, and often they are founded only after they receive assurances of a grant award. Many community action agencies, CMHCs, neighborhood health centers, and halfway houses for the mentally ill or developmentally disabled are in this category. These agencies usually depend heavily on government funds, often for 90 percent or more of their revenues.

The third group comprises nonprofit agencies that have been founded in response to community concerns. For example, "communities" of feminists founded shelters for battered women and rape crisis centers in the 1970s. Homeless shelters have been established by community activists and religious leaders who have seen unmet community needs. Typically, these agencies receive their initial revenues from private cash and in-kind donations. At some point, many enter into a contractual arrangement with government, from which they then receive a substantial portion of their income.

By 1980 the federal government's funding of nonprofit service agencies had expanded and diversified the social service system. Before widespread government funding, social services tended to be concentrated in a few types: child protection, counseling, emergency relief, and residential care for youth. The government-sponsored and new community agencies received funding for services that did not exist before, such as community living for the disabled. Many traditional agencies have also branched out into these new services through government contracts.

Federal Cutbacks and Changing Responsibilities for Service Funding

In 1981 President Reagan successfully won passage of the Omnibus Reconciliation Act. This multipurpose legislation consolidated federal grant programs for social services, devolved the administration of the programs to the states, and reduced funding levels by about 20 percent.[14] President Bush generally left the changes in place. The long-term result of these changes has been a declining federal role in funding and administering social services. For example, the federal share of total social service spending fell from 64.6 percent in 1980 to 51.1 percent in 1989.[15] The response to the changed federal role by nonprofits has varied. Many nonprofit agencies were forced to retrench and some closed. Many altered their revenue mix, relying more on state and local funds. Others raised additional revenue through private contributions or higher fees for services. In many cases the new fee income was from private and public health insurance programs rather than directly from individuals.

Although an increase in state and local funding was possible during the economic prosperity of the mid- to late 1980s, most states are now experiencing recession and are reducing their funding. Despite these cutbacks, however, the use of nonprofit agencies has not diminished in the 1980s and 1990s. State and local governments depend on the organizations to provide basic social services. And the enthusiastic support for privatization of public services by the Reagan and Bush administrations and many state and local policymakers has encouraged contracting out even more services with private nonprofit agencies (and to a lesser degree with for-profit organizations). In addition, services provided by nonprofit agencies are usually less expensive than those provided by government, although the cost advantages diminish over time.[16]

Government funding is attractive to these agencies because private charity and fee income from individuals is a relatively limited source of

14. Gutowski and Koshel (1982).
15. Bixby (1991, p. 13).
16. Smith and Lipsky (1992).

revenue. Private fundraising is time-consuming and expensive, and many newer and smaller nonprofit agencies are poorly positioned to raise significant contributions. Also, many newer agencies provide controversial services, such as drug rehabilitation or shelter for the homeless, that are unattractive to private donors. Because these agencies serve a disproportionate number of poor people, they are also unable to generate much income from service fees.

The agencies have also tapped public health insurance through medicare and medicaid, which have continued to grow sharply during the past twelve years. Although most medicare funds go to hospitals, many nonprofit service agencies have used medicaid to support counseling services, residential programs for the mentally ill and developmentally disabled, and homecare services for AIDS patients. Many nonprofit agencies, with the cooperation and encouragement of state officials, have switched their funding, at least in part, from federal or state funds from social service grant programs such as the federal social services block grant to medicaid, a shared federal-state funding program.

In some cases the federal government has also increased funding for social services to address the emergent problems of child abuse, drug abuse, AIDS, hunger, and homelessness. Many nonprofit agencies that lost federal funding in the early 1980s were able to regain it through newly created programs. This new funding is usually for research or demonstration programs for a specified period—perhaps three years—rather than a permanent commitment. Nonetheless, nonprofit agencies are able to use these short-term grants to fund their continuing operations.

The New Politics of Nonprofit Service Organizations

The explosive growth of contracting in the last thirty years has produced three important political developments relating to nonprofit service organizations: the creation of new associations to represent public policy interests of nonprofit agencies, the emergence of bargaining arrangements between government and nonprofit agencies that resemble corporatist politics, and efforts to restrict the political role of nonprofit organizations.[17]

17. Portions of this section are adapted from Smith and Lipsky (1993), chap. 9. Also see Smith and Stone (1988).

The New Organization of Nonprofit Interests

Associations representing nonprofit agencies grew significantly in influence and scope in the past three decades. At the federal level, associations such as the National Association of Community Mental Health Centers and the National Association of Community Action Agencies represent nonprofit social welfare organizations created with federal funds. Other associations such as Therapeutic Communities of America, which represents residential drug treatment programs, are not specifically linked to government programs but to the growth of government and the importance of federal regulations and policy in affecting individual agencies.

State-level nonprofit associations are also increasingly common, reflecting the rising importance of state governments in funding and regulating nonprofit services. Some associations are program specific, such as the Massachusetts Association of Home Care Providers and the North Carolina Association for Home Care.

Another type of state-level organization is the association representing a variety of nonprofit service organizations. Organizations such as the Massachusetts Council of Human Service Providers (MCHSP) or the North Carolina Association of Nonprofit Organizations strive to influence funding levels, rates, regulations, service priorities, and other issues that affect their members. They may assist members with board recruitment, agency liability, and taxes, or they may arrange joint purchasing of goods and equipment and reduced rates on insurance.[18]

In some states these associations undertake direct political action. For example, in 1990 the executive director of the California Association of Nonprofits, Robert Kardon, also served as chairperson of the National Council of Nonprofit Associations, which represents nine statewide associations and nineteen local and regional nonprofit groups.[19] The California association has been very active in trying to fight cutbacks in state funding to nonprofits. The MCHSP has also lobbied for more funding, better rates, and more favorable government regulations. Its board of directors is dominated by large new agencies that depend on government funding. The traditional agencies have more diversified funding bases and their own organizations. Also, the traditional organizations have

18. In some states, organizations initially created to advocate human services have gradually broadened to include advocacy for nonprofit concerns. The Connecticut Association for Human Services is a good example.

19. Williams (1991).

until recently tended to shun direct political advocacy on funding and rates.

In general these associations are constrained in their political advocacy by conflicting demands on their constituents and the membership's practical interest in funding, regulations, and operational concerns. As a result, association leaders focus on these practical and technical issues rather than on the merits of homeless shelter programs, the adequacy of welfare payments, or other broad policy questions. Association executives also cannot be too militant. Overly aggressive tactics may alienate key government officials who may influence funding levels and contract renewals. The leadership of the MCHSP, for instance, would hesitate to call a march on the state capitol to protest inadequate government funding because too few member agencies would participate. In addition, in the small world of nonprofits and social services, many executives are former colleagues and personal friends of state officials.

Still, nonprofit associations have had an impact on public debate on contracting, funding for nonprofit service agencies, and government regulations. State associations have campaigned to protect their programs from budget cuts and shaped regulations on contracting, charitable contributions, and social service priorities.[20] As nonprofit service providers become more organized, public officials will have a greater incentive to work with them on the details of program operation and oversight. Moreover, government administrators sometimes find that nonprofit associations can be important political allies given the austere budget climate and legislators skeptical or hostile toward government social programs. By enlisting them as allies, administrators also hope to avoid appeals to the governor or the legislature for relief from administrative decisions by disaffected nonprofit providers.

The Corporatist Politics of the Contracting Regime

The political role of nonprofit associations is reflected in a bargaining relationship with government. Unlike a relationship in which policymakers act after weighing the arguments and influence of groups competing for favor, corporatism places at the policymaking table the groups af-

---

20. For example, voluntary agencies in Massachusetts successfully pushed for legislation that excluded endowment income from revenue used to calculate rates paid to voluntary agencies by government agencies.

fected by the policy being decided. In many European countries government, business, and labor are represented in discussions on economic policy. In Germany, major social policy questions are debated by representatives of government and nonprofit groups, which provide most health and social welfare services. Public officials and executives of nonprofit agencies are in a long-term relationship; public policy is made in close consultation among the affected parties. Those participating are expected to have a stake in the agreed-upon policies. Corporatism tends to make nonprofit service providers more powerful politically but more limited in their advocacy.[21]

Claus Offe argues that corporatism increases with the extent to which the resources of an interest organization are supplied by the state, the extent to which the range of representation is defined through political decision, the extent to which internal relations between rank-and-file members and executive members of the organizations are regulated, and the extent to which interested organizations are licensed, recognized, and invited to assume a role in legislation, policy planning, and implementation.[22] The evolution of government contracting with nonprofits for the most part fits Offe's description of corporatism. Nonprofit agencies depend on government for a large percentage of their revenues. Their clients and services are increasingly determined by government as opposed to nonprofit decisions. For example, clients eligible to receive the services of nonprofit agencies are often determined by government contract language or eligibility criteria, as is the case for medicaid and the Job Training Partnership Act (JTPA). Whether or not a nonprofit agency provides drug treatment or job training is also a political decision on the allocation of government funds. Many states control the referrals of clients to nonprofit contract agencies. Increasingly, too, government officials shape the content of the service provided.

Nonprofit associations are often invited to participate in formulating policy on rates, funding levels, contract procedures, and other issues affecting their member organizations. In New Hampshire, nonprofit agencies for children have worked with state officials to draft regulations governing their program standards and rates. In Massachusetts, shelters for battered women, rape crisis centers, and day care centers worked

21. Schmitter (1979, p. 9) defines corporation as an "ideal-typical institutional arrangement for linking the associationally organized interests of civil society with the decisional structures of the states." See also Berger (1981); and Katzenstein (1985).
22. Offe (1981).

with state officials to revise regulations and procedures applicable to their programs.

Only with respect to regulating internal relations is the applicability of Offe's conditions for the development of corporatism problematic. Executives who bargain with public officials must be able to expect those they represent to accept the deals that are struck. Yet many member agencies are simply unwilling to abide by the political bargains struck by association leaders because agreeing might put their agencies at a disadvantage in the future.

One difference between American nonprofit agencies and their associations and some European counterparts is the funding relationship with government. In Germany and the Netherlands, for example, nonprofit agencies usually enjoy a monopoly in their service jurisdiction. They do not have government contracts. Instead, they are reimbursed for their normal costs in accordance with prevailing law and policy. Consequently, most have less reason to worry that government will shift their funding to another agency. European governments have also generally avoided serious funding cutbacks for social services. By contrast, government cutbacks in the United States have destabilized nonprofits and provided their local executives with incentives to look out for their individual agencies rather than be bound by agreements made by associations at the state or national level. Given this difficulty of regulating member compliance with executive agreements, corporatism may be regarded as not fully developed among nonprofit contract agencies and government.

Public officials promote corporatism to protect themselves from the results of unregulated competition among nonprofit providers.[23] In social services, this includes the uncertainty of follow-through by providers and the possible unreliability of provider supply. To promote the capacity of nonprofit providers, Peter Goldmark, then secretary of the Massachusetts Executive Office of Human Services, sponsored the establishment of MCHSP, the state's principal provider association. Massachusetts had begun the process of broad deinstitutionalization of state hospitals for the mentally ill and state schools for the developmentally disabled and the closure of all of the state's training schools for delinquent youth. But the hundreds of new nonprofit agencies created in the wake of the public institutions' restructuring created serious management problems for state administrators. MCHSP offered the possibility of efficiently resolving

---

23. Government organizing of private interests is discussed in Schmitter (1979, p. 27).

important policy questions affecting the contracting system by working with one large statewide agency.[24]

Technical issues predominate in these corporatist relationships.[25] What should be the formula for rate increases? Should shelters for battered women be required to remain open twenty-four hours a day? What should be the duration of contracts? What qualifications are necessary for agency executives? What are the minimum space requirements for day care centers? These questions have major policy implications. For example, the rate formula is crucial to how nonprofit organizations allocate their revenues and may affect their willingness to solicit private contributions. Stringent regulations for day care centers may give an edge to large nonprofit providers or for-profit providers, diminishing the importance of community-based agencies.[26] Shelters for battered women sometimes fight regulations mandating twenty-four hour coverage in the belief that the regulations undermine their goal of client independence.

Another consequence of the corporatist relations between government and nonprofit agencies is the exchange of personnel. Executives in nonprofit associations and agencies are increasingly recruited by government for their expertise and connections. Knowledge of nonprofit operations is helpful for government administrators, who depend on nonprofit agencies for policy implementation. Likewise, nonprofit agencies regard government experience as an asset for executive directors. Political influence gained through government positions can be important in negotiating contracts and making rate appeals. And good government contacts may be especially helpful to an agency, given the competition for public funding. Because of the financial strains and difficulties experienced by nonprofit agencies, executives are under increasing pressure to generate new

24. Government organizing of nonprofit providers is also illustrated by formal negotiation between government and nonprofit service agencies on social service priorities and policies. In Connecticut, state and local officials and nonprofit providers maintained a multiyear bargaining relation during the 1980s to allocate federal funds received through the social services block grant. See Connecticut (1983). A similar highly structured bargaining process was used in Massachusetts in an effort to restructure the public-private partnership program, a shared public-private funding program of the Massachusetts Department of Social Services. The formal bargaining model employed in each of these cases was the negotiated investment strategy, whose development and dissemination was funded by the Cleveland-based Kellogg Foundation.

25. The emergence of corporatist relationships and the focus on technical issues in health care has been noted by Brown (1985). Also see Brown (1983).

26. Rose-Ackerman (1983) concluded that federal day care regulations curtailed the supply of day care services and expanded the role of large for-profit firms.

funds to offset lost public or private funding or to prevent the loss of a government contract.[27]

The corporatist character of the contracting system has helped create a certain stability in service delivery. Government takes advantage of nonprofit agencies' ability to create and start programs quickly and manage their operations on a continuing basis. Arguably, the service sector has greater scope at a higher level of expenditures because of widespread contracting.[28] To be sure, nonprofit provider groups in the United States still do not exhibit as much internal discipline as their European counterparts. Nonetheless, the corporatist relations between government and nonprofit agencies have facilitated the restructuring of U.S. social services.[29]

Political Vulnerability of Nonprofit Agencies

Recent trends may in the long run undermine the corporatist relationship between government and nonprofit contract agencies. These trends include political attacks on the nonprofit sector, the fragmenting constituency for social service programs, emerging social movements, and the decentralization of social services policy.

The political attacks on the nonprofit sector have come from many quarters. Nonprofit organizations' support for many government social programs has made them the target of people who are skeptical of government programs. To many in the nonprofit sector, the recent effort by the federal Internal Revenue Service to curtail the advocacy role of nonprofit organizations seemed to confirm that they were being targeted because of their relations with sympathetic legislators and public admin-

27. This pressure to obtain new funds or contracts is one reason nonprofit executives are being forced to be "more entrepreneurial." The executives direct their energy at government because private contributions are often difficult to obtain and usually small. Government funding tends to be for a longer period and a far greater amount of money. One indicator of this entrepreneurship is that many nonprofit agencies provide services very different from those they offered in the 1970s.

28. This perspective is consistent with the work of scholars such as Harold L. Wilensky (1981) who contend that corporatist democracies are likely to have higher social expenditures than countries with fragmented, noncorporatist political arrangements.

29. Robert Salisbury (1979) argues that America lacks a corporatist tradition because of its social diversity and institutional fragmentation. However, the growth of contracting gives nonprofit providers a sense of shared mission that facilitates greater cooperation and discipline among them. At the same time, government has a greater incentive to enter into a long-term bargaining relationship with nonprofit associations and service providers.

istrators. After much protest the IRS retreated, but not before sending a clear message that nonprofits' advocacy would be closely scrutinized.[30]

Nonprofit service organizations are also defending themselves from for-profit organizations eager to enter businesses or services currently dominated by nonprofits. The for-profit organizations complain that nonprofits enjoy an unfair competitive advantage because of their tax advantages and exemptions.[31] For-profit organizations have not so far achieved any major changes in public policy, although there have been scattered victories at the state level.[32] Elsewhere, the Financial Accounting Standards Board tried to require nonprofit organizations to place a dollar value on in-kind donations when calculating annual revenue. Nonprofits fear that this cashing out of in-kind donations overstates revenues and would make nonprofits less appealing to government contract administrators and private contributors because they would appear richer than they are.[33] Finally, the Justice Department is pursuing possible antitrust violations by nonprofit hospitals and elite private universities.

Taken individually, these actions may appear to have little impact on most nonprofit agencies. Shelters for the homeless and soup kitchens are not in competition with for-profit service agencies. Most nonprofit universities are unaffected by the Justice Department inquiry. Child welfare agencies do not need to fear a similar inquiry. However, the overall effect of the political challenges is to limit the range of action by nonprofits and make their political activity more suspect. In the long run, these challenges may lead to a smaller nonprofit sector because the agencies may find it more difficult to raise revenues and fend off competitive bids from for-profit organizations.

Another destabilizing factor is that as the welfare state grows, it fragments the constituency for social programs.[34] For example, the North Carolina Home Care Association may now be in competition for govern-

30. In 1985 the Internal Revenue Service issued draft regulations defining advocacy for purposes of assessing a nonprofit organization's eligibility for tax exemption under 501(c)3 of the Internal Revenue Code. The 501(c)3 organizations are exempt from income and property taxes, and individuals can receive a tax deduction for their charitable donations to them. Under current regulations 501(c)3 organizations can devote no more than 25 percent of their revenues to advocacy. The draft regulations would have broadened substantially the definition of advocacy to include public education campaigns and other activities that many nonprofits had historically performed. See Williams (1990).

31. Bennett and DiLorenzo (1989).

32. "California Court Upholds a YMCA's Tax Status" (1990).

33. Alison Leigh Cowan, "New Accounting Proposals Create Nonprofit Anxiety," *New York Times*, July 29, 1990, p. F10.

34. Heclo (1978).

ment funds with nursing homes and hospitals and challenged by public and private insurance programs to justify its services.

Cooperation between government and nonprofit associations has also been challenged by organizations representing women, minorities, neighborhoods, and the environment. These challenges are most likely to appear where the long-term relationship between government and voluntary organizations is highly institutionalized, rigid, and too cozy. Sallie Marston and Susan Gonzales Baker (chapters 6 and 7 in this book) describe the new organizations representing immigrants and neighborhoods and their efforts to challenge existing policy.

And finally, relations between government and nonprofit organizations may be disrupted by the decentralization of social policy. Fiscal strains on state and local government are causing them to search for cheaper ways to provide services. New strategies being used by state governments include merging agencies, using for-profit providers, closing programs, and tightening eligibility. These developments are pitting nonprofits against each other and creating tensions between them and government administrators and legislators.

Citizenship and the Changing Role of Nonprofit Agencies

The emergence of widespread contracting and the evolution of the government-nonprofit relationship underscores the complexity of citizenship in a mixed system of publicly and privately provided social welfare. Contracting combines the flexibility and responsiveness of nonprofit service agencies with the financial resources of government. It may free nonprofit agencies from the inadequacies of private charity, allowing citizens greater access to social services. In this sense, contracting may strengthen citizenship as put forth by Marshall. But contracting affects the political role of nonprofit organizations and the politics of social services in fundamental ways that may compromise these social rights.[35]

First, contracting affects the political activity of nonprofit service agencies. These organizations often arise to provide alternatives to prevailing social service policies. In the past thirty years many nonprofit agencies combined this service role with political activism on behalf of battered women, juvenile delinquents, rape victims, and others. Contracting tends to channel and mute this political activity by creating divided loyalties

35. Smith and Lipsky (1993).

among nonprofit agencies. Although they may be committed to a specific mission, they depend on government funding, which discourages them from undertaking political activity that might alienate or antagonize their sponsors. Citizenship changes because the nonprofits' mediating role between the state and the individual is narrowed as they become part of government's social service system. In the long run, citizenship rights may diminish as the diversity of services decreases under the impact of more government regulation and less funding. And the limitations on nonprofit advocacy resulting from contracting make it more difficult for nonprofits to reverse or check this decrease in diversity.

Contracting may also alter citizenship because of its effect on the link between political and social rights. Marshall and many other scholars long ago contended that political rights would lead to an expansion of social rights guaranteed by government. If allowed to vote and freely participate in politics, citizens would try to insure themselves against the risk of various health and social problems through government funding, regulation, and administration.[36] To some extent contracting hampers the exercise of political advocacy by nonprofits receiving government funds. They may become less effective advocates for social rights as they become more dependent on government funding and vulnerable to government influence. The impact on social rights is likely to be most acute in the countries such as the United States that lack strong parties to act as another political voice for social programs.

Indeed, contracting has arguably checked the growth of entitlements in the American welfare state. During the 1960s and 1970s federal spending on social services rose rapidly as the government increased access to services and made more social services entitlements.[37] Initially, government contracting was an essential part of this movement. But during the 1980s, contracting increasingly became separated from the desire to expand entitlements. Government policymakers contracted with nonprofit organizations as a way of providing cheaper services, not more universally available services. The social policies of the Reagan and Bush administrations reflected efforts to return to the pre-1960s era when social services were funded primarily by state and local governments and private charity. Fewer nonprofit programs are now entitlements, and the

36. Many conservatives worry that people will seek too many entitlements from government, thus undermining individual responsibility and ultimately sapping productivity and economic growth. See, for example, Bell (1976).

37. For more discussion of the expansion of social services in the 1960s and 1970s, see Gilbert (1977) and Kahn (1972).

variation across geographic areas has increased because communities and states differ in their willingness to support these services. And dependence of nonprofits on government financing and their often precarious financial condition make it difficult for many nonprofits to advocate broader entitlements, although they can be effective advocates for their own programs. However, even when they successfully argue for their own programs, they are often faced with the difficulty of trading their own survival for eligibility criteria that shrink the pool of clients.

To ensure their survival, nonprofits are increasingly forced to become more market-oriented, which includes imposing fees and developing new revenue-producing services. Advocating broader entitlements tends to be submerged within the overall concern about organizational survival. Citizenship is diminished because social services are less available and depend more on a person's ability to pay.

Citizenship may also be restricted as the mediating function of nonprofits erodes. As they become more market-oriented, they lose their distinctive character as intermediaries between government and the market. Some begin to resemble for-profit organizations while others, in a bid to remain financially viable, aggressively seek government contracts and agree to substantial restrictions on their autonomy. As nonprofits reflect market or government norms, they may deter people from participating as either staff or volunteers. In the long run, advocacy may become more difficult.

Government accountability to citizens is also undermined when responsibility for program admission, treatment, and outcomes is lodged with private organizations. To be sure, it is possible to construct monitoring systems that allow public officials to hold nonprofit contractors accountable. But in practice, citizens do not consider nonprofit organizations to be controlled by government managers. This impression is reinforced by the perceived failure of government to invest adequately in monitoring personnel and resources. Ultimately, accountability in service provision depends on professional standards, which does not necessarily reassure citizens who depend on services provided by contract agencies, and in any event poses troublesome problems of democratic accountability.

Finally, contracting may reduce the investment of the citizenry in the public sector. Political scientists have puzzled for many years about the apparent increase of participation in single-interest politics at the same time that electoral participation is declining and American political parties are in disarray. One explanation is that as the electoral system appears unable to incorporate citizen concerns adequately, people turn to interest groups, community activities, and social movements to articulate their interests. The move toward contracting may make this trend worse. The structure of contracting tends to obscure the details of the welfare state from citizens, who may be unable to understand a system that intermingles public and private responsibilities. Private agency errors are not often regarded as public mistakes under contracting. Likewise, successful, innovative nonprofit programs funded by government are typically not viewed as products of government administrative ingenuity. In this sense contracting can be considered part of the "hollow state," described by H. Brinton Milward and Keith Provan in chapter 10, in which the government delegates key service delivery responsibilities to the private sector.

Yet, effective social services now require healthy private organizations. Contracting encourages concerned citizens to invest in community organizations to obtain effective public policies. Governments cannot always find a nonprofit organization whenever they want to provide a service. For many services the number of qualified nonprofit providers is very small; government and the citizenry need to nurture and sustain these organizations if services are to be available when needed. Contracting tends to force citizen energies into private-sector concerns. For the involved citizen the politics of social services now necessitates not only making demands on public officials but also worrying about maintaining healthy, capable private institutions.

This phenomenon underscores the paradoxes of citizenship in advanced industrial countries. The welfare state grew and matured on a model of expanding government responsibility and administration. But the model did not consider the problems caused by unresponsive and oppressive public bureaucracies or the demands of women, minorities, and other groups for greater access not only to public services but to the political process as well. Contracting is a way of marrying the resources of government with the grass roots democracy and participation of community organizations. But such a contracting bargain is unstable, so as it evolves, participation in nonprofit organizations is greater—millions across the country are board members in contract agencies—but the organizations' agendas are narrower and more defined by the government's policy agenda.

Contracting appears to have implications for citizenship different from those of other public policies involving community organizations. Susan

Gonzalez Baker notes (in chapter 7) that immigration legislation led to a new politics of immigration involving the federal Immigration and Naturalization Service and vigorous advocacy by voluntary associations and service organizations urging more liberal immigration laws. These organizations seem to have been able to escape the muted advocacy characteristic of contract agencies because most had no direct contractual arrangement with government. Although the agencies received government funds for processing immigrant applications, they had other means of support and were less vulnerable to government influence. Another difference is that the INS did not envision this program as a permanent commitment. Consequently, the agency had less incentive to be concerned with the internal operations of the immigrant organizations or their political stances.

Sallie A. Marston (in chapter 6) chronicles the development of citizen activism in Tucson as a result of the federal community action program started as part of the war on poverty. Although it was widely considered ineffective, Marston contends that the CAP actually had a lasting effect of mobilizing citizen and neighborhood groups in Tucson. The introduction of the CAP, she argues, led to greater participation in local policymaking and the institutionalization of regular and meaningful interactions with local neighborhood groups.

Unlike most communities in the United States, in Tucson the CAP was implemented through the municipal government rather than through private nonprofit organizations funded by the federal government. Although initially these nonprofit CAP agencies were politically active and controversial, most became conventional social service agencies and more politically mainstream. In Tucson, voluntary agencies have not engaged in a formal contractual relationship with the municipal government and have been less politically constrained. In this era of antigovernment sentiment, Baker's chapter reminds us that local government agencies can promote greater citizen participation and empowerment. *Public* need not mean antidemocratic or oppressive.

The chapters by Baker and Marston and my chapter suggest that public policies designed to provide a formal policymaking role for voluntary associations can have a strong empowering effect and encourage greater citizen participation, thus promoting enhanced political rights. Once these organizations become involved in formal contractual relationships with government, however, political advocacy becomes more constrained. They will remain politically active, but their activism will be focused on organizational concerns rather than broader public policy. The organizations may then be challenged by new organizations dedicated to policy reform.

Contracting, Citizenship, and Policy Analysis

Contracting has long been promoted because of its reputed efficiency in public service delivery.[38] This is understandable, given the concern of government and the citizenry for providing public services for the least cost, even though the cost savings for contracted services are often ephemeral or elusive. An important lesson provided by the contracting system is the profound consequences for citizenship. This impact presents a challenge for policy analysts charged with assessing the merits of contracting out public services. Relying on efficiency criteria in policy analysis would present only one aspect of the potential effects. Yet understanding the costs and benefits is crucial.

What appears to be needed for sound public policymaking is an appreciation of different strategies to evaluate contracting and other public policies. Rather than relying on one strategy, policymakers might develop analytic approaches that combine strategies. A consultant might be asked by a city government to evaluate a proposed contracting program not only for its possible cost savings but also for its potential impact on citizen participation, the political role of voluntary associations, and the overall decisionmaking process for public policies. Will decisionmaking be more or less democratic? Where will ultimate political accountability for contracted services reside? What options will citizens have to express their concerns about public services provided through nonprofit organizations? By answering these questions, policy analysis can become an agent to reshape policymaking and public services in a more democratic fashion.

Policy analysis can also be used to reform and improve the contracting system. Contracting can be a very good way to provide public services. However, government must approach it as a public investment that needs adequate and continuing support rather than simply as an opportunity to save money. Policy analysis can identify matters that need attention from government and the contract agency to ensure the long-term stability of the contract relationship. Policies can be developed that balance

38. Savas (1979, 1982); and Stein (1990).

government accountability for public funds with the desire of nonprofit organizations to maintain their autonomy and distinctive mission.

References

Bell, Daniel. 1976. *The Cultural Contradictions of Capitalism*. Basic Books.

Bennett, James T., and Thomas J. DiLorenzo. 1989. *Unfair Competition: The Profit of Nonprofits*. Lanham, Md.: Hamilton Press.

Benton, Bill, Tracey Feild, and Rhona Millar. 1978. *Social Services: Federal Legislation vs. State Implementation*. Washington: Urban Institute.

Berger, Peter L., and Richard John Neuhaus. 1977. *To Empower People: The Role of Mediating Structures in Public Policy*. Washington: American Enterprise Institute.

Berger, Suzanne D., ed. 1981. *Organizing Interests in Western Europe: Pluralism, Corporatism, and the Transformation of Politics*. Cambridge University Press.

Bixby, Ann Kallman. 1991. "Public Social Welfare Expenditures, Fiscal Year 1988." *Social Security Bulletin* 54 (May): 2–16.

Brown, Lawrence D. 1983. *New Policies, New Politics: Government's Response to Government's Growth*. Brookings.

———. 1985. "Technocratic Corporatism and Administrative Reform in Medicare." *Journal of Health Politics, Policy and Law* 10 (Fall): 579–99.

"California Court Upholds a YMCA's Tax Status in a Lawsuit by Owners of Health Clubs." 1990. *Chronicle of Philanthropy* (June 12):31–32.

Connecticut, State of. 1983. *A Negotiated Investment Strategy: A Joint Agreement on Principles, Priorities, Allocations and Plans for the Social Services Block Grant, October 1, 1983–September 30, 1984*. Hartford.

Esping-Andersen, Gosta. 1990. *The Three Worlds of Welfare Capitalism*. Princeton University Press.

Gilbert, Neil. 1977. "The Transformation of Public Services." *Social Service Review* 51 (December): 624–41.

Glazer, Nathan. 1988. *The Limits of Social Policy*. Harvard University Press.

Gronbjerg, Kirsten A. 1993. *Understanding Nonprofit Funding: Managing Revenues in Social Services and Community Development Organizations*. San Francisco: Jossey-Bass.

Gurin, Arnold, and Barry Friedman. 1980. *Contracting for Services as a Mechanism for the Delivery of Human Services: A Study of Contracting Practices in Three Human Service Agencies in Massachusetts*. Waltham, Mass.: Florence Heller School of Advanced Studies in Social Welfare, Brandeis University.

Gutowski, Michael F., and Jeffrey J. Koshel. 1982. "Social Services." In *The Reagan Experiment: An Examination of Economic and Social Policies under the Reagan Administration*, edited by John L. Palmer and Isabel V. Sawhill, 307–28. Washington: Urban Institute.

220   STEVEN RATHGEB SMITH

Handler, Joel F. 1990. *Law and the Search for Community*. University of Pennsylvania Press.

Heclo, Hugh. 1978. "Issue Networks and the Executive Establishment." In *The New American Political System*, edited by Anthony King, 87–124. Washington: American Enterprise Institute.

Kahn, Alfred J. 1972. "Public Social Services: The Next Phase—Policy and Delivery Strategies." *Public Welfare* 30 (Winter): 15–24.

Katzenstein, Peter J. 1985. *Small States in World Markets: Industrial Policy in Europe*. Cornell University Press.

Lipsky, Michael. 1980. *Street-Level Bureaucracy: Dilemmas of the Individual in Public Services*. New York: Russell Sage.

McMurty, Steven L., F. Ellen Netting, and Peter M. Kettner. 1991. "How Nonprofits Adapt to a Stringent Environment." *Nonprofit Management and Leadership* 1 (Spring): 235–52.

Marris, Peter, and Martin Rein. 1982. *Dilemmas of Social Reform: Poverty and Community Action in the United States*. 2d ed. University of Chicago Press.

Marshall, T. H. 1964. "Citizenship and Social Class." In *Class, Citizenship and Social Development: Essays*, 71–134. Doubleday.

Offe, Claus. 1981. "The Attribution of Public Status to Interest Groups: Observations on the West German Case." In *Organizing Interests in Western Europe: Pluralism, Corporatism, and the Transformation of Politics*, edited by Suzanne D. Berger, 123–58. Cambridge University Press.

Offe, Claus, and Rolf G. Heinze. 1992. *Beyond Employment: Time, Work, and the Informal Economy*. Temple University Press.

Peterson, Paul E., and J. David Greenstone. 1977. "Racial Change and Citizen Participation: The Mobilization of Low-Income Communities through Community Action." In *A Decade of Federal Antipoverty Programs: Achievements, Failures, and Lessons*, edited by Robert H. Haveman, 241–78. Academic Press.

Polsky, Andrew J. 1991. *The Rise of the Therapeutic State*. Princeton University Press.

Rose-Ackerman, Susan. 1983. "Unintended Consequences: Regulating the Quality of Subsidized Day Care." *Journal of Policy Analysis and Management* 3 (Fall): 14–30.

Salisbury, Robert. 1979. "Why No Corporatism in America." In *Trends toward Corporatist Intermediation*, edited by Philippe C. Schmitter and Gerhard C. Lehmbruch, 213–30. Beverly Hills: Sage.

Savas, E. S. 1979. "How Much Do Government Services Really Cost?" *Urban Affairs Quarterly* 15 (September): 23–41.

———. 1982. *Privatizing the Public Sector: How to Shrink Government*. Chatham, N.J.: Chatham House.

Schlesinger, Mark, Robert A. Dorwart, and Richard T. Pulice. 1986. "Competitive Bidding and States' Purchase of Services: The Case of Mental Health Care in Massachusetts." *Journal of Policy Analysis and Management* 5 (Winter): 245–63.

Schmitter, Philippe C. 1979. "Still a Century of Corporatism?" In *Trends toward Corporatist Intermediation*, edited by Philippe C. Schmitter and Gerhard Lehmbruch, 7–49. Beverly Hills: Sage.

Smith, Steven Rathgeb, and Michael Lipsky. 1992. "Privatization in Health and Human Services: A Critique." *Journal of Health Politics, Policy and Law* 17 (Summer): 239–44.

———. 1993. *Nonprofits for Hire: The Welfare State in the Age of Contracting.* Harvard University Press.

Smith, Steven Rathgeb, and Deborah A. Stone. 1988. "The Unexpected Consequences of Privatization." In *Remaking the Welfare State: Retrenchment and Social Policy in America and Europe*, edited by Michael K. Brown, 232–52. Temple University Press.

Stein, Robert M. 1990. *Urban Alternatives: Public and Private Markets in the Provision of Local Services.* University of Pittsburgh Press.

Tocqueville, Alexis de. 1956. *Democracy in America.* New American Library.

Walzer, Michael. 1988. "Socializing the Welfare State." In *Democracy and the Welfare State*, edited by Amy Gutmann, 13–26. Princeton University Press.

Wilensky, Harold L. 1981. "Democratic Corporatism, Consensus, and Social Policy: Reflection on Changing Values and the 'Crisis' of the Welfare State." In *The Welfare State: An Account of the Conference on Social Policies in the 1980s*, 185–95. Paris: OECD.

Wilensky, Harold L., and Charles N. Lebeaux. 1965. *Industrial Society and Social Welfare.* Free Press.

Williams, Grant. 1990. "IRS Issues Final Lobbying Rules." *Chronicle of Philanthropy* (September 18): 31.

———. 1991. "California Association: Speaking Up for Nonprofits." *Chronicle of Philanthropy* (January 15): 12.

10. The Hollow State: Private Provision of Public Services

H. BRINTON MILWARD AND KEITH G. PROVAN

"THE HOLLOW CORPORATION" was the subject of a cover story in *Business Week* in 1986.[1] The editors believed that a new organizational form had emerged and that Nike, the athletic shoe company, was the template for this new organization. The hollow corporation consisted of a lean headquarters operation with only four departments: research and development, design, marketing, and financial control. What was unique about Nike was that it had no production capability of its own. Nike shoes were made all over the world under contract with various shoe manufacturing firms.

An even more extreme type of hollow corporation is cited and advocated by Tom Peters, coauthor of *In Search of Excellence*.[2] In a recent article he advocates subcontracting anything and everything: "Subcontracting is hardly new. What's new is that major firms [MCI, Apple, and Boeing] are looking at subcontracting as a way of life." These corporations conceive of themselves as a "systems integration" unit, sitting at the center of a web of subcontractors.[3]

The hollow corporation appears to be the analog of "the hollow state." This metaphor captures what has been occurring in the delivery of health and human services in the United States. The hollow state concept is particularly useful in making sense of the specific case investigated for this chapter: the redesign of a metropolitan area's community mental health network to deal with the multiple problems faced by growing numbers of deinstitutionalized seriously mentally ill adults. Our def-

Research for this project was made possible by a grant from the National Institue of Mental Health (Ro1 MH 43783).

1. "Special Report: The Hollow Corporation," *Business Week*, March 3, 1986, pp. 56–85.

2. Peters and Waterman (1982).

3. Peters (1990, p. 13). The management literature on network organizations has begun to generate its first critical assessments of the "hollow corporation" (see Miles and Snow 1992).

inition of hollowness in this case hinges on the degree of separation of government from its output. Advocates of privatization often make the point that government can provide or arrange for citizens to receive a service without government actually producing it.[4] A government intent on privatization would decide what it wanted done and then contract with the private sector to provide the good or the service.[5]

The "hollow state" is a metaphor for the intense effort the Reagan and Bush administrations made to privatize public services.[6] Initially, this privatization consisted of extensive contracting with private nonprofit and for-profit agencies to provide public services. Government administrators monitored and evaluated these contract programs. Increasingly, though, government is now contracting with third parties for administration and monitoring, functions previously performed by government.

The increasing complexity of public services has received some attention from scholars, but little attention has so far been devoted to the implications for citizenship and democracy of this new diffuse network of public and private services. If, as many scholars have argued,[7] public services serve as an important connecting link between citizens and their government, the blurred role of the state must raise critical issues for the citizenry and the accountability of government.

The hollow state is the result of several different trends. The federal government has always relied on state and local government to deliver federally funded services. Government funding of nonprofit agencies increased during the grant-in-aid explosion of the 1960s and 1970s and continued during the Reagan and Bush administrations under the banners

4. Savas (1987, pp. 60–61).
5. "The government has taken on many functions . . . precisely because the private sector either will not do them or would not do them in a way that respects competing values such as equality, for instance, over efficiency." (Kettl 1988, p. 12). A strong state would hold its performance accountable to an array of standards—efficiency, effectiveness, personal responsibility, accountability, responsiveness, and equity—that conflict and require explicit trade-offs. These values and the trade-offs they imply would be much more difficult to achieve where services are largely delivered by third parties.
6. Variations on the concept of the hollow state have been advanced by other scholars in recent years. Jennifer Wolch (1990) uses the term "shadow state" to refer to the increased role that nonprofits play in the delivery of human services to clients. Donald Kettl (1988) and Steven Rathgeb Smith (1990) describe government contracting to third parties respectively as "government by proxy" and "the contracting regime." Lester M. Salamon (1981), following Frederick Mosher (1980), calls our attention to the growing phenomenon of "third party government." David Broder in his syndicated columns uses the term "hollow government" to describe what has happened to domestic public services.
7. Lipsky (1980); and Offe (1984).

of privatization, limited budgets, and getting government off the backs of those it regulates. Many liberals also championed contracting with nonprofit community organizations as a way of increasing citizen control and participation in service delivery.[8]

This chapter develops the concept of the hollow state through a case study of the publicly funded mental health system in Tucson and Pima County, Arizona. The focus will be the implications for citizenship and democracy of this fundamental transformation in the relationship of the state to its citizens.

The Implementation of Public Policy by Nongovernmental Entities

Control of agents in a federal system like the United States is always difficult; Madison saw this as a virtue in his "Compound Republic." Different levels of government share authority for the implementation of health, welfare, education, and many other policies. The traditional problem of control in a federal system is how to implement policy effectively when the relation between levels of government is based on bargaining rather than hierarchy.[9]

A different type of policy implementation problem is the implementation of public policy by nonpublic entities. Whether nonprofit or for-profit organizations are involved, the problem is how to control the behavior of people who are not public servants and whose loyalty, in addition to serving their clients, is either to the prosperity of their own firms or to their nonprofit calling.

Jeffrey Brudney has found evidence to support the hollowing out of the state.[10] Less than 15 percent of the federal government's budget is spent on programs it administers itself, and some federal departments support four indirect workers for every one on the department's payroll. The hollow state is not simply the federal government turning over the delivery of services to states and cities. State and city governments are in the business of creating "hollow" service systems as they turn over hos-

---

8. Organizational scholars have attempted to describe, operationalize, and model the resulting new organizational forms—often called "network organizations" or "service implementation networks"—in the public, nonprofit, and private sectors. See Chisholm (1989); Landau (1991); Lawless and Moore (1989); Miles and Snow (1986); Provan and Milward (1991); and Wise (1990).

9. Ingram (1977).

10. Brudney (1990).

pitals and mental health centers, parks, water treatment plants, prisons, and transportation facilities to nonprofit or for-profit entities.

Since the taxpayer revolt of the late 1970s, there have been major limitations on governmental spending at all levels. In addition, an anti-government zeitgeist, reflected in the Carter, Reagan, and Bush administrations, has significantly changed the way policy can be implemented. In regard to privatization, most policy analysts would recommend that government rationally weigh the costs and benefits of direct provision of a service by government versus provision of the same service by a firm or firms under contract with the government. Given the resource and capacity limitations faced by many governments today, the choice often has little to do with the merits of the case for or against privatization. It is simply a question of finding some scheme to do the job without direct cost to the taxpayer.

Barriers to revenue increases and capacity constraints are so stringent, and the privatization ethos so strong, that government is turning over to nongovernmental entities not only service delivery, but also financial control and eligibility determination for the simple reason that there are few other options.

In the case of the Environmental Protection Agency's Superfund program, contractors are actually performing the basic work of the agency. Because of severe manpower and technical constraints,

> the agency had to rely on contractors to carry out virtually every part of the Superfund program. . . . Contractors were involved not only in the actual business of cleanup, but in the minutiae of EPA management and policymaking. Contractors helped EPA respond to congressional inquiries, analyze legislation, and draft regulations and standards. Contractors even drafted records of decisions, the cental documents guiding what would be cleaned up and how. Contractors researched Freedom of Information Act requests received by the agency. They drafted memos, international agreements, and congressional testimony for top EPA officials. . . . They even wrote the Superfund program's annual report to Congress.[11]

The effect of the nongovernmental provision of public services in the long is not yet known.

We decided to explore in depth one community mental health system

11. Kettl (1993, pp. 111–12).

being run as a private franchise under contract with the state of Arizona. We make no claim as to its being representative of all such systems. While case studies are of limited utility, we decided that we needed to know much more about the new landscape of nongovernmental provision of public services as a way of generating a research agenda for exploring the effect of the hollow state on the delivery of public goods and services, which in turn affects citizens' perceptions of government.

Mental Health, Citizenship, and the Hollow State

In terms of citizenship, the mentally ill are powerless. As a target population, they are clearly among the "dependents" (chapter 4). The most notable characteristic of the mentally ill—and particularly the seriously mentally ill, who are the focus of this study—is political impotence. This impotence stems from personal disorganization and limited social skills, which render them ineffective as political actors.[12] To overcome the powerlessness of the mentally ill, there have been attempts to ensure their rights through the courts and through the creation of lobbying groups like the National Alliance for the Mentally Ill. This lobby consists of family members of the mentally ill who lobby in Washington, all fifty states, and in many communities. Based upon anecdotal evidence, their effectiveness varies a great deal. Some local chapters are inhibited by the stigma of mental illness and by the burdens of caring for their mentally ill family members. Others, like the one in this case, are skillful, effective, and potent. Like Baker (chapter 7), we also found that policy design can be shaped by effective advocacy groups.

This case explores the restructuring, by its participants, of a community mental health system that consisted of a set of largely nonprofit agencies serving, among other clientele, the adult seriously mentally ill.[13] While patient care is an important value in any system of care, the agencies and individuals who deliver these services have interests and agendas of their own. We assume that a good deal of intellectual purchase can be obtained in this analysis by assuming that in addition to normative values concerning patient care, much of the conflict among agencies, the

12. Scull (1985); and Bloche and Cournos (1992).
13. The information regarding the description of this community mental health system comes from an analysis of public documents, personal interviews, newspaper accounts, and participant observation.

state, and participants revolves around the capture and control of state- and county-provided funds to pay for mental health services.

In an earlier attempt to coordinate community mental health care in Arizona, the state government created regional administrative entities in each county to funnel state money to the set of providers of services to seriously mentally ill adults.[14] In Pima County, an existing nonprofit agency, ADAPT, Inc., was designated as the state comptroller for most mental health spending in the community. Since this agency and other nonprofit entities control the flow and distribution of mental health dollars in Arizona, they epitomize how even the direct control of state funds is not necessarily a public function.

One characteristic of a public organization is that it is publicly funded.[15] In the Pima County community mental health system, the funds were largely public, but there was little attempt to coordinate the services various agencies provided to the adult seriously mentally ill. The agencies received funds from the entity that received the money from the state, and each agency largely determined what services it would provide to its clients. In this case these publicly funded agencies did not try very hard to control how funds were spent or to account for whether funds were used effectively.

It is often assumed that organizations that receive most of their funds from one source will be highly responsive to that source. Dependence is, however, a two-way street. Organizations that are highly dependent on funding from one source may receive that funding because they perform critical functions for the funding agency or because there are no alternative providers of an essential service.

Coordination was a problem in this largely privatized system just as it has been in publicly run systems. There were problems in coordinating patient care and coordination problems between agencies. The system of mental health care had recently been further redesigned so that a newly created, state-sponsored nonprofit, Arizona Center for Clinical Management (ACCM), was responsible for a system of capitated, case-managed care that allowed the purchase of needed services from the existing set

14. The chronically mentally ill are persons who, as a result of a mental disorder, exhibit emotional or behavioral functioning that is so impaired it interferes substantially with their capacity to remain in the community without supportive treatment or services of a long-term or indefinite duration. In these persons mental disability is severe and persistent, resulting in a long-term limitation of their functioning capacities for primary activities of daily living. Such clients are now referred to as "seriously mentally ill" so as not to attach a pejorative label to these people.

15. Perry and Rainey (1988); and Wamsley and Zald (1973).

of mental health providers.[16] Thus there are two state-sponsored non-profits, ADAPT and ACCM, providing overall guidance and control for patient utilization of services and purchase of services with public funds. These changes stemmed from well-justified concerns about the low level of funding for the system and a concern that patients were falling through cracks in the previously uncoordinated system. From a theoretical perspective it is interesting that this system has little public accountability built in. All interactions, other than informal interactions, are handled by contracts that the state has with the designated entity (ADAPT), which then routes funds into the community mental health system. Thus control over who gets what services and what clients are served and exactly how taxpayer dollars are spent rests in the hands of an agency that is not directly responsive or responsible to public authority. This, for us, is the essence of the hollow state.

The idea for a case management agency to help coordinate services to the seriously mentally ill was developed by a cluster of key community mental health professionals and advocates, none of whom worked in state government. In fact, few worked for the state at all. System redesign usually assumes that those who fund services are trying to "correct" the behavior of those who provide the services to clients. Here, conversely, a group of service providers and advocates mobilized to redesign the system.

The initial concept of bringing more efficient and effective case-managed services to the county under a capitated funding model started the process that would lead to the redesign of the system. However, the passage and use of time allowed various parties to drag their feet and try to use their influence with the state to moderate the extent of the changes in the system. The resistance was due to uncertainty about how many services the ACCM case management teams would purchase for their clients. In the past, providers had been given contracts by ADAPT to provide a certain amount of services to clients. The notion of the "retail" purchase of services by a case manager for a client, as opposed to the "wholesale" purchase of a fixed number of units of service at the begin-

16. Capitated and case-managed systems control funding through a prospective payment scheme where a defined pool of funds are available on a per capita basis to a fixed set of clients. Case management means that a client is assigned to a team that includes a clinical case manager, doctor, nurse, and social service worker. Services are purchased by the team according to the client's specific needs. Services under case management include the full continuum of care of medications, day treatment, crisis stabilization, transportation, residential services, outreach, mobile crisis services, and therapy.

ning of the fiscal year, created a great deal of uncertainty for the providers. The state budget contained funds specifically allocated for the purchase of services for the seriously mentally ill that ADAPT controlled. The providers had little influence over the dissemination and administration of those funds.

Entrepreneurship and Advocacy

Case management of the seriously mentally ill population led to the change in the design of the system. One entrepreneur focused attention on this issue as a mechanism for creating a more effective and responsive system of services. Dr. Jose Santiago, a vocal and committed policy entrepreneur, had labored long and hard for a capitated and case-managed system while he was head of the psychiatric unit at the community hospital. He worked with others in the system to get the state to fund two pilot programs to test whether a case-managed system produced more beneficial outcomes than the existing system. This man of great energy, who had standing in national mental health circles and with the state legislature through both his formal and informal connections, was in a position to affect and influence implementation of a more humane and efficient mental health system in a state that had a tradition of neither. In so doing, he attempted to influence the reform of a fragmented system. However, by acting as a vocal advocate for the mentally ill, he alienated himself from many local providers. His criticisms of the system were sometimes interpreted as personal assaults. However, most consumers and their families interpreted his statements as necessary activism. He played a key role in the founding of AMISA, the local advocacy group for families of the mentally ill.

Policy entrepreneurs play key roles in decentralized service systems. They often forge informal links that bind the system (or at least part of it) together or provide the energy and ideas to get the system to adopt innovations.[17]

Discussion

This description of the redesign of a community mental health system, which lacked service delivery capacity on the part of federal, state, or local government, provides an example of a "hollow state."

17. Hull and Hjern (1987); and Milward and Laird (forthcoming).

At the beginning of this chapter we freely admitted our intellectual borrowing from the *Business Week* issue on the "Hollow Corporation." The hollow corporation's chief design feature was its lack of production capacity, but it retained responsibility for financial control, research and development, marketing, and design. Now we investigate to what extent the hollow state we studied exhibits these control functions.

Financial Control

In this case study the state does exercise some control over finance of the system through a series of contracts issued to the entity and then to the set of local providers. Based on our observations, the state uses persuasion and, on occasion, threats, to try to influence the design of the system or the behavior of the agencies that make up the system. The state can exert this influence through its control of most of the financing for the system. Unlike in the hollow corporation, this financial control does not come from the specificity of the contracts with the provider agencies, but from direct formal or informal intervention in the system through control over scarce resources.

As a result of an increase in scale and revenue, government funding shifts control from voluntary community boards to salaried employees. Nonprofits also become tied to the state budget cycle and legislative and bureaucratic politics. What emerges, over time, are organizations that are likely to be more tied to the state government and less to the community they serve.[18] The result is that systems of this nature become "producer" dominated. The members of the network of directors, staff, and state officials come to see each other as the principals of the system. This community mental health system has funded "advocate" positions to counteract this tendency. The advocacy organization for clients and their families also plays this role. This is necessary because government funding of nonprofits dampens the traditional mediating role between client and government that nonprofits have traditionally played.[19]

Research and Development

A second function of hollow corporations is research and development. There is a functional equivalent here in the pilot programs that Jose Santiago, the policy entrepreneur, persuaded the state to fund to test the viability

18. Lipsky and Smith (1989–90); and Smith (1990).
19. Smith (1990).

of the case management approach. While the results of these pilot programs were not clear cut, they provided the model and part of the justification for the adoption of the case management approach by the system and the creation of the state-sponsored case management agency.

Marketing

Marketing is a third function that is centrally controlled by hollow corporations; however, this is not something that government usually does. While government public affairs offices are very efficient at churning out justifications for agency actions and the need for increased funding, marketing is foreign to government-funded service delivery systems. This is because these systems are typically inadequately funded. This is certainly the case in Arizona, which ranks at or near the bottom in per capita funding of mental health.[20] In a poorly funded system, the incentive is not to market: the more the client load increases, the more the level of services will deteriorate. In the Tucson system, the "discovery" of more clients than the expected number almost led to the collapse of the new structure in the summer of 1990. Provider agencies were upset because a number of their seriously mentally ill clients were not on the list for case-managed services and the case management agency was initially unwilling to accept more clients than the state was willing to pay for. Thus marketing in the private sector often becomes rationing in the public or nonprofit sector.

Design

In the hollow corporation, design is critical. If you control no production capabilities, you must be very careful in designing the specifications of the products that you want to produce. Companies in many countries produce shoes for Nike at an agreed-upon design standard, cost, shipping schedule, and quality. This is precisely the problem confronting managers of the hollow state. However, in this case the difference could not be more striking. In the redesign of the system we examined, design came from the producers themselves, in reverse of the usual pattern. Case management was an idea in good currency in social services nationally, but an entrepreneur in the system was its champion along with a group advocating the rights and needs of the clients and their families.

20. Torrey, Wolfe, and Flynn (1990).

The entity system was originally created to funnel money to the providers. The fact that the system had to be redesigned only five years later is an example of how top-down system design often fails to achieve its purpose. The quality and quantity of services the system produced were poorly specified and thus needed to be redesigned. Based on our observations, one missing feature in this community mental health system is the capacity to produce information that would allow the system to increase its level of performance. The state was simply incapable of utilizing any of the information it collected from the community agencies in a way that allowed it to monitor performance or help the entities control the system they were supposed to manage. This problem may have been due to turnover in government, bureaucratic rigidity, or, what we believe is far more likely, years of budget cuts and hollowing that have simply eroded the ability of governmental agencies to be effective.

What is so interesting about this case is that while the state did not have the capacity to bring about system redesign, the contractors did. Local learning did occur, and an interdependent set of providers, with the aid of an entrepreneur and local advocates, was able to bring significant change to a community mental health system.

This case raises a number of normative issues related to the effect of hollow service systems on citizen capacity to influence public policy. The use of nonprofits to deliver taxpayer-provided public services loosens the connection between the citizen and the state, as nonprofits may not be as responsive to public demands. From a service provider perspective, that is indeed one of a hollow system's virtues. The long-run effects of this on citizenship and the willingness of taxpayers to support these systems are unclear.

State funding and the state sponsoring of nonprofits may damage the mediating role that nonprofits play in buffering the citizen from the state. This is certainly true if the nonprofits begin behaving like the government agencies—risk averse, bound by red tape, and more concerned with those who provide their funding than with their clients. Both of these issues— the effect of state funding and insulation from citizen control—are important issues that need both normative and empirical attention if we continue to use the hollow state to deliver public-provided services.

Citizenship and the Hollow State

The foregoing analysis suggests that the current restructuring of public services contains several important concerns for citizenship, democracy, and state. These include the legitimacy of the state, the accountability of private organizations for the expenditure of public funds, and citizen participation in the governance of public services.

The Legitimacy of the State

In the 1970s jails were often used in public finance classes as an example of a public service that could not be privatized. The reason given was that since the state monopolized the legitimate power of coercion in society, the power to take away a person's liberty was viewed as a function that, if delegated to a private firm, would lead to the state becoming illegitimate in the eyes of its citizens. Today the courts have not been privatized but some prisons are indeed run by private companies. In the community mental health system described here, an attorney under contract with the courts evaluates and recommends which petitions requesting that an individual be institutionalized in a mental hospital be granted. In this same system, the nonprofit entity that serves as the conduit for taxpayer dollars to provide treatment also determines who is eligible to receive services from the system.

In essence, the public character of public services is no longer obvious. Thus poor-quality services are no longer experienced as straightforward problems of government services. But the benefits of government programs, in improving the quality of life of consumers, are not credited to government either. Consequently, citizen support for publicly funded services may decline as the public's tie to government programs becomes weaker.

Accountability for Public Services

Privatization often occurs because severe capacity limitations force the government to contract for services it does not have the ability to provide. Policy design, control of the implementation process, and evaluation of the quality of the contracted services can, and often do, remain the job of the public agency. However, the capacity limitations that led to contracting out in the first place may extend to the guidance and evaluation functions of government. In the community mental health system examined here, policy design and control of the implementation process were performed by the nonprofit entity and providers. Evaluation was not performed by the state because its administrative resources were

stretched thin in responding to a lawsuit that, among other things, re-
quested systematic evaluation of the treatment services provided by the
nonprofits.

This case illustrates the new and increased complexity of the governance of social services; responsibility for managment and oversight is
more diffuse and vastly more complicated. To the extent that governments are unwilling to invest in adequate management, accountability
for the expenditure of public funds by private organizations will be compromised. And even if sufficient funds for oversight are provided, entirely
new governance structures will need to be developed.[21]

Citizen Participation and Public Services

At least part of the impetus for privatization was the desire to shift
services from public bureaucracies—which were perceived to be remote,
rigid, and unresponsive—to decentralized local organizations that were
closer to the people and presumably more responsive to the citizenry. Yet
this case study suggests that privatization may actually reduce the *potential* responsiveness of public services.

Bureaucracies can be inflexible and rule-bound, but procedures exist
for citizens to bring complaints or concerns against these organizations.
Elected officials exert oversight over bureaucratic agencies. And bureaucracies have increasingly adapted their organizational structures to include various citizen committees to provide input into the organization.

In the Tucson case study, ADAPT, which held the private franchise
that arranged for the provision of mental health services, had essentially
no citizen oversight. ADAPT's records were private and it operated as
any other not-for-profit agency. In addition the case management agency,
ACCM, was also a not-for-profit organization. Given the fact that both
service provision and delivery had been privatized, the public character
of services for the seriously mentally ill was obscured. Most citizens
would not be likely to contact the relevant government agency if they
were dissatisfied with the quality of service provided by these organizations. One possible long-term consequence could be even further alienation of citizens from the state as they experience declining levels of service
and a powerlessness to correct any problems or decide what should be
the major programmatic priorities.

21. Kooiman (1993).

Conclusion

In sum, the hollow state phenomenon has implications for both citizenship and policy design. One key design issue is what Hal Rainey calls "the irony of privatization."[22] Privatization is portrayed as a solution to government mismanagement and efficiency. The irony is that privatization is not self-implementing. The contractor must be highly competent and effective for a privatized system not to become a "nongovernmental monopoly." Effective privatization requires skilled public managers, adequate public resources for oversight, and new management techniques and structures to cope with the more complex and diverse service system.

Similarly, enhancing citizen participation in public services in an increasingly privatized system will necessitate the development of new types of government-private cooperation. Through new public-private relationships, the difficult and conflicting values of responsiveness, equity, efficiency, and effectiveness can be directly addressed.

22. Personal communication from Hal G. Rainey, Department of Government, University of Georgia.

References

Bloche, M. Gregg, and Francine Cournos. 1992. "Mental Health Policy for the 1990's: Tinkering in the Interstices." *Journal of Health Politics, Policy and Law* 15 (Summer): 387–411.

Brudney, Jeffrey L. 1990. "Expanding the Government-by-Proxy Construct: Volunteers in the Delivery of Public Services," *Nonprofit and Voluntary Sector Quarterly* 19 (Winter): 315–28.

Chisholm, Donald. 1989. *Coordination without Hierarchy: Informal Structures in Multi-organizational Systems.* University of California Press.

Hull, Christopher J., and Benny Hjern. 1987. *Helping Small Firms Grow: An Implementation Approach.* New York: Croom Helm.

Ingram, Helen. 1977. "Policy Implementation through Bargaining: The Case of Federal Grants-in-Aid." *Public Policy* 25 (Fall): 499–526.

Kettl, Donald F. 1988. *Government by Proxy: (Mis?)Managing Federal Programs.* Congressional Quarterly Press.

———. 1993. *Sharing Power: Public Governance and Private Markets.* Brookings.

Kooiman, Jan, ed. 1993. *Modern Governance: New Government-Society Interactions.* London: Sage.

Landau, Martin. 1991. "On Multiorganizational Systems in Public Administration." *Journal of Public Administration Research and Theory* 1 (January): 5–18.

236   H. BRINTON MILWARD AND KEITH G. PROVAN

Lawless, Michael W., and Rita A. Moore. 1989. "Interorganizational Systems in Public Service Delivery: A New Application of the Dynamic Network Framework." *Human Relations* 42 (December): 1167–84.

Lipsky, Michael. 1980. *Street-Level Bureaucracy: Dilemmas of the Individual in Public Services.* New York: Russell Sage.

Lipsky, Michael, and Steven Rathgeb Smith. 1989–90. "Nonprofit Organizations, Government, and the Welfare State." *Political Science Quarterly* 104 (Winter): 625–48.

Miles, Raymond E., and Charles C. Snow. 1986. "Organizations: New Concepts for New Forms." *California Management Review* 28 (Spring): 62–73.

———. 1992. "Causes of Failure in Network Organizations." *California Management Review* 34 (Summer): 53–72.

Milward, H. Brinton, and Wendy Laird. Forthcoming. "Where Does Policy Come From?" In *The Discipline of Public Administration*, edited by B. Guy Peters and Bert Rockman. Chatham, N.J.: Chatham House.

Mosher, Frederick C. 1980. "The Changing Responsibilities and Tactics of the Federal Government." *Public Administration Review* 40 (November–December): 541–48.

Offe, Claus. 1984. *Contradictions of the Welfare State*, edited by John Keane. MIT Press.

Perry, James L., and Hal G. Rainey. 1988. "The Public-Private Distinction in Organization Theory: A Critique and a Research Strategy." *Academy of Management Review* 13 (April): 182–201.

Peters, Tom. 1990. "Part One: Get Innovative or Get Dead." *California Management Review* 33 (Fall): 9–26.

Peters, Thomas J., and Robert H. Waterman. 1982. *In Search of Excellence: Lessons from America's Best-Run Companies.* Warner Books.

Provan, Keith G., and H. Brinton Milward. 1991. "Institutional-Level Norms and Organizational Involvement in a Service Implementation Network." *Journal of Public Administration Theory and Research* 1 (October): 391–417.

Salamon, Lester M. 1981. "Rethinking Public Management: Third-Party Government and the Changing Forms of Government Action." *Public Policy* 29 (Summer): 255–75.

Savas, E. S. 1987. *Privatization: The Key to Better Government.* Chatham, N.J.: Chatham House.

Scull, Andrew. 1985. "Deinstitutionalization and Public Policy." *Social Science and Medicine* 20 (5): 545–52.

Smith, Steven Rathgeb. 1990. "Managing the Community: Privatization, Government and the Nonprofit Sector." Paper presented at the annual meeting of the American Political Science Association.

Torrey, E. Fuller, Sidney M. Wolfe, and Laurie M. Flynn. 1990. *Care of the Seriously Mentally Ill: A Rating of State Programs.* Washington: Public Citizen Health Research Group and National Alliance for the Mentally Ill.

Wamsley, Gary L., and Mayer N. Zald. 1973. *The Political Economy of Public*

Organizations: A Critique and Approach to the Study of Publilc Administration. Lexington, Mass.: Lexington Books.

Wise, Charles R. 1990. "Public Service Configurations and Public Organizations: Public Organization Design in the Post-Privatization Era." *Public Administration Review* 50 (March–April): 141–55.

Wolch, Jennifer R. 1990. *The Shadow State: Government and Voluntary Sector in Transition.* New York: The Foundation Center.

Part Four
Reconnecting Public Policy and Citizenship

CITIZEN EMPOWERMENT as envisioned by Richard M. Valelly in the closing chapter of this book returns to some themes first introduced by Marc Landy. Citizens are empowered through involvement in association, deliberation, and the performance of civic duty. Rather than the freedom to pursue self-interest through economic power stressed by R. Kenneth Godwin, Valelly believes that citizen empowerment is different from individualism. Citizenship develops through association, and although associations can introduce the evils of faction, they can also be schools for democracy. Policies that reduce the costs of associational activity may help to reconnect citizens to politics. Policies developed with respect for people's competency to make decisions invite those people to invest in civic duty.

Valelly is a great deal more hopeful and positive about the potential of government to reinvigorate democracy than some of the other authors in this volume. However, the empowering policies he suggests require less radical policy change than many of the privatizing experiments already under way. Policy can selectively encourage trends such as workplace democracy. Long-standing norms can be strengthened and reinforced. Proposals already on the table can be marginally but importantly modified to better empower citizens.

The optimism of Valelly's chapter—with its emphasis on renewal—is appropriate to a volume whose authors advocate a change in policy analysis. The need and the opportunity for innovation in the construction of policies clearly exist. Criticism about the current state of modern democracies and concern about citizen cynicism and disaffection are widespread. Such radical changes as abandoning the two-party system and placing limits on legislative terms are receiving surprising support. Far less radical design changes in policies to enhance democracy, such as Valelly suggests, may well receive a welcome from elected officials.

Policy analysis for democracy should also appeal to political scientists. Since the behavioral revolution of the 1960s, many political scientists have compared observed behavior with democratic ideals. Critical political theorists, among others, have convincingly argued that policies not only do not solve problems or equitably reflect interests, they perpetuate dependency and powerlessness among citizens. The authors of this book have attempted to move beyond simply stating or criticizing findings to offer positive recommendations and strategies to improve policy designs that foster citizenship and democracy. Nonetheless, identifying policies that are likely to enhance citizenship and democracy will not be easy and straightforward. Just as measuring policy success in instrumental terms is contingent on priorities and specific criteria, whether a policy is determined to foster citizenship depends on which aspects of the concept are emphasized. Further, the effects of particular elements of design are likely to change depending on the context and target groups affected.

This final chapter not only provides an appropriate conclusion to this volume but also suggests fruitful and potentially rewarding new directions for public policy research. A fundamental tenet of public policy research has been that it be useful and contribute to improved policymaking. Yet public policy scholars have not adequately tackled fundamental normative questions of democracy and citizenship. Because the design of public policy has significant implications for how people conduct public life and fulfill their roles as citizens, policy analysts must include democratic renewal among their scholarly goals.

11. Public Policy for Reconnected Citizenship

RICHARD M. VALELLY

INTENTIONALLY OR UNINTENTIONALLY, public policies influence the individual and group foundations of democratic processes and institutions. My purpose here is to explore the design of policy for reconnected democratic citizenship. Reconnected citizenship here means some shift both at the individual level and among the publics who are involved in making any given policy work. This shift would be toward a stronger, more self-conscious approval of some or all of the distinctive norms of democratic politics (public debate, governmental competence, rule of law, political equality, and social commitment to social provision of public goods) and, just as important, the principle that collective problems can be publicly resolved.

By changing or reinforcing links between individuals and group and electoral politics, policy design can alter the very context of democratic citizenship in which policy is made. Policy analysts, policymakers, political activists, and citizens can—and ought—consciously to assess, much more often than they do now, the potential that any given policy has for involving citizens in democratically useful forms of group politics and for strengthening a sense of citizen duty. Policies that do so can enhance the broad governmental competence (and the public confidence in such competence) that is a condition for the effective political resolution of public problems.

Ruy Teixeira, in his study of nonvoting in American politics, calls for "reconnecting" American citizens to their political system. By this he means finding ways to foster both a better grasp of political institutions, processes, and issues among citizens and a significantly more positive, psychological affect toward the political system. Reconnected citizens, in his view, differ from citizens who are either indifferent toward or neutral

For valuable comments I thank Joshua Cohen, Martha Derthick, and Robert Kuttner. None, of course, is responsible for any errors of fact or interpretation.

about politics, are openly cynical, or have a weakened sense of citizen duty, that is, reject a norm of participation whatever their current evaluation of the political process. Over the past three decades many Americans have developed such attitudes.[1]

In using the term *reconnected citizens*, I mean more than citizens simply having a positive affect toward the political process. Democratic politics is something that everyone can be part of, at least electorally, and possibly more often than electorally. Without unrealistically demanding that everyone be a full-time political agent, my recommendations focus on making political participation more individually meaningful for more Americans.

Why Reconnected Citizenship?

Two broad concerns animate these recommendations and the basic inquiry into the relationship between policy design and democratic citizenship. The first has to do with America's seeming increase in organized politics bashing (for want of a better term); the second deals with the fundamental utility and rewards of democratic political community.

First is politics bashing. Fostering reconnected citizenship may constitute, I believe, a needed response to increased public discontent with politics. In 1992, fourteen states approved term limitations for members of Congress. The idea of an explicit constitutional rule for curbing deficits, espoused by Presidents Reagan and Bush, has also become increasingly popular, on the ground that ordinary legislative politics has no internal fiscal balance. Consider, too, some of the Perot movement's significance. In launching and then relaunching his candidacy, Ross Perot and those associated with him frankly espoused new mechanisms of accountability and representation that would supposedly solve not just the "mess" in Congress but the whole mess in Washington. These ideas include electronic town meetings, mass canvassing of the public mood via instant electronic referenda, and service in the presidency without pay. The Perot campaign articulated a fairly widespread desire for a special government above ordinary politics.

Such public discontent undoubtedly performs useful corrective functions in American politics. It reflects public concern over very real features of contemporary American politics and holds open the promises of more

1. Teixeira (1992, chap. 2). The term *reconnected* can be found on pp. 154–55; for reform proposals giving a flavor of Teixeira's view of reconnectedness, see pp. 156–82.

collective dialogue and political accountability.[2] But collective problems cannot actually be addressed if there is no public patience with ordinary democratic government and politics. Politics ought not to be a dirty word or connote that the dominant reality of American politics is a giant rent-seeking scam run by the organized at the expense of the unorganized.

Effective policymaking—the public and efficient provision of public goods—requires tolerance of the characteristic limits of the policy process, not a desire for "big fixes," such as new constitutional rules or plebiscitary presidencies. Effective policies require feedback, assessment, and modification when warranted; such feedback, assessment, and recasting depend on public patience; and public patience ultimately comes from public loyalty to and confidence in ordinary political and policy-making processes. Policy initiatives in the 1990s, when the public has become aware of a series of social, environmental, and economic problems, demand a sturdier foundation than impatient discontent.

American politics is now haunted by the specter of inflated expectations and mass disappointments with broad policy initiatives to correct such widely perceived problems as the health insurance crisis. A subtle harm to constitutionalism and, ultimately, to political democracy, to say nothing of the prospects for really solving public problems, might result from the organized politics bashing that is now a real and growing force.[3]

Careful attention to how policy can generate reconnected citizenship may therefore be a way of avoiding such dangers. There are other ways, of course, such as revitalizing local government. But national policy gets made regularly; every day large numbers of creative people are thinking about setting the national policy agenda, shaping the policy process, influencing implementation, and working to fight future battles over policy. Analyzing how artfully to redirect this ongoing policy process may help to change the rage, discontent, or simple apathy with and about government and politics that many Americans feel. Success in doing this, in turn, might well strengthen the social foundation of public approaches to common problems.

Public policy for reconnected citizenship has a second and separate justification. In an important sense, fostering reconnected citizenship

2. Jeffrey Schmalz, "Americans Sign Up In Record Numbers To Cast A Ballot," *New York Times*, October 19, 1992, p. A1, provides anecdotal evidence of the Perot campaign's impact on citizen awareness of issues.

3. See, for instance, President Clinton's May 14, 1993, press conference. An interesting report in this connection is Dennis Farney, "Bedroom Communities Want Clinton to Solve Their Problems, Too," *Wall Street Journal*, May 5, 1993, p. A1.

would help to lay the "seed corn," so to speak, of political community and of the arts and skills of political cooperation and mutual political association (hereafter referred to as *associationalism*). These arts and skills help democratic polities avoid fratricidal conflict, suboptimal social and economic development, and social tendencies to authoritarianism or leader worship.[4]

Through its ordinary processes democratic politics often seems to continually reinvigorate these arts and skills. Recent theorizing about the relationship between individuals and collective institutions and processes has come to appreciate that preferences and behavior shift as individuals cross boundaries between marketlike areas of life and communal and political areas of life. Voting, for instance, becomes paradoxical and irrational in strictly egoistic terms, hence the recognition in political science of the role of a sense of duty. More basically, different domains exist and people recognize this as they shift back and forth between them.[5]

But even if people adjust as they shift between "the market" and "the public square," suggesting a stable coexistence of domains, association-alism and the norms supporting it require nurturance, given what is known about the difficulty of collective action. Self-interest and egoism are powerful forces; at some point one domain might colonize or conquer the other. In the 1970s it was widely feared that politics had killed the market, but the opposite fear—that self-interest more often than not blocks cooperation for the supply of public goods—is equally plausible. Self-interest and egoism can and do play positive roles. As an example, some approaches to environmental regulation recommend establishing markets in pollutants that would adequately price the negative external-ities of production and thus rapidly accelerate progress toward meeting environmental standards. But self-interest and egoism, or simple indif-ference toward politics, can gradually corrupt a community's capacity to address its problems. In a society as powerfully individualistic as Amer-ican society, it is almost impossible to "overnurture" associationalism and public-regarding norms.[6] We may well constantly run, as a society,

---

4. For a recent statement, see Putnam (1993) generalizing from Putnam, Leonardi, and Nanetti (1993).

5. See Hirschman (1982) and Kelman (1987, especially chaps. 10–11). For more ana-lytic treatments, see Margolis (1982), and Riker and Ordeshook (1968). I thank Janice Fine of the MIT Political Science Department for reminding me of the basic links between the less analytic and more analytic works cited here.

6. This was Tocqueville's basic point in *Democracy in America*.

an associational deficit. Public policy for reconnected citizenship would help to lay "seed corn" for a stock of socially valuable skills and behaviors perhaps continually in danger of depletion. Public policy for reconnected citizenship has not only a short-run justification—balancing the potential dangers of contemporary politics bashing; it also has a long-run justification—contributing to the diffusion of norms and skills that any democratic polity needs.

Policy Messages and Citizen Status

My approach to analyzing policy for reconnected citizenship borrows from the work of other authors in this volume: Helen Ingram and Anne Schneider's work on, as they aptly put it, "the subtle messages of policy design," Deborah Stone's account of the role that "causal stories" play in policy processes, and Janet Weiss's work on public information campaigns.[7] Public policies can contain several kinds of messages about public purposes and citizens' role in their realization. First, they can send signals about the people who are involved in making the policy work—what Ingram and Schneider have called the "target populations" of a given policy, that is, the specification of "who is to do what, how, and for what reason." In selecting target populations, further, a policy and its design implicitly tell a "story" about both the problem or problems that the policy is meant to address and the causal role of the target populations in solving that problem.

For instance, in a case discussed further below, a policy encouraging European-style works councils within industrial firms would signal that one of the causes of a public problem, uncertain or possibly declining industrial competitiveness, is how firms use the problem-solving skills of their work forces—and therefore would also signal a less well-recognized problem, namely, poor standards for workplace relations. Therefore, to realize a common national goal—increased competitiveness—workers become a "target population" conceived of as agents of a public solution to the problem of uncertain competitiveness. Their very agency also addresses a related problem—poor standards for workplace relations between workers and management.

This is an illustration of a policy whose design would signal to its target population the public recognition of a public problem, shared by many Americans; it thus "constructs" a target population as the agent

7. Chapters 4 and 5 in this volume and Stone (1989).

of a common purpose, through participation and representation, in local, workplace problem-solving processes. Not only does such a policy design help place people in valued problem-solving roles, but it also underscores that public goals are realizable.

Policy design can thus signal to citizens that effective government is possible and it involves ordinary people. Key conditions of democratic political order—competent government and political accountability—are reinforced. Strengthening these conditions reinforces another democratic norm—deliberation. Political deliberation, whether in legislatures or in carpools, means little if government is ineffective or unaccountable. But deliberation means much more if the prospect of effective government is genuine. Policy for reconnected citizenship, in other words, involves ordinary citizens in publicly constituted processes that address real problems and also strengthens their stake in democratic politics.

These points are suggested through illustration. After treating general issues in democratic theory, a case study of the "employment involvement" trend in industrial relations considers how to redirect an existing trend in a democratically desirable direction. Next a case study of an environmental policy seeks to uncover the democratic value of an existing policy. Finally, a case study of legislation to improve voter turnout seeks to show what a policy proposal already on the legislative agenda may well need in order to maximize its intended democratic goal. The first two cases are about designing associationalism; the last treats how to clarify for citizens some of what is involved in electoral choice.

Recasting Associationalism

One of the key things that public policy for reconnected citizenship can do is affect the group system. But how easy is citizen involvement in group politics? And what does democratic theory say about the desirability of group politics? Without addressing these questions, seeking to influence associationalism in the name of reconnected citizenship might seem either pointless or, worse, factional.

The Relative Ease of Associationalism

Early pluralist theorists, such as David Truman, emphasized how quickly groups arose, and they underscored the inherently inclusionary character of the group system, picturing it as an arena for broad representation of a wide variety of interests and values. This view suggests that associationalism comes easily to citizens. Such a seemingly Panglossian view of the group system came under several kinds of attack, ranging from Mancur Olson's formal and logical demonstration of both the difficulty of collective action and the strength of the microeconomic incentives to avoid associational activity, to arguments emphasizing the highly uneven distribution of resources necessary for competition for public resources within the group system. In E. E. Schattschneider's famous phrase, "the flaw in the pluralist heaven is that the heavenly chorus sings with a strong upper-class accent." The cumulative force of these attacks apparently required very substantial modification of early views of group politics.[8]

In recent work, however, Jack Walker went far toward showing that the group system is as dynamic in its evolution as early pluralists suggested, although for reasons far different from those initially emphasized. Walker constructed the first reliable "census" of interest groups across time. He found that the older view of "stable unrepresentation" (due to scarce distribution of political resources) no longer captures interest group politics.[9] At any point in time in a democratic system political resources do have a highly skewed, underlying distribution consistent with the socioeconomic inequalities of a capitalist society. The underlying scarcity of resources for effective group politics—time, skills, and money — appears to erect a high "threshold" for associational activity. But Walker considered the variety and scope of government's regulatory and policy initiatives, as well as the array of private institutions and actors, including government, foundations, and the media, dedicated to solving policy problems and to diffusing information about policy issues.

Actors in public and private institutions are constantly, if often unintentionally, rearranging the group system, for instance, by changing the structure of opportunities for organization, by providing valuable resources, or simply by deepening lines of conflict. For example, when the Kennedy administration established state-level commissions on the status of women, it laid the basis for the formation of the National Organization of Women. Similarly, liberal foundations helped to finance the black voter registration drive of the early 1960s in the deep South. This accelerated social change but also intensified factionalism within the civil rights movement. Injection of resources and change in political oppor-

8. Truman (1951); Olson (1965); and Schattschneider (1975).
9. Walker (1988); and Gamson (1968).

tunities thus regularly restructure patterns of collective action. An important aggregate, unintended consequence has been that—with the exception of the long decline of organized labor—gaps in group representation have closed steadily since the 1930s. In short, the group system is dynamic, shifting, and relatively open—not unchanging and closed to newcomers. While associationalism hardly comes as easily to citizens as pluralist theorists first claimed, it comes more easily than the reactions to pluralism suggested.[10]

The Relative Desirability of Associationalism

But is a trend toward increased associationalism desirable? If not, why reinforce it or further stimulate it? From at least two perspectives increased associationalism could easily seem questionable. The first is neoclassical liberal theory, which considers the collapse of the separation between market and state that is embedded in the interventionist, welfare state a central feature of modern politics. It has generated innumerable forms of government-conferred privilege for producer and social groups—farmers, workers, industrial sectors, the aged, and those in need of low-cost housing. The development of the social standards that are demanded by these groups simply piles up labor costs, causing capital to move toward lower-cost countries, and menaces the fiscal balance required for providing truly essential public goods.[11]

From a more neo-Madisonian political perspective, there is widespread evidence of the mischiefs of faction. To whatever degree the group system is more dynamic than once thought, there still is a threshold of entry. Groups consequently have an advantage over ordinary citizens in shaping the political agenda. "Overrepresented" minorities thus generate governmental goods for their private benefit and spread the costs to the unorganized majority. "Pork" may be generated, agencies may be "captured," agenda-setting in specific policy domains may be ceded to organized groups, and, through the political economy of campaign finance, the integrity of legislators and legislative processes compromised. Groups may exploit either citizen activism or legitimate citizen concerns while actually operating as little more than sophisticated, direct mail operations with high overhead. Or, if they influence presidential nominating rules

10. Walker (1988); see also Walker (1991).
11. For thinking about objections to associationalism I found Cohen and Rogers (1992) very useful.

of the major parties in their favor, they may undermine the capacities of parties to offer majoritarian policy platforms.[12]

The total results of such rent seeking and faction not only threaten the norm of equity in access to public privileges and in the incidence of public burdens (as in the case of spreading the costs of narrow benefits), but also threaten the foundations of governmental competence (as in the case of "pork" or agency capture). Yet the prospects both of equity and of governmental competence are fundamental conditions of a democratic order. Without them, public debate about public purposes would become trivial. Thus groups seem constantly to threaten a democratic order.[13]

But democratic theory does not speak with one voice about groups and associationalism. It also holds that groups and associations can be "schools of democracy." Associationalism builds a certain kind of civic virtue. As John Stuart Mill argued, participation is educative: a person has to "weigh interests not his own; to be guided, in the case of conflicting claims, by another rule than his private partialities; to apply, at every turn, principles and maxims which have for their reason of existence the common good."[14]

A distinction that Tocqueville drew between "self interest well understood" and "individualism" is also helpful here. Tocqueville, in *Democracy in America*, pondered the character of the political virtue that democracy requires of its citizens. He suggested that "self interest well understood" was a form of democratic virtue strong enough to sustain a widely held ethic of caring, to some degree, about public concerns. He contrasted this with an antipolitical attitude, "individualism," and worried about the disconnection from politics and from the associationalism of democratic politics that is implied by "individualism." Associationalism, in his view, nurtured self-interest well understood.[15]

Second, associations can empower and encourage those who can easily become discouraged and disfranchised: landless farmworkers, the disabled and handicapped, veterans of an unpopular war, women discriminated against in the workplace and in courtrooms, and ordinary, hardworking blue-collar men and women. Despite formal political equality,

12. An especially striking example of several of these problems can be found in Erik Eckholm, "Alarmed by Fund Raiser, The Elderly Give Millions," *New York Times*, November 12, 1992, p. A1, which describes Richard Viguerie's activities in direct mail fundraising for groups supposedly monitoring social security policy for the elderly. See also Hansen (1991); Hirschman (1970, chap. 6); Moe (1989); and Polsby (1983).
13. McConnell (1966); Hansen (1991); Page (1983); and Romer and Weingast (1991).
14. Pateman (1970, p. 30).
15. Tocqueville (1969, pp. 506–28).

their "voices," even if articulated, are often indistinct or inaudible to "the mainstream."

Electoral politics, especially presidential electoral politics, would seem to correct for "deaf democracy." Voting is not a costly activity: everyone one can do it, the handicapped and the healthy, men and women, rich and poor. Also, the presidential constituency is national. Presidents tend to care about the macroeconomy, national strength, and such broad issues as strengthening self-reliance, equality, inclusion, and some measure of social justice. Hence the interest in responsible parties and activist presidencies found among such critics of pluralism as E. E. Schattschneider and Grant McConnell and their legatees in American political science. And, broadly speaking, as Steven J. Rosenstone and John Mark Hansen show, strong party politics, which involves mobilization of the electorate, tends to reduce class bias in representation.[16]

But electoral politics can also be subtly unrepresentative. It tends toward the aggregation of interests, toward broadest common denominators. And mandates are notoriously found in the eyes of the beholders. Electoral outcomes provide very imprecise signals to policymakers; the information they convey is always mediated by the policy activists, pollsters, and political professionals within and without major campaign organizations. The articulation of interests and "voicing" of group politics, particularly protest groups, make up for such intricate exclusion, removing ambiguity and doubt about interests and needs, and, in so doing, betokening inclusion and equity. Strong party and electoral politics are perhaps most representative, therefore, when there is also a strong group system.[17]

If, therefore, democratic theory delivers conflicting judgments about groups and associationalism—finding democratic education and honorable representation in group politics as much as it finds faction—then ruling for one or another view obviously becomes an empirical and prudential matter. The proof of associationalism is in the political pudding, as it were. Sometimes democratic education and inclusive representation ensue; other times, faction prevails. Joshua Cohen and Joel Rogers have advised, accordingly, a deliberate politics of association. Using standard policy tools, they mean to recast group politics so that its processes converge simultaneously on democratic education, more inclusive rep-

16. Schattschneider (1975); McConnell (1966); and Rosenstone and Hansen (1993).
17. Schlozman and Verba (1987).

resentation, and more effective policy. The basic idea here is that groups have an unrecognized function to perform in tailoring policy initiatives to local circumstances. In a wide variety of settings they can help ordinary people to act as the experts "on the ground." Such policy design can, indeed, add to governmental competence.[18]

To exemplify this recommendation, I will focus on industrial relations and on an emerging form of representation in environmental regulation.

Recasting Representation in Industrial Relations

By now it is commonplace to hear a summons for public policy to encourage workplace democracy. Such calls occur in a context in which it is widely (although hardly universally) assumed that labor has rights, that is, that industrial democracy, in principle, is socially valuable. But key issues now are international economic competitiveness, particularly concerning newly industrializing countries, such as Korea or Taiwan, and seemingly well organized social systems of production, such as Japan's or Germany's, and increasing international wage competition. Thus calls for employee involvement (or EI) typically recognize that, given this new context, the social standards for protecting a measure of industrial democracy need to be recast.[19]

Indeed, public policy already seemingly encourages workplace democracy and many private initiatives appear to institute it. The tax code currently encourages employee stock ownership plans; by the late 1980s several thousand firms, covering millions of employees, had some kind of employee ownership, and several hundred of these were majority-owned. In addition, several national agencies have responsibilities for "facilitating the formation of worker cooperatives and worker buyouts."[20] During much of the 1980s the U.S. Department of Labor assisted in the creation of more participatory workplace systems.

In the private sector, corporate experimentation with worker participation has been very widespread, partly out of competitive necessity (also, in part, to shed or to deter unionization). In the 1980s corporate America was a prime agent of experimentation in new organizational structures and more flexibility in the workplace. Some form of employee participation had come to between one-third and one-half of U.S. firms

18. Cohen and Rogers (1992, p. 425).
19. The best short discussion, scholarly or popular, is Metzgar (1992).
20. Bachrach and Botwinick (1992, pp. 104–05). See also Rosen (1991).

by the mid-1980s. Larger firms may have adopted it more willingly than smaller firms.[21]

The effect of these changes on efficiency is as yet unclear, although the cumulative evidence regarding the few genuine cases of EI suggests real gains. More relevant to my purpose here, there has been very little discussion of the political consequences.

The effect on citizenship of increased public and private investment in EI appears to have been, at best, slight. Worker-owned and worker-managed companies do tend to reinforce voting in national and local elections. Workers in such companies also seem a bit more likely to encourage friends or neighbors to vote, to contact public officials about an issue, to write letters to editors, to work with others to solve some community problem, to attend meetings of the city or town council, and to attend a public hearing of a government agency, such as a school board.[22]

The meager political effect of the extensive experimentation with EI is surely explained to some extent by its largely cosmetic character. Overall, the 1980s were marked more by harsher employer treatment of unions and by less focus on employee job security, pension rights, and fringe benefits than by consensual establishment of workplace democracy. If the experimentation had led to fundamental changes in workplace hierarchies, then it is much less likely that one would have seen in the late 1980s and early 1990s both a rash of corporate efforts to replace striking workers permanently and widespread "downsizing" and "reengineering" of work forces. Only a handful of corporations witnessed significant efforts at genuine reform: the Saturn division of General Motors, Xerox, Ford Motor Company, and a few others. Others, such as Eastern Airlines and Caterpillar, saw new management teams dismantling successful EI systems, with, at best, dubious gains.[23]

21. Cutcher-Gershenfeld, Kochan, and Verman (1991); Heckscher (1991); Kochan and McKersie (1990); and Bachrach and Botwinick (1992, p. 102).

22. See Greenberg (1986, chap. 5). Greenberg reviews the scant positive, empirical literature on the subject of workplace democracy's political effects at pp. 119 and 123. Greenberg cautions that certain forms of workplace democracy, in particular worker-owned cooperatives, tend to make workers, quite rationally, given the market challenges such co-ops face, more aggressively self-interested.

23. See Kelley and Harrison (1992) and Harrison (1991, p. 74). On the state of labor relations, see Hoerr (1992). On Xerox, see Cutcher-Gershenfeld (1991), the result of doctoral work at the MIT Sloan School of Management. Saul Rubenstein, of the Sloan Ph.D. program in industrial relations, is currently preparing a similar study of Saturn. For Ford

Clearly, therefore, there is room for public policy, in particular policy that tends to institute the kind of genuine reform that currently exists in only a few firm-level oases in the American workplace economy. The Commission for the Future of Worker-Management Relations appointed by Secretary of Labor Robert Reich suggests that the 1990s may see some push for revitalized industrial relations.[24] A promising proposal would tie the reform of pension laws or tax expenditure benefits to establishment of employee participation committees (EPCs) in firms larger than twenty-five employees. The National Labor Relations Act of 1935, and its statutory and administrative amendments, are implicitly seen in this proposal as somewhat limited, although by no means obsolete. Along with basic unionism new forms of workplace representation may be necessary. These would build on recognition of the multiple ways in which industrial representation has grown up outside the administrative framework established by the NLRA, for instance, in the federal courts, which now increasingly govern a variety of workplace issues (for example, women's reproductive rights, workplace safety, and pension benefits of bankrupt companies).

EPC members would be rank-and-file employees elected by their co-workers through secret ballots. EPCs would consider not only wages, benefits, hiring, and training, but product and process innovation and the introduction of "best industry practice" technology. Finally, they would administer federal workplace safety programs in ways that would eliminate the need for the inspectorates that business has found so meddlesome.

A key feature of the EPC idea is that it be autonomously funded through joint worker and firm contributions. In other words, in return for tax credits or other incentives, firms would be required to partly fund EPCs. This funding would help EPCs secure expert assistance and advice from unions, consulting firms, academics, and other EPCs. To the extent that this incorporation of expertise generated firm-level allocative effi-

Motor Company, see Neal Templin, "A Decisive Response to Crisis Brought Ford Enhanced Productivity," *Wall Street Journal*, December 13, 1992, p. A1. On "re-engineering," see Al Ehrbar, " 'Re-Engineering' Gives Firms New Efficiency, Workers the Pink Slip," *Wall Street Journal*, March 16, 1993, p. A1. For an equally chilling glimpse at the corporate shedding of labor, see Joann S. Lublin, "Ranks of Unemployed Couples Multiply, Devastating Double-Income Households," *Wall Street Journal*, May 7, 1993, p. B1.

24. For examples of the debate inspired by the commission's establishment, see Estreicher (1993); Rothstein (1993); and Stone (1993). See also Cohen and Rogers (1992, pp. 455–58).

254   RICHARD M. VALELLY

ciencies, incentives for passing the cost of funding EPCs on to consumers would diminish.[25]

Genuine, robust codetermination, which probably means also helping autonomous unionism to reemerge in many workplaces, would also have two political dimensions that firms might accept because of the promise of internal efficiencies. These are restoring or substantively implementing protective rights that have not been vigorously enforced in the past decade, such as rights to a safe work environment, and, second, the development of new participation rights in the form of significant worker participation in decisions historically considered to be management prerogatives.[26] Change along these two dimensions would surely be contentious. One of the fundamental origins of the Caterpillar strike of 1991–92, for instance, was management opposition to growing union involvement in historic management prerogatives. But workplace democracy may well possess key economic strengths: flexibility in responding to market change and higher product quality. It was precisely along these dimensions that Japanese companies mounted their most effective challenge to firms in other countries in the past two decades.[27] Obviously, the prospect of reaping efficiencies might well constitute insufficient inducement in a corporate culture that has nurtured only superficial changes in workplace relations and that credits recent success in export competitiveness to cost cutting through shedding labor or forcing down the wage bill. But many Americans may be genuinely interested in economic democracy.[28]

EPCs might help to restore confidence among much of the industrial work force that setting social standards, such as protective rights in the workplace, is not an exercise in futility. The confidence of industrial management in broad social standards may be increased, and managers

25. For more on EPCs see Weiler (1990).
26. Bachrach and Botwinick (1992, chap. 9) and Metzgar (1992).
27. Cutcher-Gershenfeld (1991) details some of the efficiency advantages. Womack, Jones, and Roos (1990) detail the firm-level characteristics of Japanese industrial competitiveness in a leading economic sector, auto-industrial manufacturing.
28. A 1975 survey found that 65 percent would favor working for a company that is employee owned and controlled; 52 percent would support a plan "in which employees determine broad company policy"; and 66 percent said they did not work as hard as they could "because they aren't given enough say in decisions which affect their jobs." Christie (1984, p. 125). The survey is obviously dated, and I am not aware of more recent data, but we now have a better sense that public opinion is surprisingly stable. See Page and Shapiro (1992, chaps. 1–2). Still, a repeated survey would be required before drawing any satisfying inference.

might see that such standards need not be overbroad or burdensome but can be adjusted to local needs in light of local knowledge and capacities. A possible second-order effect of reformed workplace relations is the construction of a certain context for reconnected citizenship. A public policy encouraging the establishment of EPCs implicitly treats those participants in EPC formation and maintenance as competent: able to manage the overlaps between workers' interests and management interests in productivity, flexibility, and workplace safety and judge the need for new rights. It is a policy that tends to "construct" people in a certain way.

In doing this, a policy encouraging workplace democracy that is much more genuine than has so far appeared with most employee involvement programs of the 1980s establishes nationally sanctioned patterns of small-scale governance. Such national encouragement of small-scale forms of governance might well reinforce citizenship for large-scale governance. Involvement in making truly consequential decisions at the local level in a publicly designed and publicly evaluated process may invite other forms of associationalism beyond the workplace, and it may betoken a strengthened capacity of individuals for involvement in other processes of consequential decisionmaking. It may promote reconnected citizenship even as a specific policy issue is addressed in ways that meet the interests of the various actors in, or concerned about, the policy domain. A second, similar example follows.

Recasting Representation in Environmental Regulation

Environmental regulation today explicitly provides for group representation, such as public comment on rulemaking. Yet such group representation is subject to the criticism that it impedes effective decisionmaking, partly explaining, in turn, a notorious delay in achieving environmental goals. Putting regulation together with a key feature of democracy, group representation, seems to be a recipe for the frustration of public goals and the undermining of governmental competence in this particular policy area.

One example, however, the 1986 Emergency Planning and Community Right-to-Know Act (EPCRA), seems to provide evidence for a different and hopeful view of the relationships between groups and regulation. Certain of its characteristics have the potential to improve environmental standards while arguably revitalizing civic consciousness in local communities around the country.

256   RICHARD M. VALELLY

In 1986, in response to the disaster at the Union Carbide facility in Bhopal, India, Congress passed EPCRA as Title III of the Superfund Amendments and Reauthorization Act of 1986, modeling it in part on an earlier New Jersey right-to-know statute. EPCRA requires the Environmental Protection Agency to release what is known as the Toxics Release Inventory (TRI), which lists the quantity of 320 carcinogens released by industrial plants across the country.[29] The TRI, in principle, provides information on what a factory is emitting, how much, and into what medium (land, water, or air) and what chemicals are currently stored and whether there is a record of spillage.

In fact, TRI is unknown to the general public, even in areas where general community concern about toxic emissions is known to exist, is woefully incomplete due both to its flawed, data-gathering mandate and imperfect corporate compliance, and has few internal, systematic checks on the reliability of the data it reports. While EPA has made improvements to how the information in TRI is released, via on-line database, CD-ROM, fiche, and other media, obtaining the information is prohibitively expensive for an ordinary citizen. Corporations, indeed, purchase most of the TRI data for their own use. Finally, there is some fragmentary evidence that TRI encourages corporations in compliance with the EPA reporting program to juggle their data in order to appear as if they are reducing emissions at a greater rate than they actually are.

Nevertheless, TRI has spurred citizen protest, involvement by state environmental regulators, state legislative activity, and very strong voluntary compliance among leading companies, principally the Monsanto Corporation, to meet locally set targets for reduction of emissions. Much of the transmission of its information occurs through the existing system of environmental advocacy groups. The process is in line with the revised view of the group system's developmental dynamics, which states that associationalism, while not easy, is certainly easier than the critics of pluralism in the 1960s and 1970s suggested, and that governmental provision of a resource crucial for collective action (in this case, information that would otherwise be impossible or irrationally time-consuming for any given group, not to mention the ordinary citizen, to obtain) is a key stimulus to associationalism.

Environmental advocacy groups computerize and process the dense information in the TRI, circulating their reformatting of the data, which

29. My treatment of this statute is based on Shenkman (1990); Randolph B. Smith, "A U.S. Report Spurs Community Action By Revealing Polluters," *Wall Street Journal*, January 2, 1991, p. A1; and General Accounting Office (1991).

are then picked up by local media or local activists. Although the evidence so far is fragmentary, it does seem that this mechanism has triggered the ad hoc formation of local citizen groups, which then work with local companies, state regulators, and, when companies are unionized, a plant's unions.

Local dynamics are hardly free of conflict, can create tensions, and are marked by sometimes irate citizen protest. Managers in many companies evidently believe that the information in the TRI can be and has been put to misleading uses. But the bottom line seems to be genuine progress, in several communities, on first developing and then implementing local environmental standards.

A striking feature of EPCRA's politics is the policy's implicit evaluation of citizen capacities to understand a scientifically complex issue, in this case the level of acceptable risk to a community due to toxic emissions from a local plant. It assumes that citizens should be able to control politically the level and kind of toxic emissions occurring in their communities. For some, this optimistic evaluation of citizen capacities may seem mistaken. Scientific literacy is not widespread in the United States, and it is widely believed among the technologically and scientifically literate that citizen incompetence probably precludes citizen involvement in key regulatory issues.

Yet the threshold for effective citizen involvement may not be very high at all in the sense that ordinary citizens may be able to make reasonable choices after only brief exposure to thinking about complex issues. A recent study paired roughly equal, randomly selected samples of ordinary citizens and scientists, for whom uncertainty, probability, and hypothesis are familiar concepts even though they were not experts in the issues treated by the study. The study exposed the citizen sample to a questionnaire, a twenty-minute film, and forty-five-minute group discussions of complex policy issues led by moderators, followed (at a second, later session) by another brief film recapitulating issues treated in the earlier session and a readministration of the questionnaire. It found that for the most part both samples, layman and scientist, considered the same policy issues similarly. These included solid waste disposal and reducing the threat of global warming from carbon dioxide emissions due to coal and gasoline consumption in home heating and transportation. The differences that did exist between the two groups seemed plausibly related to factors other than scientific literacy. The study hardly settles the wisdom or illogic of citizen involvement in scientifically or technologically complex policy issues. But it does suggest that renewal of the system of representation may not have to be restricted to certain kinds of issues deemed "suitable" for the average citizen.[30]

EPCRA's potential for reconnected citizenship is striking for the absence of an inspectorate intervening in local circumstances. A common complaint about bureaucracies is that they impose broad standards but are unable to customize these broad standards, so to speak, to account for local circumstances. This is not meant to argue against bureaucracies or standards. The TRI obviously could not exist without bureaucratic collection of the information that goes into the inventory and efforts to enforce corporate compliance with reporting. Relatedly, the capacity of citizen groups in a given locale to have articulate demands at all about permissible standards clearly depends in part on an earlier, national history of a public search for broad environmental standards. Mentioning the common complaint about bureaucratic incapacity to take account of local conditions is meant only to underscore a feature of contemporary regulation that can and does generate a certain amount of public cynicism, both about governmental competence and, more generally, about the very possibility of effective regulation. EPCRA thus seems to have a potential for encouraging public confidence in the public purpose of environmental regulation. If so, that points toward reconnected citizenship.

A second and related feature of EPCRA's politics is the implicit emphasis on small-scale governance. The design of this policy constructs a target population in such a way as to endow it with competence to address responsibly a public problem about which there is widespread concern, namely, the release of toxic chemicals. The design of the policy further assumes that a key cause of the problem is public ignorance about such release and that, therefore, a key remedy must be government provision to citizens of the information they need. Small-scale governance not only involves people in solving a problem that many actors in the policy domain, for different reasons, have an interest in solving; it also has a tendency to lay the "seed corn" of reconnected citizenship. To the extent that people govern on a small scale, the possibilities grow for the transfer of skills engendered in one area to another, small-scale context, or to involvement in electoral politics and in the associational life of groups or movements with national goals.

In considering how policy design can recast associationalism, I have stressed that such design has the potential to "construct" citizens as participants in local forms of representation—in the workplace and in

30. Doble and Richardson (1992).

communities—that in turn effectively address widely recognized public problems. But for several reasons a discussion of policy design for reconnected citizenship must also explore whether and how policy can influence a revitalization of the electoral process.

First, for those who are part of the stronger group politics that is envisioned here, group politics might well be perceived—by some fraction of them—as oriented toward broad goals if electoral politics is also seen as meaningful and valuable. Second, some fraction of those who are not now involved in group politics may become more interested if electoral politics is perceived as more vital. The two domains, group and electoral, may renew each other. Associationalism ought to be seen as a continuum, and policy for reconnected citizenship ought—and can—attend to reconnecting all along this continuum.

Recasting Voter Registration: The Role of Public Information

As is well known, voter turnout in U.S. presidential elections (defined as the ratio of actual to eligible voters) dropped about 13 points between 1960 and 1988, and it dropped in other national elections as well. To be sure, the 1992 presidential election seems to have reversed the trend noticeably, but given the amount of measurement error in estimates produced on or right after election day, and given the weight and variety of social and political forces that appear to have produced the decline, it will not be clear whether there really was a significant reversal until well into 1993, and, in any event, far from clear that it can stand as a lasting reversal.[31]

Nonvoting, indeed, is pervasive in American electoral politics. Minorities of active voters determine the outcomes of gubernatorial, state legislative, county, mayoral, and municipal council elections, as well as state and local referenda. While there are exceptions, the rule seems to be that the smaller the constituency, the smaller the active voting public.[32]

The question of whether and how to reverse decline in just one category of electoral activity, national elections, proves to be a genuinely complex matter. Any resolution of it depends in part on properly conceptualizing the decline and on properly specifying its causes. Neither facet of the issue is (nor is likely to become) free of enduring controversy.

31. For a brief introduction, see Valelly (1990).
32. The theoretical framework for this proposition is laid out in Peterson (1981).

260 RICHARD M. VALELLY

Even more controversial are evaluations of whether turnout decline makes or has made any real difference for the representation of public policy preferences, and thus for who gets what from government.

Even if one concludes that turnout decline can partly be reversed through choices that are plausible and possible in the contemporary political context, it turns out that simply returning to the status quo as of about 1960 will probably require at a minimum an ambitious mix of strategies: reform of campaign finance, reform of print and broadcast media coverage of the electoral process, and changes in procedures for voter registration. Even so, historically deep-seated features of how parties compete with each other and how they mobilize (and fail vigorously to mobilize) voters would inhibit the full potential effect of this mix of reforms.[33]

Still, agency-based registration (the "motor voter" bill), a key accomplishment of the 103d Congress, is an important step. Voters register to vote when they are also interacting with a state agency, such as a motor vehicle registration board. Under this reform states are also provided with resources for using an unbiased procedure for regularly cleaning their voter lists. Agency-based registration lowers the costs of voter registration to an individual radically by "folding" them—as Teixeira has pointed out—into another set of costs, like those of, say, registering a car. The potential effect on turnout is estimated between 4 and 10 percentage points.[34]

Little attention seems to have been paid, though, to the need to alert citizens—as they interact with an agency—as to *why* motor voter registration seems easier. There is a role here for a public information campaign. Such a campaign could reinforce the norm of citizen duty that seems clearly important in motivating a decision to vote at all.

A narrow microeconomic approach to voting would lead any voter to conclude that the ratio of costs of voting—time involved in registering and voting, for instance—far outweigh the real benefit to the individual of voting. The decision to vote depends, in other words, on political norms. And, having decided to vote, an average voter is unlikely to vote on narrow pocketbook grounds. Such voting is less frequent than voting based on broad retrospective or prospective evaluations of the performance of politicians ("have they, or has he or she, made America or the state or the district better or worse off?"). Yet the role of political norms

33. McGerr (1986); Rosenstone and Hansen (1993); and Coleman (1992).
34. Teixeira (1992, chap. 4).

in the decision to vote—and perhaps in the act of voting—has become attenuated. Policy design can play a key role in replenishing the force of norms in voting; it can lay the "seed corn" of associationalism in its broadest sense.[35]

The National Election Study used to ask survey questions that sought to tap citizens' sense of obligation to participate in spite of factors that made it seem hard or unpleasant. Because so little change seemed to occur, most of the survey items were dropped after 1980, but the one that was retained—whether one ought to vote even if one did not care much about an election—showed a very substantial drop of 17 points (59 to 42) between 1980 and 1988. The *Washington Post* has asked citizens whether they thought that their vote mattered. In 1980 its survey found that 91 percent responded yes, but by 1991 that number dropped to only 73 percent.[36]

Under these circumstances, agency-based voter registration may not play as effective a role as it could without an effort to address the decline in a sense of citizen duty. When citizens register to vote while doing something else at an agency, they can be provided with a brief analysis of what many political scientists refer to as the "turnout problem."

Providing information will cause controversy, and formulating its content may (perhaps ought) to require a special federal commission that incorporates the advice and input of the fifty secretaries of state, as well as expert advice on what is known about the consequences and effectiveness of public information campaigns. This is a policy tool whose use inevitably raises broad questions about how to safeguard against government manipulation of citizens.

But an information campaign might include coverage of the change in turnout since 1960, a brief international comparison of turnout in the United States and in other countries (a feature that will inevitably arouse concern since turnout is much lower in the United States than elsewhere) and further analysis showing, though, that the United States differs much less from other countries in rate of turnout among *registered* voters. A public information campaign would emphasize the clear evidence that once registered, voters tend to vote. Fourth, it could also emphasize what

---

35. This proposal seems consistent with Teixeira's own sense of the unexplored role of information in changing citizen motivation: "Though it may be implausible to expect a characteristic like party identification (partisanship) to increase much in intensity . . . it is quite plausible . . . to expect levels of information-oriented characteristics to increase . . ." (1992, pp. 156–57).

36. Teixeira (1992, pp. 55–56).

political scientists have tended to find, namely, that turnout does not benefit one party or the other. Fifth, an information campaign could summarize the arguments that hold that the "turnout problem" is exaggerated. Finally, it could suggest further reading, pro, con, or mainly informative, and a brief statement of a key rationale for voting, namely, that active voters tend to know more about what their government is doing than inactive voters or habitual nonvoters.

Thus the design of agency-based voter registration could be altered so that it incorporates a particular policy tool, the public information campaign, so as to reinforce or reawaken a sense of citizen duty, as defined above. Janet Weiss reports that public information campaigns appealing to existing, widely held norms are the most successful.[37] This may be because an individual's awareness of the relatively uncontroversial nature of these norms makes it easier for him or her to pass along or to discuss with others—family members, coworkers, and friends—the contents of a public information campaign. Agency-based registration thus has a potential for more fully replenishing—without manipulation and in a way that is respectful of citizens—the norms that motivate voting.

Otherwise, agency-based registration may subtly signal to citizens that citizenship is mainly a matter of calculating costs and benefits ("If we lower the costs to you won't you please vote?"). If so, this would hardly be a way to lay "seed corn" for strengthening democratic politics. Through espousing a sensitivity to how policy design affects citizenship, one sees that a simple issue of apparent detail—whether to provide information about the "turnout problem"—raises the question of how to maximize the broad, democratic utility of a public policy.

Conclusion

Policies are often evaluated as to whether they get the job done well and at what price. But policies and their design can also alter the very democratic context within which policymaking and policy evaluation take place. Like others in this volume I have argued here for an approach to policy analysis that is more sensitive to consciously strengthening democracy than most contemporary policy analysis. Through illustration I sought to show that policy analysts and policymakers alike can ask important questions about and of policy trends and initiatives. Other examples would surely occur to a group of legislators or administrators.

37. Chapter 5 in this volume.

How can an existing trend be redirected in a normatively desirable direction? The discussion of building on the employee involvement movement of the 1980s by encouraging works councils sought to answer this question. Does this or that policy have an unappreciated democratic value? The discussion of the surprising effect on group representation in environmental regulation of the Emergency Community Planning and Right-to-Know Act addressed this question. What does a policy proposal already on the legislative agenda seem to need in order to meet its intended goal? By exploring the role of a public information campaign in agency-based voter registration policy, I sought to answer this question.

Concerns about strengthening both the meaning of democratic citizenship and the continuum of associational life that stretches between simply deciding to vote and fairly engaged participation in a citizen's movement or in a group stood behind these questions. Thinking through how to lay the "seed corn" of associational norms and political skills can inform, indeed articulate, policy analysis and recommendation. Policy design can construct citizens as competent to address public problems. It can do so by providing for representation in local problem-solving processes. Such representation provides for small-scale governance that, in turn, can foster reconnected citizenship in other areas: other groups and more frequent voting. The problem-solving features of local representation that can be encouraged by policy also reinforce a norm of governmental competence. Public confidence in the realizability of such a norm is crucial to democracy and its deliberative character. Otherwise, public cynicism can steadily grow. Finally, public policy can reinforce existing norms that are crucial for reconnected citizenship, such as the sense of citizen duty that can motivate electoral participation.

Even if policy design can in fact attend to the task of laying "seed corn," ought it to? Tocqueville claimed that knowledge of association is, as he put it, the "mother of all other forms of knowledge," a dictum implying that strong, mutually respectful, "bottom-up" patterns of democratic participation and associationalism help nations to become more prosperous and decent.[38] His claim for a correlation between such forms of participation and national strength makes sense, in fact, out of the cases explored here. Real, not ersatz, employee involvement arguably makes firms stronger and more competitive, and to the extent that firms are stronger, then sectors and the economy as a whole are stronger. Participation may well be crucial, also, to environmental problem solv-

38. Tocqueville (1969, p. 517).

ing. Finally, while the link is less obvious in the case of strengthening the norms that motivate voting, stronger links between citizens and the electoral process are crucial for creating basic public respect for political approaches to common problems.

Democratic renewal through public policy and other initiatives is, in fact, already on our national agenda. The American polity is in the midst of a widespread sense of public discontent with politics unrivaled since the late nineteenth century. Democratic systems have many internal sources of renewal, not least the constant recognition among citizens that the norms governing the "market" areas of daily life differ from the norms that are sovereign in the "public square." But the careful design of public policy is not often seen as a strategy of renewal. This chapter—this volume—urges us to take public policy for democracy more seriously.

References

Bachrach, Peter, and Aryeh Botwinick. 1992. *Power and Empowerment: A Radical Theory of Participatory Democracy.* Temple University Press.

Christie, Drew. 1984. "Recent Calls for Economic Democracy." *Ethics* 95 (October): 112–28.

Cohen, Joshua, and Joel Rogers. 1992. "Secondary Associations and Democratic Governance." *Politics and Society* 20 (December): 393–472.

Coleman, John J. 1992. "Economics, Recession, and Party Decline: American Parties in the Fiscal State." Ph.D. dissertation, Massachusetts Institute of Technology.

Cutcher-Gershenfield, Joel. 1991. "The Impact on Economic Performance of a Transformation in Workplace Relations." *Industrial and Labor Relations Review* 44 (January): 241–60.

Cutcher-Gershenfeld, Joel, Thomas Kochan, and Anil Verman. 1991. "Recent Developments in U.S. Employee Involvement Initiatives." In *Advances in Industrial and Labor Relations: A Research Annual,* edited by Donna Sockell, David Lewin, and David B. Lipsky, 1–32. Greenwich, Conn.: JAI Press.

Doble, John, and Amy Richardson. 1992. "You Don't Have to Be a Rocket Scientist . . ." *Technology Review* 95 (January): 51–54.

Estreicher, Samuel. 1993. "Employee Voice in Competitive Markets." *The American Prospect* (Summer): 48–57.

Gamson, William A. 1968. "Stable Unrepresentation in American Society." *American Behavioral Scientist* 12 (November–December): 15–21.

General Accounting Office. 1991. *Toxic Chemicals: EPA's Toxic Release Inventory Is Useful but Can Be Improved.* Report to Congress. GAO/RCED-91-121.

Greenberg, Edward S. 1986. *Workplace Democracy: The Political Effects of Participation.* Cornell University Press.

Hansen, John Mark. 1991. *Gaining Access: Congress and the Farm Lobby, 1919–1981*. University of Chicago Press.

Harrison, Bennett. 1991. "The Failure of Worker Participation." *Technology Review* 94 (January): 74.

Heckscher, Charles. 1991. "Can Business Beat Bureaucracy?" *The American Prospect* (Spring): 114–28.

Hirschman, Albert O. 1970. *Exit, Voice and Loyalty: Responses to Decline in Firms, Organizations, and States*. Harvard University Press.

———. 1982. *Shifting Involvements: Private Interest and Public Action*. Princeton University Press.

Hoerr, John. 1992. "Is the Strike Dead?" *The American Prospect* (Summer): 106–18.

Kelley, Maryellen R. and Bennett Harrison. 1992. "Unions, Technology, and Labor-Management Cooperation." In *Unions and Economic Competitiveness*, edited by Lawrence Mishel and Paula B. Voos, 247–86. Armonk, N.Y.: M.E. Sharpe.

Kelman, Steven. 1987. *Making Public Policy: A Hopeful View of American Government*. Basic Books.

Kochan, Thomas A., and Robert B. McKersie. 1990. "Human Resources, Organizational Governance and Public Policy: Lessons From a Decade of Experimentation." Working Paper 3184-90-BPS, Alfred P. Sloan School of Management, Massachusetts Institute of Technology.

McConnell, Grant. 1966. *Private Power and American Democracy*. Alfred A. Knopf.

McGerr, Michael E. 1986. *The Decline of Popular Politics: The American North, 1865–1928*. Oxford University Press.

Margolis, Howard. 1982. *Selfishness, Altruism, and Rationality: A Theory of Social Choice*. Cambridge University Press.

Metzgar, Jack. 1992. "'Employee Involvement' Plans." *Dissent* 39 (Winter): 67–72.

Moe, Terry M. 1989. "The Politics of Bureaucratic Structure." In *Can The Government Govern?*, edited by John E. Chubb and Paul E. Peterson, 267–330. Brookings.

Olson, Mancur. 1965. *The Logic of Collective Action: Public Goods and the Theory of Groups*. Harvard University Press.

Page, Benjamin I. 1983. *Who Gets What From Government*. University of California Press.

Page, Benjamin I., and Robert Y. Shapiro. 1992. *The Rational Public: Fifty Years of Trends in Americans' Policy Preferences*. University of Chicago Press.

Pateman, Carole. 1970. *Participation and Democratic Theory*. Cambridge University Press.

Peterson, Paul E. 1981. *City Limits*. University of Chicago Press.

Polsby, Nelson W. 1983. *Consequences of Party Reform*. Oxford University Press.

Putnam, Robert D. 1993. "The Prosperous Community: Social Capital and Public Life." *The American Prospect* (Spring): 35–42.

266   RICHARD M. VALELLY

Putnam, Robert D., Robert Leonardi, and Raffaella Y. Nanetti. 1993. *Making Democracy Work: Civic Traditions in Modern Italy.* Princeton University Press.
Riker, William H., and Peter C. Ordeshook. 1968. "A Theory of the Calculus of Voting." *American Political Science Review* 62 (March): 25–42.
Romer, Thomas, and Barry R. Weingast. 1991. "Political Foundations of the Thrift Debacle." In *Politics and Economics in the Eighties,* edited by Alberto Alesina and Geoffrey Carliner, 175–214. University of Chicago Press.
Rosen, Corey. 1991. "Employee Ownership: Performance, Prospects, and Promise." In *Understanding Employee Ownership,* edited by Corey Rosen and Karen M. Young, 1–42. Ithaca, N.Y.: ILR Press.
Rosenstone, Steven J., and John Mark Hansen. 1993. *Mobilization, Participation, and Democracy in America.* Macmillan.
Rothstein, Richard. 1993. "New Bargain or No Bargain?" *The American Prospect* (Summer): 32–47.
Schattschneider, E. E. 1975. *The Semisovereign People: A Realist's View of Democracy in America.* Reprint. Hinsdale, Ill.: Dryden Press.
Schlozman, Kay Lehman, and Sidney Verba. 1987. "Sending Them a Message— Getting a Reply: Presidential Elections and Democratic Accountability." In *Elections in America,* edited by Kay Lehman Schlozman, 3–26. Allen and Unwin.
Shenkman, Ethan. 1990. "Right-to-Know More." *The Environmental Forum* 7 (July–August): 20–27.
Stone, Deborah A. 1989. "Causal Stories and the Formation of Policy Agendas." *Political Science Quarterly* 104 (Summer): 281–300.
Stone, Katherine Van Wezel. 1993. "The Feeble Strength of One." *The American Prospect* (Summer): 60–66.
Teixeira, Ruy A. 1992. *The Disappearing American Voter.* Brookings.
Tocqueville, Alexis de. 1969. *Democracy in America,* edited by J. P. Mayer, translated by George Lawrence. Garden City, N.Y.: Anchor.
Truman, David B. 1951. *The Governmental Process: Political Interests and Public Opinion.* Alfred A. Knopf.
Valelly, Richard. 1990. "Vanishing Voters." *The American Prospect* (Spring): 140–50.
Walker, Jack L. 1988. "Interests, Political Parties, and Policy Formation in American Democracy." *Federal Social Policy: The Historical Dimension,* edited by Donald T. Critchlow and Ellis W. Hawley, 141–70. Pennsylvania State University Press.
———. 1991. *Mobilizing Interest Groups in America: Patrons, Professions and Social Movements.* University of Michigan Press.
Weiler, Paul. 1990. "Who Will Represent Labor Now?" *The American Prospect* (Summer): 78–87.
Womack, James P., Daniel T. Jones, and Daniel Roos. 1990. *The Machine That Changed The World.* New York: Rawson Associates.

Index